Surviving
Betrayal

Surviving Betrayal

Hope and Help for
Women Whose Partners
Have Been Unfaithful

365 DAILY MEDITATIONS

ALICE MAY

HarperSanFrancisco
A Division of HarperCollins*Publishers*

HarperCollins books may be purchased for educational, business, or sales pro-
motional use. For information please write: Special Markets Department,
HarperCollins Publishers, Inc., 10 East 53rd Street, New York, NY 10022.

HarperCollins Web Site: http://www.harpercollins.com
HarperCollins®, ☘®, and HarperSanFrancisco™ are trademarks of HarperCollins
Publishers Inc.

FIRST EDITION
Designed By Joseph Rutt

Library of Congress Cataloging-in-Publication Data
May, Alice.
Surviving Betrayal : hope and help for women whose partners have been
unfaithful : 365 daily meditations /Alice May. — 1st ed.
ISBN 0–06–251804–6 (paper)
1. Adultery—Psychological aspects. 2. Betrayal—Psychological aspects.
3. Wives—Psychology. 4. Wives—Religious life. 5. Affirmations. I. Title.
HQ806.M365   1999
306.73'6—dc21   99–37159
01 02 03 ❖/RRD(H) 10 9 8 7 6 5 4 3 2

This book is dedicated with love and gratitude to Lynne, who first lit the path to God; to Dianne, who walked me through the crisis; to Kay, who loved me through it; to Becky, who had no idea she was teaching me that helping someone else helps me, too; and for showing up when I needed them most, to Kathy, Deb, Carol, Marsha, Nancy, Denise, Evelyn, and, of course, the three Susans. Whatever I have to share came from all of you, and from God.

MY STORY

I DIDN'T CRINGE WHEN I CELEBRATED MY FORTIETH BIRTHDAY.
I told my friends I'd felt forty all my life and couldn't wait to finally feel
comfortable in my own skin.

Thankfully, at that time, I had absolutely no idea how God intended
to accomplish that.

Two months later, my mother was dead, I'd discovered that my husband was having an affair, and I'd collected every painkiller left in my
mother's condo, fully intending to swallow them.

Things grew bleaker as I discovered just how insane one person can
become while trying to monitor, control, or change the behavior of
someone else. I started following my husband to make sure he was going
where he said he was going. When that didn't work, I spent money I
needed for the mortgage payments to have him followed. I eaves-
dropped on his telephone conversations. I opened his mail and searched
his office. I was obsessed. I *had* to know the truth.

I don't know why I bothered. As soon as I found out the "Truth of the
Day," I would confront him with it, then gratefully and eagerly listen to
his vows that things would be different. But nothing changed. How
could it have?

I spent years in this frantic, suspicious, anxious state before I could
really face what was going on: I was married to a man obsessed with
affairs and pornography.

My husband's sexual compulsions brought me to my knees. I felt I had
hit an emotional, spiritual—even a physical—bottom. I couldn't sleep. I
worried constantly. I felt I had lost my very soul. My state of mind was a
far cry from that fortieth birthday when I thought I had the world by the
tail.

Sure, my husband was soul-sick, but I, too, had become emotionally and spiritually ill. I felt shattered in every way imaginable and couldn't see any way to return to normal. How was I to regain my lost self-confidence, my enjoyment of life, my trust in my husband and myself? How could I do those things when I couldn't even leave the house without panicking? How could I decide whether we had a marriage worth working on when I couldn't even decide what to wear each morning?

I was devastated. I was angry. I knew beyond a doubt that I could never again trust anyone. I felt less a woman than I'd ever felt. I felt betrayed not only by my husband but by God—especially by God. How could such things happen? Where had God been?

The only thing I knew for certain was that I had to talk to other women who had been where I was. Women who knew the pain of infidelity, who knew the isolation and the breakdown of intimacy that come when sexual betrayal enters a relationship. Finding those women so I could learn how they made it out of the darkness became my new obsession.

I had little luck with my search. It's no surprise that women don't talk openly about this kind of betrayal. I kept digging. I made telephone calls. I wrote letters. The closest support group meeting I could find was a half-day away. So I got on the phone again, running up a long-distance bill talking to women all over the country who had survived betrayal. Their solutions spoke to my broken heart, but I was still hungry to look another woman in the eyes and see myself, to listen to her story and hear my own.

I eventually scheduled a meeting in my den, quietly getting the word out in my community in a variety of ways, wondering if anyone would show up, knowing I couldn't hang on alone much longer.

The first night, two other women came, as bewildered and devastated as I was. I was so grateful I cried. For the first time in months, I began to believe I might survive. The second week, there were three of us. Within six months, there were seven of us, women no longer willing to play the role of victim in an unhealthy situation that everyone wants to keep secret. Today we have a dozen regular members, with new women showing up each month.

We are healing together, finding help and hope and spiritual solutions to our problems. Together we are regaining parts of ourselves we never expected to know again—our self-confidence, our joy, and our ability to laugh and love, to name just a few. Some of us are still married, some have ended the relationship that brought us together, and some are still in the process of finding answers. But we are all healing. We have all been changed by our experiences, and for the better.

Today, although I am now closer to fifty than forty, I know I'm attractive and desirable. I also know that's a lot less important than I once imagined it was. I've learned how to love my husband without expecting him to be the source of all my happiness. I've learned to let go of fear. I've rediscovered God and know how to live my life by spiritual principles such as honesty and forgiveness and personal responsibility. I've learned how to make choices that lead to serenity. I've learned how to get the love I need. Some of it I get from myself, which is something I had always had trouble doing before.

And I've learned a little bit—more all the time, I hope—about healthy sexuality.

With the help of the women I've met along my healing journey, I've learned that no matter how low and degrading the events in my life seem to me, there is hope. I've learned that the worst parts of my life will be transformed and made beautifully whole. Because of my experience and the experiences of many others, I know now there is hope for all of us who are looking for a way out of the darkness.

It is my hope that my experience and those of my fellow survivors can help you find a new source of strength. The lessons that come out of this most devastating ordeal can be the most profound gifts of a lifetime.

Alice May
December 1999

WHAT YOU FEED WILL GROW

Betrayal takes many forms.

Some of us have been betrayed with pornography or prostitutes, fantasies with which we can't compete. For some of us, the other woman takes on many faces—one-night stands, the co-worker, our best friend, or faceless names on the Internet.

All forms of sexual betrayal reflect unhealthy emotions in our partner. And because we are touched by it daily, we, too, become emotionally unhealthy. *Our* illness shows itself in many ways also. We obsess, we rage, we stalk, we withdraw, we bury ourselves in denial or work. The one unavoidable constant is our pain.

But we can choose what to do while we're in our pain.

We can try to ignore it, to bury it so deeply inside that for the moment we can't feel it. Others of us may focus on our pain, magnify it, hanging on to our victimhood.

Or we can choose to focus on the behaviors that will free us from our pain, behaviors that will bring us relief, healing, recovery. We can choose counseling or prayer. We can focus on forgiveness. We can find the support of healthy people who understand our pain because they've been where we are.

What we feed will grow; let us feed recovery.

TODAY I WILL RESPOND TO THE UNHEALTHY CIRCUMSTANCES IN MY LIFE WITH HEALTHY BEHAVIORS. I WILL FEED MY SPIRIT. I WILL BEGIN THE PROCESS OF HEALING.

WHAT'S WRONG WITH ME?

What's wrong with me, that the lies went on so long and I didn't have a clue?

What's wrong with me, that I picked a man like this in the first place?

Once the denial has ended and we see the truth, we sometimes begin to ask ourselves questions like these.

How could I have been so stupid?

Questions like these are simply one more way to blame ourselves. And we don't deserve the blame for a situation we didn't create. We didn't cause his behavior.

Let us repeat that as often as we need to in order to convince ourselves: *We didn't cause it.*

But sometimes we still need to understand why we were so easily deceived, why we stayed in denial as long as we did. That is how the process of spiritual healing can help. The healing journey asks us to look at ourselves, to take the focus off our partner long enough to find the face of our own dysfunction. We seek the truth about what made us such perfect partners in this dance of deceit. And when we know the truth, we no longer need to be a part of the deception.

TODAY I BEGIN A JOURNEY THAT WILL HELP ME SEE WHY I AM IN THIS RELATIONSHIP. I WILL BEGIN THIS JOURNEY NOT TO BLAME MYSELF, BUT TO TAKE RESPONSIBILITY FOR MYSELF AND MY HAPPINESS. I DIDN'T CAUSE THIS MISERY. BUT I CAN CAUSE IT TO END.

EMOTIONAL NUMBNESS

Most of us experience some degree of emotional numbness as the truth about our partner unfolds. For most of us, this numbness is temporary and protective. We will feel more as it is safer for us.

For others, the numbness has become a key tool for coping with life's pain.

Remaining emotionally numb for the long term is damaging. We lose touch not only with our negative emotions but with our positive ones as well. We may be saved from feeling the raw anguish of betrayal, but a part of us is also shut off from life's joys.

The real danger, however, is that when we become numb we allow the pain to continue. We do nothing to protect ourselves. We no longer draw back instinctively when we are burned.

When that happens, we end up more severely burned.

On this journey, we will find others who understand our circumstances; we will listen to their stories. We will hear their pain even if we can't fully understand it. Eventually, we will share our stories. We will learn to use the tools of acceptance and choice and self-examination. Eventually, our numbness will begin to be replaced by emotion.

This hurts. Our first instinct may be to flinch, to retreat into numbness again.

If we are committed to healing our lives, we will find the courage to move forward. We will be delivered from our half life to a full life. And the joys of a full life outweigh the temporary discomfort we will experience on the journey.

I WON'T GET FROM THIS PLACE OF NUMBNESS TO A PLACE OF TRUE EMOTION WITHOUT EXPERIENCING THE PAIN I'VE SUPPRESSED. BUT I CAN GET THROUGH IT. I CAN REACH JOY AND FREEDOM.

ALICE MAY

THE HEALING PROCESS

Healing is a process. A simple process. Simple, not easy.

Beginning now, our anger and fear and pain are calling us to a journey. A healing journey, a never-ending journey that leads us toward a life of peace and emotional security. To a heart that is healed and whole.

The process is not a formula and will unfold differently for each of us. But a few simple, enduring principles will guide our progress.

The first of these is surrender.

All we need to begin our journey is a willingness to acknowledge the mess our lives are in today. We can admit defeat. We have battled another person's demons, and that is a fight we are doomed to lose. Now we can see that, and we are willing to ask for help. Surrender is a relief.

Once we get that honest, once we've tried everything we know to try and nothing has worked, we are ready to seek the help of others who have traveled this painful path. Some of us may even be ready to seek help from God. When we ask for help, from whatever source we seek it, we will receive everything we need for this first stage of our journey.

TODAY I SURRENDER ANY LINGERING BELIEFS THAT I CAN HAN-DLE MY DIFFICULTIES ALONE. I RECOGNIZE AND ACCEPT MY LIM-ITATIONS. I AM WILLING TO ACCEPT THE HELP OF OTHERS, THE HELP THE UNIVERSE OFFERS, PERHAPS EVEN THE HELP THAT COMES FROM A POWER GREATER THAN HUMAN POWER.

WHY GOD?

Some of us wonder how strengthening our spiritual lives can help at a time like this. Infidelity is a worldly problem and its aftermath doesn't leave us with the time or the energy or the emotion to work on a connection with God. That, we may think, will have to wait for a better day.

One answer is that the problems we face are too debilitating for human power to handle alone. We need help. *Big* help. Another answer is that infidelity is essentially a spiritual disease. A person who is unfaithful is spiritually anemic, and his disease affects the entire family.

On a more down-to-earth level, of course, the final answer is that we have tried everything else we can think of to do. We've pleaded and threatened and seduced and raged and withdrawn and manipulated. We have emptied our bag of tricks trying to change our partner's behavior.

None of it worked.

For many of us, there is only one place to turn. And that is to God.

We may have little practice in allowing God into our lives. Maybe we still aren't convinced that a spiritual solution is the answer. Either way, we need new tools that will enable us to recover our spirits. Even those of us who already live a life of faith sometimes realize that we aren't as connected to a higher source as we need to be to survive the crisis.

But we can be, if we are willing. And if we are willing, we will begin to understand why spiritual solutions work even in such worldly circumstances.

TODAY I WILL BE OPEN TO SPIRITUAL SOLUTIONS. THAT DOESN'T MEAN I HAVE TO BELIEVE IN ANY KIND OF GOD TODAY, OR EVER. IT SIMPLY MEANS THAT TODAY I RECOGNIZE THAT MY SPIRIT HAS BEEN DAMAGED AND I AM READY FOR MY SPIRIT TO HEAL.

ALICE MAY

THE LAST TO KNOW

The friends and family who knew the truth but never told us may look to us like accomplices in our betrayal. If they cared about us at all, how could they leave us in the dark? Surely they owed it to us to tell.

Being the last to know is humiliating and infuriating.

Today our challenge is to understand that friends and family who do not tell are making the best decision they can in a very difficult situation. They are caught in the middle. They are betraying someone they care about, risking somebody's anger, no matter what they do. We can't count on friends or family members to have a clear picture of our inner lives, thus making such a decision simple and straightforward.

Today we are also beginning to understand that we may have thought we were ready for the truth before it came to us. But rarely is that so. Most of us see the truth as soon as our hearts and spirits are prepared for the struggle ahead. The signs are there. We will read them when we are ready. Others do us no favors by forcing us to look at something we aren't yet ready to face.

We will work to let go of our anger at those who knew but didn't tell. We will understand that their silence was the best decision they could make. And it may have been the best decision for us as well.

TODAY I WILL TRY TO SEE THAT MY FRIENDS AND FAMILY HAVE NOT WRONGED ME. I DON'T NEED TO EXTEND MY ANGER TO INCLUDE THEM.

STOP BELIEVING THE LIES

When the pain is great enough, we can stop believing the lies.

We've all heard the lies. We've built our lives around them. We've made ourselves emotionally—and sometimes physically—ill over them.

All men do this. It really doesn't mean anything.

This will never happen again.

This would never have happened in the first place if I were thinner/more fun/prettier/less inhibited/younger.

I'm imagining things. It isn't happening.

Sometimes we believed the lies because the truth sounded too preposterous. Or because we'd heard them so long they had the ring of truth. Sometimes we believed them because we weren't yet strong enough to look the truth in the eye.

When the pain overwhelms us, the time is right to move into truth and healing. At first, it may be hard to know when we're hearing the truth and when our fear is asking us to believe more lies. At first, the truth may hurt so much that denial looks attractive once again.

But once we've glimpsed the possibility of recovering from a loved one's unfaithfulness, we can't turn away from it. We can't turn back. We can only move forward, and through to a place where the truth—our truth—finally heals our pain.

All men don't do this.

This never has to happen again.

This has nothing to do with how thin or pretty or fun or uninhibited or young I am. I didn't cause this.

I didn't make this up. I'm not crazy.

TODAY I WILL ACCEPT ONLY THE TRUTH. I WILL NOT LIVE BY UNTRUTH ANY LONGER. I AM STRONG ENOUGH TO SEEK THE TRUTH.

ALICE MAY

SEEKING A SOURCE OF HOPE

We don't all have a relationship with God. And just because our lives are in crisis doesn't make us ready to find one—in fact, for some of us this blow merely confirms our worst suspicions about God.

Yet we're being asked to turn to some source of strength outside ourselves. We're being asked to seek help and courage and healing from that source.

Some of us will call that source God. Others of us can't do that today.

On my own journey, I didn't want anything to do with God at first. I didn't think much of the way God was running the universe. The only scrap of belief I had was in the healing power of love. I vaguely sensed that all people are linked by some kind of universal love that could see us through our lives.

For those of us who aren't willing to turn to God, there are countless other ways to tap into strength and hope that are beyond our power to achieve alone. One woman I know speaks to the Wise Woman within her, the one she had ignored for so long; another finds a Universal Spirit in nature; another simply relies on the support of the group of women who are seeing her through this crisis. And one person who doesn't trust the God she learned about as a child directs her prayers to a higher power she calls Gladys.

Each of these people has simply become willing to look for answers from a higher spirit, a spirit undiminished by the pain of betrayal. And as they do so, they begin to heal. They begin to believe there is a power that will serve them well, if they are willing to reach out for help.

TODAY I WILL TURN TO A SOURCE BEYOND MY LIMITED HUMAN POWERS FOR HELP. WHETHER I CALL THAT POWER GOD OR UNIVERSAL SPIRIT OR THE WISE WOMAN WITHIN, I WILL BE OPEN TO THE DIRECTION AND HEALING I WILL RECEIVE.

Surviving Betrayal

ALLOWING HIM TO GO

When his infidelity first came out into the open, my husband announced that he wanted to separate, that it was all over. I reacted by doing everything I could think of to convince him otherwise. I used every kind of logic, every emotional ploy, every bit of pressure I could bring to bear to get him to change his mind.

I lost my self-respect, and I certainly didn't change his mind.

Wanting him to stay was part of my insanity. And part of his was that he remained adamant about leaving until I gave up and said, "Fine. Go. Now." Then he decided to stay.

The point is that we cannot change our partner's mind if he is determined to go. We are free to tell him why we think our family would be better off if we stayed together. But even if we manage to get him to stay put against his will, he will be gone in spirit. We will have accomplished very little except to give him one more reason to resent us.

If he is determined to leave, we are better off letting him leave, keeping our own dignity intact. As hard as it is to allow him to walk away, giving him room to make his mistakes gains us so much more than trying to control him. Because trying to control him merely confirms his conviction that we are the reason he is so miserable in the first place.

Let him go if he insists it is what he wants. Wrap yourself in dignity and treat him with respect as well. If he returns, you will have the satisfaction of knowing it is because he understands now that you are the one he wants to be with. If he does not return, you will have minimized the conflict. Either way, you will not have degraded yourself.

SOMETIMES THE ONLY THING I CAN DO TO MAINTAIN MY SELF-RESPECT IS THE THING THAT HURTS THE MOST AT THE MOMENT. I WILL FIND THE COURAGE TO LET HIM GO IF THAT IS WHAT HE INSISTS HE WANTS.

ALICE MAY

RESURRECT OUR SPIRIT

He may choose behaviors that degrade him, but those behaviors don't have to degrade us as well.

His behaviors don't have the power to bring us down, unless we choose to let them. His behaviors don't have the power to destroy our spirit, unless we choose to let them. They may hurt us, but they cannot destroy us without our cooperation.

What sometimes happens when we live long enough with another person's dysfunctional, unhealthy behavior is that we grow unhealthy ourselves. We begin to choose behaviors that demean us, that destroy our spirit. Some of us drink too much to dull the pain. Or we seek revenge in the arms of other men. Some of us snoop and spy. We comfort ourselves with too much food or deprive ourselves of necessary nourishment. We cling to compulsive behaviors of our own until we are numb to the pain.

When we do this, we have degraded ourselves. We don't need him to do it for us.

It is time to stop degrading ourselves.

TODAY I CAN EASE THE PAIN BY DOING HEALTHY THINGS FOR MYSELF THAT HELP ME LEARN AND GROW. I CAN MAKE THE CHOICE NOT TO DEGRADE MYSELF.

RELIEF FROM THE PAIN

How long will it hurt?

What most of us want more than anything is for the pain to stop. And we want it to stop now. But we eventually learn there is nothing healthy we can do to make the pain go away quickly. Healing is a gradual process. And anything we do to force an immediate solution is likely to create more pain in the long run.

How long will it hurt?

Sometimes it will hurt until our partner realizes his mistake and works on repairing the damage. Sometimes it will hurt until we make up our minds to accept the reality of what has happened. Sometimes it will hurt until we've finished the normal grieving process. It may be a week, a month, a year. Or more. Sometimes we think the pain has eased and something happens to open the wound again.

How long will it hurt?

The truest answer is that the healing process is different for each of us, and the outcome isn't predictable. There are no shortcuts and no sure-fire formulas. Live with the pain, accept its reality, and practice healing behaviors, until the hurt begins to ease. The way is not over, but through.

TODAY I WON'T LOOK FOR A QUICK FIX FOR MY PAIN. I UNDER-STAND THAT HEALING WILL TAKE TIME. I UNDERSTAND THAT NO ONE CAN TELL ME HOW MUCH TIME IT WILL TAKE. I WILL STOP EXPECTING IMMEDIATE RELIEF.

THE NEED TO KNOW EVERYTHING

How much do we really want to know?

Some of us are certain, at first, that we need to know every detail of his sexual behavior. Others can't bear to hear it. In this painful new territory we travel, the experiences of others can guide us. Here is wisdom from other women who have survived betrayal:

- "Having all the information in the world never did enable me to take action, to say, 'Enough!' The only way I got there was by working with other women and learning to trust God with my marriage."

- "Do I know that he's told me everything? No, he hasn't. I know there's more, but I don't want to know the details. I only want to know that he's trying to change and to make this marriage work."

- "I had a counselor who said, 'Don't go there.' But I felt that the nightmares I would create in my mind would be a lot worse than the truth. So I asked him for all the details, and I wrote it all down. For a while, that was my insurance policy. But eventually, his willingness to tell me everything and to go over it as many times as I needed to gave me confidence that he was ready to get honest. Last Christmas, we made a ceremony out of burning all my records."

Perhaps we can examine our motives. Do we want something to hold over his head? Or do we want to know the worst so we can put it all behind us? Understanding our true motives is often a key to resolving a difficult dilemma.

TODAY I WILL GET HONEST WITH MYSELF BEFORE I DECIDE HOW MUCH I WANT TO KNOW ABOUT MY PARTNER'S BEHAVIOR. I WILL MAKE A DECISION BASED ON WHAT WILL FURTHER MY HEALING.

ADMITTING THAT YOU CAN'T CONTROL HIM

To begin our journey into healing and spiritual growth, we must first admit that we cannot control our partner's sexual behavior, wherever it takes him and however much pain it causes us. We must acknowledge our helplessness in the face of our partner's betrayal.

And for most of us, the idea that we can do nothing about our situation is terrifying.

Surely, we think, there is something we can do. We can behave provocatively enough to make him want only us. We can lose a little weight. Have a face lift. We can open his credit card statements and make sure he isn't spending money where he isn't supposed to. We can destroy his pornography or harass his girlfriend or enlist ministers, parents, siblings, and friends to apply pressure.

None of those things worked to keep our partner faithful. But we told ourselves that the next little bit of insanity we tried would be the tactic that worked.

We know today that the beginning of our healing is to give up the idea that we can change him—to give it up wholeheartedly, holding nothing back. If we hold on to one shred of hope that we can fix things, we've made a decision to live in the problem a little longer instead of moving forward to live in the solution.

WHEN I FINALLY ADMIT MY POWERLESSNESS OVER HIS CHOICES, THE WEIGHT IS LIFTED FROM MY SHOULDERS. I HAVE SURRENDERED THE PROBLEM, AND THAT MAKES ME READY TO ACCEPT THE SOLUTION.

UNMANAGEABLE LIVES

For many of us, the recognition that our lives are spiraling out of control is what drives us to seek help in coping with someone else's infidelity or other compulsive sexual behaviors.

When we decide we've had enough, it is because we've been brought to our knees, broken by the weight of the burden we've carried.

What are some signs that our lives are beyond control? Some of us become physically ill. We can't eat; we have headaches or ulcers or chest pains. We have panic attacks. Some of us have isolated ourselves so that no one else can get close enough to see the ugliness in our lives. Some of us can't work, can't keep house, can't be around our children without screaming, can't deal with life without a little wine or a lot of fudge ripple.

We are falling apart, and sometimes we can't even see it. If we do see it, sometimes the only way we can imagine to put ourselves back together is to redouble our efforts to do the very things that are killing us in the first place.

We can't kid ourselves any longer. If we don't seek help, if we don't commit ourselves to finding a new way to cope, this unmanageability will kill us.

The way to stop kidding ourselves is to *give up everything we've been doing. It doesn't work. We don't have the answers. We are powerless.*

Once we've admitted that, we're on the path to finding the source of true power.

TODAY I SEE HOW OUT OF CONTROL MY LIFE HAS BECOME WHILE I'VE TRIED TO CONTROL SOMEONE ELSE. I WILL GIVE UP ONE THING I'VE DONE OVER AND OVER BECAUSE TODAY I CAN SEE THAT IT WON'T WORK NEXT TIME ANY BETTER THAN IT WORKED LAST TIME OR THE TIME BEFORE THAT. TODAY I WILL TRY SOMETHING NEW. SOMETHING HEALTHY.

KEEPING SECRETS

Secrets are a safe hiding place for emotional disease. Secrets enable us to lie to ourselves and keep us isolated from the truth. Secrets drive a wedge between us and everything healthy in life—friends, family, even our own emotional well-being.

We don't admit to ourselves that our partner has been unfaithful. We don't admit it to others. We don't admit how much drinking goes on in our home, or the incest in our family of origin. We believe that our secrets are so ugly that no one could understand. We believe that if we hide the truth, it no longer has power over our lives.

Once we begin seeking the truth, many of us who have ended up in chronically unhealthy relationships discover that we have spent much of our lives fostering secrets. Keeping the secrets under wraps was so much easier than dragging them out of the closet.

When we connect with others who share the same secrets, we learn that one way to rob a secret of its power over us is to expose it.

We can tell the truth to others who share our problems, and we won't be judged. We can tell the truth to them, and the world will not come to an end. We can tell the truth, and we are free. When we shed light on our secrets, we can see them for the first time for what they are: a trap that ensnares us in our own sick thinking.

TODAY I WILL BEGIN TO ROB MY SECRETS OF THEIR POWER BY EXPOSING THEM TO THE LIGHT OF SOMEONE ELSE'S UNDER-STANDING. I WILL FIND SOMEONE I TRUST AND SHARE ONE, SMALL SECRET. AND I WILL FEEL THE RELIEF.

WHO IS YOUR HIGHER POWER?

If we entrust ourselves to the care of a loving God or higher power, we can be sure that whatever we need for today will be provided.

The problem is that many of us have turned our partner into our higher power.

We may not like the sound of that. Of course, we know our partner isn't a God. Far from it. But the hard reality is that many of us have given our partner control of our lives.

We do that in so many ways. We believe that if we make him happy, then we will be happy. We believe that we will be safe as long as he is taking care of us. We think that we will always have the love we need as long as he is around, no matter what kind of behavior we must endure. We think that if we mold ourselves to meet his needs, all will be well. And worst, we believe that his love is denied to us because *we* are somehow at fault.

No matter how many times we've been proven wrong, we cling to these old beliefs. The focus of our lives, the goal of our existence, is to hang on to this person whom we have made the center of our universe.

And anything that becomes the center of our universe has become our higher power.

If we made a list of all the qualities we want in a God, would we include dishonesty, unreliability, weakness, immaturity, imperfection, and lack of compassion? If this isn't the kind of higher power we're looking for, isn't it time we stop allowing our partner to fill that role in our lives?

IT IS TIME TO LOOK FOR A HIGHER POWER WHO WILL NEVER BETRAY ME, WHO WILL ALWAYS LOVE ME UNCONDITIONALLY, AND WHO WANTS ONLY THE BEST FOR ME.

LOVING FEELINGS

Loving him at a time like this feels so wrong. So weak. So self-destructive. Surely a strong, confident woman could walk out without regret.

But sometimes, even in our pain, we feel the love. And that is okay. That doesn't make us wrong or weak. It isn't a cause for shame.

None of our feelings are wrong. Feelings are not facts, they are not defects in our character, they do not brand us in any way. They are simply a reflection of what is in our hearts. And at times like this, our hearts are bound to be filled with more conflicting emotions than we know how to handle.

It is okay to be confused about how we feel. It is okay to be sure that we love him one minute and to know without a doubt that we hate him the next minute. These are only feelings. And even though others may have told us that our feelings are wrong, they are not. We are free to have our feelings and to sort through them over time.

If we feel love today, if we remember the good times even when our pain overwhelms us, we don't have to judge ourselves. Hope is not a weakness. And love is never shameful.

I CAN FOCUS ON MY HEALING TODAY WITHOUT JUDGING MYSELF FOR ANY OF MY EMOTIONS, INCLUDING ANY LOVING FEELINGS I MAY HAVE FOR MY PARTNER.

BUILD A NETWORK OF SUPPORT

Don't expect your friends to be understanding and supportive at a time like this. Some will and some won't. Most will disappoint you at some point during this process, simply because this problem is so overwhelming that it stirs up the worst in all of us at one time or another. So the less you expect, the less likely you are to lose a friend at a time when too much is already lost.

We can learn to choose carefully the people in whom we confide. People who don't know us that well but who know our circumstances from the inside out because of their own personal history can be more objective and therefore more helpful than our best friend since high school.

With the help of a counselor or a minister or even a local women's organization, we can make contact with people who share our circumstances. We can build a network of support, start meeting with others who are willing to seek positive solutions to one of life's most painful circumstances.

With the right network of supportive friends, we can be more tolerant and understanding when our longtime friends are too opinionated or too protective or too angry to really be there for us.

TODAY I WILL TAKE SOME ACTION TO CONNECT WITH OTHERS WHO HAVE EXPERIENCED WHAT I AM GOING THROUGH. I WILL LOOK FOR SUPPORT FROM THOSE WHO UNDERSTAND BECAUSE THEY'VE WALKED THE SAME PATH.

SURRENDER YOUR LOSS

When we first learn that we've been betrayed by someone we love and trust, that event takes on such magnitude that it leaves room for little else in our hearts. It becomes the sun around which everything in our personal universe revolves.

We define ourselves by what someone else has done. We live our life under that shadow. We forget that the rest of our life continues, and that many parts of it need not be destroyed by this single event.

My partner's infidelity is but one event in my life. I also have work I enjoy, even if concentrating on that work is harder for a while. I have others who love me, as well as others whom I love, and I do them and myself a disservice if I suddenly act as if their love means nothing because one person has disappointed me. I have the quilt my grandmother made, a favorite CD, and my cat's squeaky voice when she rubs against my ankles, all of which bring me comfort and joy and moments that feel warm and safe. I have a best friend who walks with me and points out the delights in my neighborhood—the purple chair sitting on someone's porch, the clown face drawn on the sidewalk in fat pink chalk, the tiny crocus buds as they nudge up out of the ground in late winter.

And I still have my faith in the hand of a loving God, acting in my life to ease my pain.

Even if something we've long treasured has been taken from us—for the moment or forever—our life is still full of gifts and grace.

TODAY I WILL SURRENDER MY LOSS AND SPEND TEN MINUTES IN A QUIET, PEACEFUL PLACE REMEMBERING ALL THE BLESSINGS THAT REMAIN.

ALICE MAY

BEING SEXUAL AFTERWARD

One of the hardest questions to answer as we try to cope with infidelity is what place physical intimacy has in our relationship.

Do we make love with a man who has betrayed us? If we don't make love, are we giving him justification to act out sexually again? Are we crazy to still want this man?

One way I've learned to get at the answers is to ask another question I've learned from women who seek spiritual solutions to their pain: *What are my motives?*

If we check our motives whenever we wrestle with a dilemma, the solutions present themselves with less struggle.

Do we want to be sexual to express our love and our hope for healing our relationship? Or do we consider being sexual out of fear that he'll go elsewhere if we don't? Do we think we can control his behavior by our behavior in bed?

Do we want to abstain from making love because our hearts are too bruised to feel any love at the moment? Or do we abstain to punish him, to rub his nose in his guilt every night?

Checking our motives requires honesty, and honesty isn't easy after a period of living in denial and dysfunction. But if we seek it sincerely, discussing our situation with someone who has been where we are today and listening to our own wise spirit, we can trust that the right answers—the honest answers—will present themselves.

SOMETIMES MAKING LOVE IS THE RIGHT ANSWER. SOMETIMES ABSTAINING IS THE RIGHT ANSWER. WHICHEVER PATH I TAKE, IF I'VE DONE IT WITH THE BEST INTENTIONS, I'M NOT WRONG, I'M NOT INADEQUATE, I'M NOT CRAZY. I AM SAFE.

LETTING GO

When you get to the end of your rope, let go.

You don't have to hold on until your hands are raw and your shoulders scream in pain. You don't have to hold on even when you think you're the only one keeping the world from slipping over the edge. You don't have to hold on simply because you don't know how far down you'll fall if you let go.

Let go. Release your grip. Turn loose of your problems, your fears, your certainty that only you can salvage the situation.

Let go. Once you let go, you'll find that hitting bottom is the easy part.

It was hanging on that caused all the pain.

TODAY I WILL EXPERIENCE THE RELIEF THAT COMES WITH LET-
TING GO OF ONE SMALL PART OF MY LIFE, SOMETHING I'VE BEEN
GRIPPING SO TIGHTLY IT HURT. I WILL TELL MYSELF I CAN'T FIX
THE SITUATION AND I WILL LET GO.

ALICE MAY

ABANDONMENT

Abandonment feels like death. Or worse.

In fact, for many of us, death sometimes sounds like a better alternative than abandonment.

When our partner betrays us or leaves us for someone else, that often feels like the most devastating abandonment of all. Some of us have even felt that burying our partner would be easier than watching him leave for someone else. Being a widow attracts sympathy and dignity and honor. Being the discarded partner, we feel, strips us of every bit of our worth.

Abandonment is so intense that the pain is almost physical, like a withdrawal from that which sustained us. We actually believe we might die. On some deep level, we believe we cannot survive without this person.

It isn't so. We can survive.

When this person is out of our life, we will continue to breathe in and out, to eat and sleep and wake. In fact, the truth is that when this person is out of our life, we can finally learn to do more than survive. We can learn to live again. We can make room for our spirits to grow.

TODAY I WILL REMEMBER THAT OTHERS MAY TAKE THEMSELVES OUT OF MY LIFE, BUT THAT DOES NOT MEAN I DON'T HAVE A LIFE. IT DOES NOT MEAN THAT I HAVE BEEN ABANDONED BY ALL THAT IS GOOD AND WORTHWHILE IN MY LIFE.

WHEN THE PAIN IS RAW

What do I do now? Where do I turn? What am I supposed to feel?

When we first learn of our partner's actions, we are so shocked or numbed or disbelieving that we hardly know how to behave. Asked what they wish someone had said to them when their circumstances were fresh, women had this to say:

- "There is hope. You can survive this. It's not an overnight thing, but hang on to that hope. That's what people did say to me. And when I left my first meeting of our support group, it was the first time in months I'd really believed I could survive this."

- "It's not a good idea to make decisions while you're bleeding to death. Give yourself six months, and don't make any decisions about your situation, unless you're in danger. At first, most of us don't know what we want, and we don't have the strength to do it if we did."

- "Find someone who has been where you are and listen and ask questions and listen. It's a comfort just knowing we aren't crazy, that our emotions are normal under the circumstances."

- "Cry. Throw things. Talk until you're hoarse. Let your feelings out. I kept it all bottled up because I still thought it was important to look in control on the outside. It isn't."

We all want answers today, but sometimes the best help is in knowing that we aren't unique in our circumstances or our feelings. There is comfort in hearing from women who have survived. There is comfort in their experiences, in their strength, and in their hope.

TODAY I HAVE MORE OPTIONS THAN I REALIZED. I CAN DEAL WITH MY EMOTIONS OPENLY, I CAN TALK AND LISTEN TO OTHERS, I CAN WAIT BEFORE MAKING DECISIONS. AND I CAN HAVE HOPE.

ALICE MAY

IMPRISONED BY RESENTMENTS

Hanging on to a resentment, someone once said, is like drinking poison and hoping it will kill someone else.

That reminds me that if I cling to my anger and ill will over the wrongs I feel someone has done to me, the one I hurt the most is myself. When I relive, over and over in my mind, the moments when I've been deceived and humiliated, when I let myself mentally toy with those times, who am I injuring? Does the person I am obsessing over even have a clue what is going on in my head?

No, that person is free. I am the one imprisoned by my resentment.

The mind is so powerful that when we re-create an event in our thoughts, our bodies react as if the event were happening now. Experience that the next time you watch a movie. You know you're watching performers act out a script. But your body exhibits the symptoms of fear or anger or passion or joy depicted on the screen. In the same way, when we relive an old wound, we can tie our guts in a knot. We can give ourselves blinding, throbbing headaches. Our hearts will race, our blood will boil. All because of our thinking.

We can't change the past, but we can change our thinking. We can think healing thoughts. We can think of mending and renewal and take the actions that make it reality. We can think forgiveness. We can think gratitude for what we do have today, instead of bitterness over what we've lost.

When we do that, we, too, are free of whatever wrong others have done us.

TODAY I WILL RECOGNIZE THE IMPORTANCE OF NOT POISONING MY SPIRIT BY HANGING ON TO OLD ANGER. I WILL SEEK HELP IN DEVELOPING NEW TOOLS FOR LETTING GO OF RESENTMENTS.

LIVE IN TODAY

Women who have reached the other side of this process encourage us to take things one day at a time. To live in this moment. To keep our heads where our feet are.

When we want to obsess over the past or the future, we can bring ourselves back to the present by asking, *What can I do about that right now? Is there some action I can take? A decision I can make today? A telephone call to set a solution in motion? Something concrete I can accomplish right this minute?* If there is, we do it.

If there is nothing we can do, we let it go, either through prayer or by talking to someone else until we have a clearer perspective. If there is no action we can take, the only positive action open to us is let the problem go for this moment. If we feel a connection to God or a higher power, we can surrender the situation to that power.

Then, whether we've taken some action or surrendered the problem, we can move on to the rest of this day's concerns. Preparing for a staff meeting. Dealing with a sink full of dirty dishes. Returning telephone calls or paying bills or volunteering at the kids' school. If we surrender yesterday and tomorrow, we find that we once again have energy for today. We no longer feel overwhelmed and scattered and out of control.

TODAY IS MANAGEABLE, AS LONG AS I STAY HERE. I WILL TRY NOT TO RETURN IN MY MIND TO YESTERDAY'S PROBLEMS OR TRAVEL AHEAD TO FEARS ABOUT TOMORROW. I WILL DEAL WITH THIS DAY, OR THIS HOUR, OR THIS MOMENT, IF THAT IS ALL I CAN MANAGE.

FORCING DECISIONS

When our life lies in pieces at our feet, what most of us want to know is how to put it back together. We want answers, and we want them now.

Do I leave him? Do I stay? Do I fight to get him back from the other woman? Do I forgive and forget?

Making decisions is never easy. Doing so at a chaotic turning point in our lives is almost impossible. Our minds are on overload. Our hearts are bruised. Our best judgment—you know, the part of us that once said this was a man we could trust with our hearts—is suspect. What do we do? Where do we turn? And how soon can we get out of this turmoil?

If we force ourselves to make decisions at times like this, we may find ourselves living with the consequences of poor judgment somewhere down the line. We may grow the most in times of pain and unrest, but we don't do our best thinking then.

At those times, we can pause, take a deep breath. We can listen to others who have shared our problem. We can remind ourselves over and over that it is okay to live with uncertainty, to put one foot in front of the other even when we can't see where that foot is going to land.

But we don't do anything irrevocable. We don't make a hasty decision. We don't listen to that frantic voice in our head that says we've got to do something *now*. Instead, we sit still until the clamoring voice dies down and we can once again hear the still, quiet voice of our heart.

THE VOICE OF MY INNER WISDOM COMES TO ME FROM SEREN-ITY, NOT CHAOS. TODAY I WILL WAIT FOR THE NOISE TO DIE DOWN BEFORE I ACT. WHEN I DO, IT IS MORE LIKELY THAT I WILL ACT OUT OF WISDOM.

DWELLING IN THE DARKNESS

All that is best and brightest in our world is born in darkness.

This pattern repeats itself again and again in nature. The butterfly must spend time in the cocoon before it is born as a shimmering creature of light and color. The tulips of early spring endure an entire winter underground, in the cold and the darkness. Even infants need time in the darkness to prepare for the miracle of their birth.

Growing from the darkness into the light is nature's way.

And so it is with our spirits, with our souls. Our job in this lifetime is to grow our souls, and we don't do that in bright sunshine. We do it in those bleak midnights when even the prayer of daybreak is beyond us, requiring more emotional energy than we have to imagine. We grow our souls when life breaks us, leaves us bereft and without hope, on our knees in the dark.

We begin the process of becoming the person we want to be at times when we finally accept that we can't even see the far edge of our darkness.

I WILL REACH OUT NOW, FOR IT IS ONLY WHEN IT'S DARKEST THAT I CAN BE WILLING BOTH TO ACCEPT HELP AND TO CHANGE.

COMING UNHINGED

The truth is, trying to cope with a problem too big to handle alone has made us crazy. We act crazy. We think crazy. Deep inside, we are beginning to wonder whether we are slowly but surely going insane.

Our partner has called us crazy often enough. Maybe it's truer than we want to believe.

My dictionary defines sanity as soundness of mind or soundness of judgment.

I only have to remind myself of all the ways in which my actions were out of control to realize that living with sick thinking eventually made my thinking sick, too. My thinking, my actions, my life were haywire. I was operating out of an unsound mind. I see ample evidence of that when I look at some of the things I did in reaction to my husband's infidelity.

I once decided that spending the rest of my life in prison for murdering the other woman wouldn't be so bad. On that day, I had clearly lost any soundness of mind or judgment I might once have had. That was only one of many examples of my insanity.

But the process of spiritual healing promises us something. It promises that we can recoup our emotional health. It promises the possibility of freedom from our particular brand of crazy thinking.

That promise has come true for me, as a result of working on spiritual solutions to healing. It can come true for all of us.

I DON'T HAVE TO GIVE IN TO IRRATIONAL THINKING OR UNSOUND JUDGMENT TODAY. MY JOURNEY TOWARD PEACE AND HEALING PROMISES THAT I CAN REGAIN MY EMOTIONAL HEALTH. TODAY I WILL REMEMBER THAT PROMISE.

SIMPLE BELIEF

The idea of turning to faith for healing frightens some of us. We've been betrayed so often and so easily that believing in anything is frightening. Many of us feel that God has abandoned us; otherwise, none of this would have happened. Some of us never believed in God in the first place.

How can we believe, now of all times?

What helped me begin this process was hearing how some people differentiate between belief and faith. Faith is knowing without doubt, even in the absence of concrete evidence. A very tall order for someone whose life is shattered. But the process of finding help and hope through spiritual solutions doesn't ask us to have faith. It asks us only to believe.

Belief is simply acknowledging a possibility.

Is it possible there is some power greater than us in the world? Is it possible that other people who were betrayed as we were have become whole again, have learned to laugh again, learned to love again, by turning to some power greater than their own? I have seen, in groups of women who have struggled with this problem, that the answer is yes.

Yes, something or someone has made them whole.

Is it possible that what worked for them can work for you?

If you can acknowledge that small possibility, you've moved a little further down the path to recovery and spiritual growth. A little closer to sanity.

TODAY I DON'T HAVE TO HAVE FAITH. TODAY I ONLY NEED TO BELIEVE THAT OTHER WOMEN HAVE BEEN SUPPORTED BY THEIR FAITH AT TIMES LIKE THIS. TODAY I ONLY NEED TO BELIEVE THAT WHAT WORKED FOR THEM MAY WORK FOR ME AS WELL.

THE POWER IN SURRENDER

Surrender is not passive. It is not submissive. It is not another way of losing control of our lives.

There is power in surrender. There is power in saying, *I will no longer waste my energy, my time, my emotions on parts of this world that are not mine to fix in the first place.*

There is power in refusing to sink deeper into the morass of someone else's problems. Courage and strength are required to give up the losing battle to control another person's behavior and take up, instead, the struggle to deal with our own inner selves.

There is even power in acknowledging our pain and our fear in the face of life-altering difficulties. Because there is power in truth, enough power to overcome the impotence of denial.

There is power in surrender because it prepares us to stop doing all the things that never worked and makes room for new solutions that do work, that have worked for others.

TODAY I WILL SURRENDER. I WILL GIVE UP THE STRUGGLE TO FORCE MY RELATIONSHIP INTO THE MOLD I WANT IT TO FIT. I WILL SURRENDER AND FIND THE REAL POWER THAT LIES IN FACING REALITY.

WILLINGNESS

Are you willing to change?

Are you willing to ask for help?

Are you willing to do things differently just because other women tell you that doing things differently helped them heal, gave them their lives back?

Are you willing to believe there is some force or being or presence in this universe with more power than you have? And are you willing to believe in the possibility that this power could help you solve your problems? Are you willing to seek that power—whether you can call that power God today or can rely only on something as tangible as the power of other women when they band together for their common comfort?

Are you willing to believe in the possibility of healing?

Are you willing to hope?

TODAY I WILL WORK ON ANSWERING AT LEAST ONE OF THOSE QUESTIONS WITH A YES. OR I WILL AT LEAST SEEK THE WILLING-NESS TO DO SO. THAT WILL BE ENOUGH TO GET ME STARTED ON THE PATH.

SERENITY AS A GOAL

What is our goal?

Do we want to win our partner back? Do we want to make him pay for all the pain he's caused? Do we want to rein him in and keep him under tight control? Or do we simply want to regain his love and put it all behind us?

The problem with all of those goals is that they are out of our hands. We have no power to make any of them happen because they are all dependent on and focused on the behavior of another person. And when we focus on someone else's behavior, when we want to change another person, we lose ourselves.

So what is our goal?

Let's try making serenity our goal.

The way we do that is by remembering that nothing in our life— *nothing*—is more important than our serenity. Because when we have serenity, our life feels good. Our life *is* good. When we have serenity, our problems become manageable. With serenity, we can see the solutions and not just the problem. We are calm. We are in touch with our wise inner spirit. We are not living in yesterday's pain or tomorrow's fears, but living fully in this moment. Serenity is the cornerstone of healing, of rational decisions, of positive change.

JUST FOR TODAY, I'LL KEEP FOCUSED ON MY GOAL. I WILL REFUSE TO ALLOW ANYTHING TO BECOME MORE IMPORTANT THAN MY SERENITY.

THE FAMILY OF WOMEN

I spent much of my life not trusting other women. I spent forty years feeling disconnected from other women and from my own womanhood.

Is it any wonder that some of us have felt that way? Other women, we've been taught, aren't to be trusted. They are predators, after our men. Other women are our competition, our enemy, the measuring stick by which we always come up short.

On my healing journey, I have made profound connections with other women. And in doing so, I have discovered the strength of my feminine side as well.

Women who have been where we are and struggled to the other side using spiritual tools can be trusted. They will understand us and nurture us and share their own painful journeys with us, all in the name of helping us heal. They will listen to us cry and teach us to laugh. They will peer into the darkest corners of our souls without judging us or betraying us. They will tell us when we are making progress, even when we can't see it ourselves. And they will gently guide us to awareness when we are hindering our progress, even when we don't want to see it ourselves.

They will hold us up, and they will teach us to fly.

They will open their arms and welcome us into the family of women no matter how long we've turned our backs on them.

TODAY I WILL TRUST WOMEN WHO HAVE CONNECTED WITH THEIR OWN HIGHER SPIRIT TO TEACH ME LOVE AND TRUST AND CONFIDENCE IN MYSELF. THERE IS HEALING AND JOY IN THE FAMILY OF WOMEN.

ALICE MAY

A PLEA FOR HELP

I hoarded all the painkillers left in my mother's medicine cabinet after she died and I discovered my husband's infidelity. Having those pills was my safety net, my way out. I also hid a small handgun in the bottom of my sock drawer, like a hedge against a hopeless existence.

Sometimes suicide beckons.

We grow weary of the struggle. Maybe, we think, it is time to end it.

Whether suicide is a fleeting idea or a possibility that takes real shape in our minds, its presence in our thoughts is a signal that we need help.

If you think life is not worth living, pick up the telephone. Call a trusted friend, a minister, a counselor, a mental health hotline. Connect with another human being and share your despair. This is not the time to pretend that you are coping. Even if you aren't yet comfortable with prayer, consider asking God to help you through another person. Then call.

And if you have reached the point of making plans, circumvent those arrangements. Tell someone you trust what you've been thinking and ask her help in short-circuiting your course of action. Flush the pills or ask a friend to dispose of the gun or have the garage door dismantled until the danger is past.

If you've ever been prone to do things solely for other people, do it now if no other motivation works. Think of the lifelong pain your death would cause your children or your parents or your siblings.

If suicide sounds like an easy way out, ask for help. Today.

And remember that no matter how weary you are of the struggle, this will pass. Things will change. Life is worth living. You may not feel it at this moment. But you will again. Soon. That is a promise.

IF I AM THINKING DESPERATE THOUGHTS TODAY, I WILL REACH OUT. I WILL GIVE THINGS A LITTLE MORE TIME TO WORK OUT, AND TAKE SOME ACTION TO FEEL BETTER IN THE MEANTIME.

Surviving Betrayal

YES, BUT . . .

In the beginning, when people tell us how they recovered from infidelity, the first words out of our mouths are sometimes, "Yes, but . . . "

When we are encouraged to consider certain changes in our lives or our beliefs or our innermost selves, our fear of the unknown prompts us to say, "Yes, but . . . "

Those two words are often followed by excuses or justifications. They signal our reluctance to examine our circumstances and to take action to change them. They are words of fear, and they do nothing to improve our circumstances. They shackle us to the notion that our case is different, that we have nothing to learn from anyone else, even someone who is serene in the face of problems that are driving us insane.

The ways others found help may not apply to you. But you will never know for sure unless you take the time to listen, unless you remain open to the idea that you and I feel the same beneath the surface no matter how different our particular circumstances seem.

If you find yourself saying, "Yes, but . . . ," make an effort to open your mind and heart to whatever is being offered. And if the new ideas you hear don't seem to apply to you today, you may find that they come to mind later. Later, further down your path, you may remember what was shared and understand how you can use it.

TODAY I WILL LISTEN WHEN OTHERS SHARE, SO I CAN HEAR WHAT I NEED TO HEAR, EVEN IF I DON'T RECOGNIZE TODAY THAT I NEED TO HEAR IT.

ALICE MAY

PERSONAL BOUNDARIES

Some of the spiritual tools I'm learning to use were meaningless to me at first. I didn't know how to live one day at a time. I didn't know how to let go. And I had no idea what personal boundaries were.

The women who were guiding me told me what unhealthy boundaries looked like, so I could begin to identify them in my life. That awareness was the first step toward change.

They asked me whether I sometimes talked too intimately with people I didn't know well. They asked whether I ever violated my personal values or rights to please someone else. Did I accept food, gifts, touch, sex that I didn't want? Did I let others direct my life or describe my reality? Did I believe that others could or should anticipate my needs, or expect others to fill my needs automatically?

At the time, many of those actions seemed like normal behavior to me. They were not. They were signs of trouble. They indicated that my judgment wasn't always good when it came to my interactions with others.

Once we are aware of specific ways in which we give ourselves away, we can begin to change. We can behave differently. We can respect ourselves more. We can encourage the respect of others. Healthy interactions can begin with healthy boundaries.

TODAY I WILL BE AWARE OF MY TENDENCY TO EXHIBIT POOR PERSONAL BOUNDARIES. NOW THAT I AM AWARE, I CAN TAKE ACTION TO CHANGE.

A PLAN OF ACTION,
NOT THOUGHT

We cannot think our way into a happier, healthier, saner way of life. We can gather knowledge, analyze, philosophize, engage in inner debate. In fact, I've done all that. Over and over again.

It never worked for me.

But if we have a plan of action designed to lead us to a more spirit-filled life, we can change. We can change from the inside out. We can change our feelings and thoughts and motives, and with them our life.

But we get there by acting, not thinking.

I talk to so many people who say things like, "Oh, we'd all like to change, but who knows how?" Or, "This is who I am. It's impossible to change at this late date."

We can change. We can become different people. But we don't do it by thinking about it. By wishing or hoping. We do it through action.

We can put a plan of action to work in our lives today. We embarked on our healing journey when we made a decision to give our spirits room to grow. Now we can carry out that decision with action. We can begin a self-assessment to identify our weaknesses and strengths. We can do our part to heal relationships by examining our motives and actions on a daily basis, looking for times when we're out of sync with the spirit of good in the world. We can pray. We can help others, especially others who also want a plan for changing their lives.

We will be transformed. Through our actions, we will become new people.

TODAY I WILL WORK ON THE ACTIONS THAT IMPROVE MY LIFE. I CAN DO MORE THAN WISH AND HOPE THINGS WILL CHANGE. I CAN ACT.

ALICE MAY

TALKING TO YOUR CHILDREN

What do we tell our children?

Sometimes, when our hearts are full of anger and empty of love, we want to tell them everything. We want to turn them against the man who has hurt us. We forget that man is their father.

Sometimes, when our hearts are full of fear, we want to hide the truth from our children.

Is either option the action of a kind and loving parent?

Can we sacrifice our children's love and trust in a parent for the sake of spite, even if we call our retribution justice?

On the other hand, can we leave them alone with their doubts and suspicions, a place we know all too well? Children, even the youngest, know when something is wrong. Their busy minds will supply explanations if we don't.

Each situation is different, and each child is different. No simple solution applies in every case. We must ask others for guidance. We must look for ways to talk to our children that are as open and honest as possible without causing unnecessary wounds. We can't promise them happily-ever-after. And we can't use them in our struggles with our partner. But we can acknowledge problems without sharing details, when doing so would be appropriate for their level of maturity. We can talk about what we're doing to work on the problems. We can reaffirm our love for them and assure them that they haven't been the cause of our problems.

TODAY I WILL MAKE A GENTLE AND LOVING DECISION ABOUT HOW TO TALK WITH MY CHILDREN. I WILL NOT SHUT THEM OUT, AND I WILL NOT TELL THEM THINGS THEY ARE TOO YOUNG TO HEAR. I WILL DO MY BEST TO BE SURE THEY KNOW THAT MY LOVE AND SUPPORT ARE AVAILABLE TO THEM, ALWAYS.

LOVING YOUR BODY

Why is it that one of the first things we do when we've been betrayed is blame our bodies?

We turn against our physical self, hating it for all its imperfections. No wonder he wanted someone else, we tell ourselves. And if we leave him, who else would want us in the shape we're in?

I was in the midst of this physical identity crisis on my first trip to Great Britain a few years ago. During an airport layover, I purchased a British magazine. Thumbing through it, I came across an ad for women's jeans. The ad featured a half-dozen women, nude from the waist up. They were professional models, of course, but they looked like regular women. There wasn't a siliconed, lifted, airbrushed breast in the bunch.

The ad riveted me. I kept looking back at it. I stuffed the magazine in my bag and dragged it all the way home to the States with me.

You see, not a single woman was perfect. Some had broad hips and breasts like small pears. Some had wasp waists, and others didn't. Some had heavy breasts, some were tiny and turned up. But as imperfect as they were by Victoria's Secret standards, they were all beautiful.

The idea stunned me: A woman could be less than perfect but still beautiful.

I never forgot those women. And I gradually stopped studying myself so critically in the full-length mirror. I started walking regularly. Eating better. I started making the most of the body I was born with.

It has taken time, but now I love my body. It's strong and healthy and takes good care of me now that I take good care of it.

TODAY I KNOW I AM BEAUTIFUL, IN ALL MY IMPERFECTIONS. I ALSO KNOW THAT IT DOESN'T MATTER WHETHER ANYONE ELSE SEES IT. REGARDLESS OF OTHERS' PERCEPTIONS, MY BEAUTY IS REAL.

ALICE MAY

MORNING-AFTER REMORSE

Beware of his remorse.

Remorse is a common reaction for people who have done something they know hurts people around them—especially if they've been caught. An alcoholic in recovery will tell you that one of the most common feelings the day after a drunken spree is remorse. He will also tell you that he was 100 percent sincere when he vowed it would never happen again.

But it usually did.

Until a person is wholeheartedly ready to change, remorse may be short-lived. It may last until the furor dies down or the memory fades or the next opportunity presents itself.

And that may be true even if the remorse is absolutely sincere.

So beware of morning-after remorse. Don't let it lift you up with sky-high hopes. Keep your head and remember that what counts is genuine change over the long haul.

TODAY I WILL BE LESS SUSCEPTIBLE TO HEARTFELT WORDS WHOSE PRIMARY PURPOSE AND MOST POWERFUL EFFECT MAY BE SIMPLY TO MELT MY HEART AND TO SAVE HIS BACKSIDE.

WHEN OTHERS BLAME YOU

The losses sometimes seem to come in waves. In addition to losing our dreams, our confidence, our belief in the man we thought we knew, we may also lose other friends and family at this time. Some of the people we care about may blame us for the problem.

Some of us are close to his family, and it will hurt if they turn their backs on us to show their support for him. Sometimes even our children blame us for what is happening. And some of our friends will suddenly be too busy for us, or even openly hostile.

The impact of bad choices is never limited only to those who made them. The effects ripple out, rocking many lives. One of those effects may be more loss for us, as people choose sides or scramble to get out of the way.

We may feel as if we'll never stop reeling from the blows.

Even those of us who have felt that we lost every single person who mattered to us in the aftermath of betrayal have survived. We have found ways to cope and people to support us. We have found comfort and peace of mind.

We can mourn. We can get busy with healthy activities. We can connect with others who fill the gaps in our lives. We can search our hearts for compassion or patience or a tiny bit of forgiveness for those who can't be there for us. We can make wise, positive choices even when others can't.

TODAY I WILL TRY NOT TO JUDGE THOSE WHO REJECT ME. I WILL TRY TO SEE THE FEAR THAT LIES BENEATH THEIR ACTIONS. I WILL PRACTICE FORGIVENESS AND PATIENCE.

TAKING ADVICE

People who are absolutely certain what we should do about our problems are often the last people we should listen to. They are sometimes people who struggle with their own issues surrounding the need to control or fix others.

However similar our circumstances may look on the outside, however many emotions we may share, I don't have the right answers for you. And you don't have the right answers for me. If I try to tell you what to do, my advice is going to be based on what worked for me when I was learning my particular life lessons. Or it's going to be based on my fears, my insecurities, my shortcomings.

Because of that, we don't *give* or *take* advice on this path to spiritual healing.

What each of us is looking for are the answers that will move us forward on our particular journey and help us grow in the directions that are right for us as individuals.

In this process, we learn to share our experience, our strength, and our hope. We learn to say, "This is what worked for me," not, "This is what you should do." We offer support. We listen. We encourage. We love each other through our problems.

TODAY I WILL SEEK PEOPLE WHO KNOW THEY HAVE ONLY THEIR OWN ANSWERS. FOR THEY WILL BE MY BEST GUIDES AS I SEEK MY ANSWERS.

FILLING EACH OTHER UP

The first night there were three of us—women betrayed brought together by unlikely circumstances we might once have called coincidence.

When they showed up at my door, I cried because I knew I could not get through this alone. With their arrival, I knew I wouldn't have to.

We spoke of our pain and focused on solutions. Eventually, we laughed at the things that hurt us most. We kept one another pointed in the direction of healing. Some nights there were only two of us. But that was enough. We were filled up when we left.

Today there are twelve of us. We call ourselves the Serenity Group. We still laugh and pray. We support the newcomer when she walks through the door, offering her a box of tissues and hope. She reminds us how far we've come and keeps us humble by proving all over again that no life is immune to tragedy.

Some of us come and go, not yet ready to face the daunting task of confronting and conquering our worst fears and our most painful problems. Others of us come and stay, knowing we have found a home in the loving embrace of our sisters in pain. And those of us who stay become strong.

TODAY I WILL REMEMBER THAT I NEVER NEED TO BE ALONE AGAIN. I AM WILLING TO FIND COURAGE AND HOPE IN THE COMPANY OF OTHER WOMEN.

DECIDING TO CHANGE

I recently took out winter clothes that had been stored for the summer. Before hanging them in the closet, I tried on everything to see what still fit.

I discovered that every pair of pants I'd worn the year before was too long by three or four inches.

That's no surprise. I'm 5'3", and pants usually need shortening when I buy them. What stunned me was the realization that I'd worn my pants that way the previous winter without making any effort to shorten them. I'd simply rolled them up to the correct length and told myself they looked cuffed.

They didn't look cuffed. They looked too long. They looked like pants worn by someone who couldn't be bothered to change something in her life that didn't fit.

As I try to heal from the effects of infidelity, I've learned that if nothing changes, nothing changes. My pants won't suddenly fit all by themselves. My life won't suddenly get better all by itself. People who have deceived me or broken my heart over and over again are not likely to change their behavior for no good reason.

If we want our life to change, it must begin with ourselves. We must decide what is unacceptable to us. We must decide what action we're going to take if unacceptable behavior continues. We must decide to become emotionally healthy.

SOMETIMES, IF ONE THING CHANGES, EVERYTHING CHANGES.

LET GO OF THE PAST

Leaving the past behind is a critical part of our spiritual journey. We don't heal, we don't move with freedom and joy into the future if we're still lugging baggage from the past.

Here is what others have done to leave the pain behind:

- "I have to allow myself to grieve the past before I can let it go. The broken dreams, the unkept promises—I have to grieve it all, and I don't judge myself or rush myself as I go through the process."

- "My husband hid his serial infidelity for years. I had no idea how many affairs he had, how much money he spent on prostitutes. It wasn't until I could accept him as a sick person, and not a demon, that I could forgive. With that came a real release."

- "I stay in this day. I pay attention to this day's work. The more todays I pile up, the further I get from the past and the less power it has over me."

- "Letting go of the past wasn't possible for me until I spent a few months working on my self-discovery and I saw who I really was, who I had become because of the past, and who I could become if I was willing to change."

Grieving, forgiving, living in the moment, working on our own growth. If we do those things, we wake up one morning and realize the past no longer has a hold on us because we no longer have a hold on the past.

TODAY I AM READY TO LET GO OF THE PAST. I WILL USE SOME OF THE TOOLS THAT HAVE WORKED FOR OTHER WOMEN AND RELEASE MY HOLD ON YESTERDAY'S PAIN.

ALICE MAY

SELF-WILL

All my life, I've relied on the wrong things to make my life run smoothly.

I've depended on husbands who couldn't manage their own problems, much less mine. I've escaped into novels, staying absorbed hour after hour in fictional problems to avoid my own very real crises. I trusted alcohol to make me feel good when things looked bleak, and food to comfort me when no one else would. I worked so hard I had no time to think or feel. I ran three miles a day until that quit working, so I upped my mileage to four a day, then five, then seven. The day I ran eleven miles and didn't want to stop I knew running wouldn't work any longer either.

Mostly, however, I relied on the most powerful tool I had: my own self-will.

I was smart enough, tough enough, persistent enough to win out over any difficulty in my life. I was a survivor. And I was all I needed.

My husband's infidelity broke me so completely that I knew I could never again stand on my own. I knew I couldn't survive without help.

My complete surrender opened the door to a real source of power. I no longer had to play God. Instead, with the loving help of people who shared my pain, I learned to trade my self-will for the will of a higher source, which never steers me wrong.

TODAY I WILL CONSIDER THE POSSIBILITY THAT LIVING IN GOD'S WILL COULD HAVE BETTER RESULTS FOR ME THAN CONTINUING TO BE GUIDED BY ONLY MY LIMITED SELF-WILL. I CAN TRY THIS IN ONE SMALL AREA OF MY LIFE AND SEE WHAT HAPPENS.

IDENTIFYING GOD'S WILL

As we embark on a spiritual journey, we may worry about how we'll recognize God's will. Unless God taps us on the shoulder and points out the burning bush, how will we know?

Three things can help us identify God's will before we take action.

First, we can compare our action to what we have learned so far about the character of the God or higher source we are turning to today. Is this action or decision in keeping with the character of God as we understand it today? How would we characterize this choice, and does it fit what we believe about the nature of good in the world?

Second, are there confirming circumstances, moments of synchronicity when the universe seems to support our decision? For example, when we are considering a career change, do we meet someone by happenstance who is already in that field and who shares valuable insights? Does the flow of the universe shed light on our decision and bring a situation to fruition or do we find it necessary to manipulate the circumstances?

And third, do we feel inner peace regarding our decision or action?

If God's will is truly at hand, at least two of these three factors will be present.

For example, we may feel a measure of something we label inner peace as we contemplate revenge. But we will probably find it hard to reconcile our decision with the character of a higher spirit. And chances are good we've got to do a lot of manipulating to bring about a good case of revenge.

Knowing God's will isn't always easy. But a little honesty in applying certain principles helps us gain clarity.

I MAY NOT ALWAYS BE ABLE TO SEE THE BEST COURSE OF ACTION. BUT IF I AM SINCERE IN TRYING TO MAKE CHOICES THAT SUPPORT MY SPIRIT, I WILL HAVE DONE ALL I NEED TO DO TODAY TO NURTURE THAT SPIRIT.

ALICE MAY

THE GIFT OF FORGIVENESS

Forgiveness is a gift we give ourselves.

We don't forgive others to make ourselves look good. We don't forgive others to make them indebted to us, to make them change, or even to make them squirm. We don't even do it to let them off the hook.

We forgive others because it soothes us, heals us. We forgive others because we'll always need forgiveness ourselves. We forgive others because our imperfection gives us compassion for others whose imperfections have gained control of their lives.

We forgive others because we deserve to live a life unclouded by bitterness or unresolved rage.

Forgiveness is the gift of freeing our souls.

We can give ourselves that gift any time we choose, by forgiving others whose actions have harmed us. Forgiveness is a process, and we begin that process by deciding to free ourselves by forgiving others. We carry out our decision by saying the words "I forgive" each day until they reach our hearts. We carry out our decision by recognizing that forgiveness does not imply our approval. We carry out our decision by recognizing another's humanity.

If we take those actions long enough, our hearts will be filled with forgiveness.

TODAY I WILL FREE MYSELF FROM ONE MORE PART OF MY PAIN BY MAKING A DECISION TO FORGIVE THOSE WHO HAVE HURT ME. I WILL BEGIN SIMPLY, WITH THE WORDS "I FORGIVE."

FEELING OVERWHELMED

The path out of our misery often feels overwhelming.

If we are ever going to feel better, we must talk to others, pray, examine our own behavior, see a lawyer, straighten out our finances, get the kids to the dentist, and prepare meals that are low-fat, high-taste, and no-fuss.

We can't do it all. It's too much. Way too much.

When we feel that overwhelmed, we've forgotten to keep it simple.

Keep it simple.

We can do only one thing at a time. Luckily, all we *must* do is one thing at a time. We don't have to cross everything off our to-do list in one day, or even one week. We have as long as we need. All we must do now is the next right thing. If we slow down, take a deep breath, and ask for guidance, it's surprisingly easy to see what we need to do next. Then we do it. We don't worry about what comes after that.

We simply do the next right thing.

Then we can breathe again, ask for guidance again, move forward again. One thing at a time, keeping it simple, never overwhelmed, because we're doing only one thing. This moment's thing.

WHEN I KEEP IT SIMPLE, EVERYTHING THAT NEEDS TO BE DONE GETS DONE. THE ONLY THINGS THAT DON'T GET DONE ARE THE THINGS I ONLY THOUGHT NEEDED DOING. AND I CAN LET THOSE THINGS GO.

ALICE MAY

UNCERTAINTY ABOUT LOVE

We don't have to know how we feel about love right now. Our love has been shaken to the core, and we don't have to set everything right today.

We may feel our love so deeply now that it's threatened. We may remember all the ways that this relationship has been good for us and may fear losing that love. Or we may feel that every bit of love we've experienced has been a fraud. We may find ourselves thinking more of hate than of love.

We may feel all those things, all in the same day. The same hour.

Having all the answers about our deepest emotions when we're in the middle of turmoil isn't a realistic expectation. We can be gentle with ourselves right now and give ourselves permission to feel all the extremes of our emotions. We can trust that our hearts and our spirits will eventually lead us to the right answers about love.

ALL I NEED TO KNOW TODAY IS THAT LOVE HAS NOT BETRAYED ME. A FLAWED HUMAN BEING—FLAWED EVEN AS I AM FLAWED— HAS BETRAYED ME. BUT LOVE IS A FORCE FOR GOOD IN MY LIFE. I WILL BE LED BACK TO LOVE.

TENDING YOUR RELATIONSHIPS

In the days after my life fell apart, a good friend suggested that I walk every day. She further suggested that each day I make note of all the colors in nature, or that I note all the scents and fragrances I encountered on my route.

I didn't realize at the time that she was asking me to open myself to a higher presence in my life. But my awareness of her motives wasn't necessary for her suggestion to work.

On my walks, I passed a rose garden in a nearby park. The roses were all colors, some with a faint scent, others with a sweet and overpowering fragrance. My heart was so battered, I didn't pay much attention most days. But in a dutiful effort to follow suggestions that had helped others, I lingered in the rose garden.

As I forced myself to sniff the varied blooms, I was reminded of my grandmother's roses. She had labored over them every year. She had carried buckets of water from her well. She had pruned and fed and fussed. And each year, the prickly bushes produced lush, redolent blooms.

Those results didn't come from neglect. Grandmother's roses didn't grow in unnourished soil, with no effort invested.

I'd never wanted to bother with roses myself; I'd seen firsthand how much trouble they were. But as I stood there in the rose garden, I realized how much delight I'd been missing because I wasn't willing to make the effort.

And I began to wonder whether marriages weren't like rose bushes. They require some effort, some nurturing, some attention. A good relationship is no more likely to thrive in rocky soil than a neglected rose is.

FOR MY RELATIONSHIP TO BLOOM, I AM WILLING TO DO MY PART
TO TEND IT.

ALICE MAY

51

HOW IMPORTANT IS IT?

When we live long enough with unhealthy behavior, our thinking becomes distorted. One of the ways it shows up in our lives is that we lose our perspective about what's really significant and what's a minor irritation.

In my case, being overdrawn at the bank could become a major crisis, so major that I once broke a desk drawer over it. Forgetting to turn on the stove to boil water for pasta could ruin the rest of the night. I could rage for an hour, sending my family searching for a quiet place to hide.

Or as a friend says, "I get to the point where I can't tell the difference between a lump in my oatmeal and a lump in my breast. One is a minor irritation. The other is life-threatening. And I forget which is which."

Now I try to save myself the emotional strain of reacting to every minor irritation as if I've discovered a lump in my breast.

TODAY I WILL REMIND MYSELF THAT MOST OF THE UNPLEAS-
ANTNESS THAT CROPS UP IN MY DAY IS NOTHING MORE THAN A
LUMP IN MY OATMEAL.

FAITH IS NOT ESSENTIAL

I didn't believe in God when the problems in my marriage first surfaced. Didn't believe and didn't want to believe.

The process worked anyway. I didn't have to become a believer overnight, and I didn't have to accept any particular beliefs in order to begin the journey to healing. I had to believe only that I was not the most powerful force in the universe.

As big a mess as my life was in, that was not too hard to believe.

Some who come to our group today have no relationship with God when they arrive. No one tries to force a particular kind of belief on them. Some of them place their trust in our group, developing a little faith in our collective power to heal together. Those of us who were non-believers are asked only to be a tiny bit willing to believe in the power of something outside ourselves.

Invariably, anyone who does this finds her own particular source of healing. She may never set foot in a church or synagogue, and that is okay. She may find all she needs from some other source that has nothing whatsoever to do with religion.

EVEN IF I AM NOT WILLING TODAY TO BELIEVE IN SOME SPIRITUAL FORCE GUIDING THE WORLD, I CAN WATCH AND LISTEN AS OTHERS GROW AND CHANGE. PERHAPS THEIR EXPERIENCES WILL LIGHT THE WAY FOR ME TO FIND WHATEVER I NEED TO HEAL.

FEAR MASQUERADES AS CONTROL

Being told that I was the strong one, the one who had everything under control, was the ultimate compliment.

Today I know that being in control is not about being strong. It isn't about being a survivor or keeping a lid on the turmoil or even knowing what is best for my loved ones.

Control is about fear.

The need to control is about our fear that we won't have enough. Our fear that we are not enough. That no one will love us just as we are. It's fear of being alone. Fear of having more pain than we can handle.

If we are in control, the unhealthy voices in our heads tell us, none of those things will happen. If we are in control, everything will turn out right.

But that is a lie.

The very notion that we can control the things that we fear is a lie. We cannot make things turn out in ways that guarantee our safety, our being loved, our being cared for. The truth is that the things we try hardest to control are the things that will probably cause us the most hurt, sometimes even the things we will lose first.

The conviction that we can control our life is not an asset. It's merely a sign of our fear. We can learn to relinquish that fear to our true source of power.

TODAY THERE IS NOTHING I NEED TO FEAR AND NOTHING I NEED TO CONTROL.

WAIT

When in doubt, don't.

Indecision is a natural state when our life is in turmoil.

Who should we tell among our friends and family? Should we see an attorney? Move out? Forgive and forget? What should we tell the children?

When our world has been thrown into chaos, deciding how to set things right again is a tougher job than most of us are up for. Whatever choices we make, we second-guess ourselves. What seems absolutely certain today may seem like madness tomorrow.

When in doubt, don't.

Make as few life-changing decisions as you can while your head is still spinning. Wait for your head and heart to calm down and speak the same language. Wait for certainty, for serenity. Wait for doubt to be replaced by a confidence that some higher power is guiding your decisions. The wait may seem to go on far too long. You may decide you've missed the message from God. Keep waiting. When the time is right for decisions, you will know what to do. You won't miss the message. When in doubt, don't.

BEFORE I MAKE DECISIONS AND TAKE ACTION, I WILL WAIT UNTIL I AM SURE OF MY CHOICE. I WILL WAIT UNTIL MY HEAD AND MY HEART ARE IN AGREEMENT. IF I HAVE DOUBTS TODAY, I WILL WAIT.

ONE DAY AT A TIME

For this one day, we can relax and know that our problems will be solved one by one, bit by bit. We don't have to tackle everything at once.

For this one day, we can turn our attention to all the other parts of our life—children or friends, job or home, our favorite pastime—and know that for this day our partner is not the center of our universe.

For this one day, we can give ourselves permission to do only a fraction of the things we normally expect of ourselves. When we are under tremendous stress, we don't need to heap more on ourselves. We can respect our bodies' limitations.

For this one day, we can turn to others when our thinking threatens to become fearful or obsessive. We can share where we are and listen for the wisdom when others share how they've handled similar situations.

For this one day, we can remember that the solutions to all our problems begin with the actions we take today.

TODAY I WILL STAY IN THIS MOMENT AND TAKE THE POSITIVE STEPS TOWARD HEALING THAT ARE RIGHT IN FRONT OF ME.

ACCEPTANCE IS NOT APPROVAL

A cornerstone of the spiritual life is acceptance. Acceptance is necessary for serenity and for personal growth.

We don't like the sound of accepting our partner's inappropriate sexual behavior. To accept, we may think, means to approve, to turn a blind eye, to put up with indefinitely. Haven't we already done those things and made ourselves crazy in the process?

Acceptance is not approval. Acceptance is merely acknowledging what is, admitting the facts of a situation. Acceptance is being in the midst of this moment's reality—with whatever grief or discomfort or anger accompanies it—without struggling against it.

We accept the truth that our partner has engaged in sexual behavior that has left us hurt, angry, ashamed, betrayed. We accept that whether he changes his behavior is up to him and not us. We accept that whether he is even sorry for his behavior is out of our hands.

We accept what is.

When we do that, the outer turmoil has no real power to destroy our inner peace.

When we do that, we can begin to see the difference between the things we cannot change—his sexual behavior, his feelings for us, the outcome of our relationship—and the things we can change, with guidance—our attitudes, our reactions, our behavior.

WHEN I ACCEPT THE REALITY OF THE CIRCUMSTANCES IN MY LIFE, I OPEN THE DOOR FOR CHANGE.

CELEBRATING LOVE

The world celebrates romance—in books, songs, movies, advertising. Everywhere we look, we are told that romance is essential to our happiness.

Thinking about that may overwhelm us with bitterness or rage or hopelessness.

We don't have to allow this obsession with the myth of romance to become a source of bitterness to us. We can choose bitterness, of course. Or we can choose a healthier response.

We can choose to focus on something else this day. We can gently focus our attention and our energy on all the examples of deep and abiding love that do exist in our lives, whether it's our higher power's love for us or our love for our children or the best friend who stands by us no matter what or the sister who always defends us to the rest of the family.

While the world worships romance, we can learn to see love in a new way, a way that nurtures and lifts up all those it touches. We can begin to see that romance may be fun, but it isn't a solid place to plant our feet.

ON THIS DAY, I CHOOSE TO CELEBRATE LOVE. I AM WILLING TO SHARE MY LOVE WITH THOSE WHO WILL TREASURE IT.

A NEW KIND OF SEXUALITY

Some days we hate sex. If it weren't for sex, we wouldn't have been betrayed. We wouldn't have cared so much. We wouldn't feel so devalued in a society that seems to value sexuality above all else.

Some days we don't care if we're ever sexual people again.

I spent months after learning of my husband's infidelity thinking I never wanted to be sexual again. I spent months examining my own sexual history, which revealed a lifetime of sexual dysfunction. Sex as weapon, as punishment, as perceived power.

I wanted to cut sex out of my life.

Today I see that what I can do instead is define a new kind of sexuality for myself. A sexuality that is based on a healthy balance of giving and receiving. A sexuality that is about joy. A sexuality that is both light of heart and weighty with sacred intimacy.

But we don't get to healthy sexuality by force of will, by pressuring ourselves. We get there by being open to what will be revealed during our healing journey. We get there by being patient while we are being transformed by our healthy approach to difficult circumstances. We get there by letting go of expectations about what direction this transformation will take.

TODAY I AM WILLING TO BE PATIENT AND TO LET MY SEXUALITY EVOLVE INTO THE GIFT I'VE REFUSED TO ACCEPT FOR SO MUCH OF MY LIFE.

LOW EXPECTATIONS

What happens when we *expect* another person to behave in a certain way?

If that person does exactly as we expect, we are happy. All is right with our world.

If that person disappoints us—arrives later than we expected, doesn't give the gift we expected, doesn't live up to promises as we expected—then our world is suddenly off-kilter. We feel miffed. Or wounded. Or deeply betrayed.

And all because of what that person did. Right?

Not necessarily.

Our discontent occurs when the things we desire don't happen the way we want them to. Our unhappiness occurs when reality doesn't match our expectations. When we expect other people to place our needs and desires above their own, we place ourselves in a position to be disappointed.

If we keep our expectations surrounding others low, the things people do hurt us less. If we wait to see what each day brings instead of having our own master plan, we have less cause for discontent. We can accept *what is* more easily. And we're not spinning from reaction to reaction when people behave in ways that have nothing to do with us and everything to do with their own wants and needs.

MY EXPECTATIONS ARE MY PROBLEM, NOT SOMEONE ELSE'S. WHEN I KEEP MY EXPECTATIONS LOW, THEY AREN'T SUCH A PROBLEM FOR ME EITHER. TODAY I WILL RECOGNIZE HOW EXPECTATIONS BLOCK ME FROM SERENITY.

ASSESSING YOURSELF

As we continue our healing journey, we find ourselves growing calmer and more certain that we are on the track to better days. Our surrender is moving from our head to our heart. When that happens, it is time for us to take the next step in our journey.

It is time for self-examination.

At this stage, we examine our lives to see how our attitudes and actions have contributed to our unhappiness. We catalog our strengths and our weaknesses, to assess who we have become and how we live our lives.

The idea of looking at our own shortcomings may seem strange to us, especially if we're only beginning to learn that our present circumstances aren't our fault. While we did not cause the infidelity, we're only human. We've lived out destructive patterns of our own. We've brought pain to ourselves and others.

And right now, the only thing we can change is ourselves. We can begin the process of cleaning up our side of the street.

Why is that good? Because it takes the focus off him. It gives us positive actions to take at a time when we may otherwise feel helpless and uncertain about what to do next.

TODAY I WILL LOOK AT MYSELF. I WILL MOVE FORWARD BY DOING SOMETHING POSITIVE IN MY LIFE: EMBARKING ON A GENTLE BUT HONEST SELF-EXAMINATION.

GETTING HONEST

A part of our healing is to become more honest with ourselves. We learn, through reflective self-examination, to see more clearly our motives, our weaknesses, our self-defeating habits.

One of the ways we do this is by opening up to and accepting the counsel of someone who has already walked the path we are on. Another woman who has sought spiritual solutions to marital or relationship problems can bring a wealth of wisdom to our circumstances.

In turning to this woman, we are committing to a willingness to hear the truth about ourselves, if it is offered in love and not in criticism and blame. We are asking her to be gentle but honest, especially if we try to mask or mitigate what is really going on with us. We don't need a mentor who will let us be dishonest with ourselves, who will not lovingly point out to us that certain actions are not in our best interests.

TODAY I WILL BE WILLING TO HEAR THE TRUTH ABOUT MYSELF FROM SOMEONE WHOSE ONLY AGENDA IS TO HELP ME GROW.

THE PERFECT WIFE

Must we be perfect wives in order for our husbands to be happy with us?

The answer, of course, is no.

Our husband's discontent with our partnership has more to do with what is going on inside him than with the external circumstances of our marriage. Even the most perfect of wives have husbands who stray. Even the least perfect of women have partners who are faithful.

When we realize that, we can remember that there are no perfect wives and that our imperfection is not a reason for our spouse's straying. We will never be perfect. Neither will he. Neither will our marriages.

Our imperfection does not justify his unfaithfulness, and the fact that we are using our present circumstances as an incentive to change and grow does not imply that we're on a campaign to become perfect. One of the gifts we give ourselves at this time is permission to be ourselves. Even if we are committed to growth, we can first accept ourselves and all our limitations.

I AM NOT BEING ASKED TO BECOME THE PERFECT WIFE. EVEN AFTER I MAKE PROGRESS ON MY SPIRITUAL PATH, I STILL WON'T BE A PERFECT WIFE. I WON'T EXPECT MYSELF TO BE. BUT I WILL HAVE BETTER TOOLS FOR THE ROLE THAN I HAVE TODAY. AND THAT IS GOOD ENOUGH.

TOOLS FOR RELEASING RESENTMENTS

Sometimes our resentment, our recycled anger, is so powerful that nothing we do seems capable of dissipating it. We're drowning in it, dying a slow death, and we're powerless to change it.

The healing journey teaches us a number of tools for ridding ourselves of the most powerful resentments. One tool is to focus on *our* role in our unhappiness. This helps us see that our attachment to certain outcomes, or our overwhelming need to have others behave exactly as we want them to, may be a major source of our misery. We can then begin to accept things as they are; we can give up trying to control other people or circumstances. And either of those actions increases our serenity and opens the door for real solutions.

Examining ourselves also points up patterns in our lives that led us to choose the people who have hurt us. Then we can break those patterns.

We are no longer victims. We are learning to see our role in our present circumstances. And that gives us the power we need to seek peace of mind.

TODAY I WILL TAKE ONE SMALL STEP TO RID MYSELF OF NEGATIVE FEELINGS. I WILL LOOK AT MY ROLE IN MY UNHAPPINESS. I NO LONGER WANT TO POISON MY LIFE WITH RESENTMENTS, BITTERNESS, AND OLD ANGER.

SURE-FIRE SOLUTIONS

When I first confronted my husband's infidelity, what I wanted was a list of sure-fire, no-fail, money-back-guaranteed techniques for getting him to clean up his act.

I was told to pray.

I'd never heard anything so pointless in my life.

The women who suggested prayer seemed confident that it had worked for them. I decided I wouldn't actually pray but could make them feel better by saying I did. Then I remembered their faces. Their eyes and their smiles weren't dulled by the pain and emptiness I felt. They were alive, inside and out. They were happy, something I couldn't imagine ever being again.

I wanted what they had. And prayer, they told me, had been part of the answer for them.

So I prayed. Against my will almost. And certainly against my better judgment. I did it not so much because I believed it would work as because I didn't have a better plan. All my plans had failed or backfired. At least prayer wasn't likely to make things worse.

When I prayed, things began to change. Without a particle of faith on my part, things began to change.

TODAY I WILL CONSIDER USING PRAYER AS A TOOL TO SEE ME THROUGH MY PRESENT DIFFICULTIES. I CAN PRAY EVEN IF I HAVE NO FAITH THAT IT WILL WORK, EVEN IF I'M ONLY PRAYING TO EMPTY AIR. UNLIKE SOME OF THE THINGS I'VE DONE TO FEEL BETTER, PRAYER CAN'T HURT ME.

UNANSWERED PRAYERS

Why pray, some of us wonder, when it's clear that God is ignoring us, denying us, abandoning us to pain?

I find the answer to that, as I've found many other answers, from others who have been on the spiritual path longer than I have been. They tell me my prayers need never go unanswered. The trick is to remember how to pray.

Today I pray for two things. I pray to know God's will for me. God's will. Not mine. And I ask to be given whatever I'll need to carry that out.

Today I don't ask God to save my marriage. I don't ask God to keep my husband out of the arms of another woman. I don't even ask God to take away my pain.

I ask for help staying on the path to a spiritual solution. I ask for help working out my marriage in whatever way is best and healthiest for me. I place my husband in the hands of his higher power. I seek help in learning the lessons my pain brings, so that I can grow.

TODAY MY PRAYERS WILL BE ANSWERED BECAUSE I WON'T PRAY FOR SPECIFIC OUTCOMES. IF I PRAY ONLY FOR WHAT IS BEST, FOR SOLUTIONS THAT FURTHER MY GREATER GOOD, MY PRAYERS WILL ALWAYS BE ANSWERED.

PROGRESS, NOT PERFECTION

Spiritual healing teaches us that we can be serene even in the midst of chaos. It tells us we can live one day at a time, unencumbered by yesterday's hurts or tomorrow's fears. It tells us we can find a gentle and loving higher spirit, which we can trust with our lives.

Our new way of life even tells us *how* to achieve these things: by sticking close to people who share our problems and who live by spiritual principles such as prayer and meditation and working with others; and by putting those same principles to work in our lives, with their help.

What the spiritual life does *not* tell us is that we have to get any of it perfect.

Even as we strive to live calmly, we can blow our tops over things big or small. We can obsess over our fears and rage over the past. We can turn away from our emerging spirits or not talk to a soul for a week at a time. We can abandon our spirituality completely, but it will not completely abandon us. Because the life of the spirit does not require us to be perfect. It only asks us to be willing.

We can take a thousand steps off the path, but it takes only one step to bring us back to the path. One prayer. One phone call. One devotional or inspirational reading. And we are back on the path to healing.

Whatever progress I make today is perfect for me at this moment. Absolute perfection is not necessary on this journey. A little progress is good enough. In fact, it is perfect.

ACCEPT HELP

A beginner on the path to spiritual healing once asked, "How do I conduct the self-assessment I'm being asked to make?"

A woman who had been around a while replied, "By doing whatever is suggested by someone else who's done it before."

That's the key to this entire process. Spiritual growth is not a self-help program. It's a journey on which some of us learn for the first time in our lives, or the first time in a long time, how to accept help from a safe source instead of always giving help to or demanding help from those who may not be emotionally safe for us.

We're in this together. Someone has gone ahead of us on the path and knows where to beware of the twists and turns. Someone else can say, "This is what I did. It helped me. If you want to try it, it might help you, too."

TODAY I WILL REMEMBER THAT I CAN'T FISH MYSELF OUT OF THE DEEP WATER. I NEED HELP. TODAY I WILL LOOK FOR A LIFELINE FROM A SAFE SOURCE.

LIVE IN THE SOLUTION

You don't have to live through this alone, as those of us who found other women to share the journey have already discovered. Through ministers, counselors, and others, most of us can find a few people who want to band together for support.

When you begin meeting, remember that healing lies not in focusing on the problem but in focusing on the solution.

We come together to find a common solution to our problem. We are not there to wallow indefinitely in our pain and victimhood. We are not there to tell others how to live or to have others tell us how to live. We are there to heal and to support one another.

We focus on the process of healing: a commitment to practicing a new way of life, a discovery of our self-defeating life patterns, a willingness to support one another. We focus on prayer and forgiveness. We stay away from advice and judgment. We bring to each meeting the tools of honesty and compassion. We are willing to gently bring the meeting back into focus if the discussion degenerates into a litany of our partner's transgressions.

We use our time with other women as the opportunity to surround ourselves with positive energy and to invite grace into the room. In such a setting, we find serenity and growth.

TODAY I WILL REMEMBER THAT I CONNECT WITH WOMEN IN SIMILAR CIRCUMSTANCES TO FOCUS ON PERSONAL GROWTH AND HEALING, NOT TO REMAIN STUCK IN MY PROBLEMS. ALTHOUGH I WILL SHARE MY DIFFICULTIES, I WILL NOT DWELL ON THEM.

ALICE MAY

PAINFUL LESSONS

A friend in despair because she couldn't let go of all the old baggage from her husband's unfaithfulness, which had happened years before, asked, "Why does God have to make all my lessons so painful?"

It seemed a reasonable question. She and I had held one another's hands for months as she struggled to overcome her anger, her mistrust of God, the eating disorder she'd used alternately to attract and repel men. With every inch of progress she made came another six inches backward into denial, into self-pity, and, worst of all, into self-loathing.

Why, indeed, was God making all her lessons so painful?

The answer eventually presented itself. The pain of the betrayal certainly was very real and not easily overcome. But the pain lingered because she could not change her old, unhealthy behaviors. My friend struggled against her problems by herself. She continued to cling to her old familiar coping mechanisms with every bit of fear and compulsion and self-will she could muster.

She isn't alone in that. I've done it. Most of us have. And the longer we try to be self-sufficient, the more painful our circumstances can get. The lessons are hard because we refuse to learn them until we are presented with them over and over again. We will be brought to our knees emotionally if we don't see that the only way out of our misery is to give up our old ways of handling life's problems.

Once we have surrendered wholeheartedly, the pain eases.

TODAY I WILL BECOME WILLING TO CHANGE THE OLD BEHAVIORS THAT CAUSE ME PAIN. I WILL ACCEPT HELP IN MAKING THOSE CHANGES. I WILL FIND RELIEF.

ABSTAINING FROM SEX

Sexual abstinence, in the first weeks and months after learning the extent of my husband's sexual acting out, seemed like a protective measure. It was detachment in the only way I could manage—physically and emotionally. If he didn't touch me physically, he couldn't hurt me emotionally.

Still, abstinence was frightening because I didn't know where it would lead.

I discovered that it left us without a safe territory to retreat to when life's difficulties intruded. In the past, when we disagreed, when he felt out of sorts, when I had my feelings ruffled, when bad news came, we had used sex to draw closer, to bridge the gap. We had used sex as a path back to what passed for intimacy.

Without sex, we had to learn new paths to intimacy.

We had to learn to break the silence and talk, even when it felt threatening to do so.

We had to learn to look one another in the eye.

We had to learn to hold one another in the darkness.

We had to face the fear that what we had wasn't strong enough to survive without using sex as a bandage to cover our problems.

And when we had learned those things, we could begin applying the newfound wisdom to our problems and using our sexuality only as a way to express our love.

TODAY I WILL SEE THAT MY SEXUALITY IS A GIFT FOR EXPRESSING MY LOVE AND ENHANCING MY INTIMACY WITH MY PARTNER. I WILL REMEMBER THAT SEX IS NOT A SUBSTITUTE FOR LOVE OR INTIMACY.

WHAT MAKES A GOOD PARTNER?

What—realistically—is a kind and loving partner?

Is he someone who supports our decisions, who backs us when we take a stand? Someone who loves us, warts and all, and doesn't hold it against us every time we fall short of perfection? Someone who doesn't mind being around our neurotic sister or our needy mother, who accepts our friends? Someone who lends a hand when we're overwhelmed and keeps us warm at night? Someone who helps us grow emotionally, without judging us?

Is he someone who makes love with enthusiasm but doesn't mind when we'd rather wait? Someone faithful and gentle and honest?

All these qualities, and more, might be part of our idea of a kind and loving mate. But instead of judging how he measures up, perhaps we could take a moment to see how we measure up. Let us apply those questions to ourselves and learn from the answers.

Our efforts to be kind and loving may not change him at all. They may or may not make our marriage better. But focusing on our own strengths as a partner can change us. And if that's the only good that comes out of this sad situation, we will have gained tremendously.

TODAY I WILL SEE HOW I MEASURE UP AS A PARTNER. I WON'T DO IT TO BEAT MYSELF UP, BUT BECAUSE I AM READY TO MAKE CHANGES FOR THE BETTER IN MY LIFE. I DON'T HAVE TO BE THE PERFECT PARTNER, BUT I AM WILLING TO LEARN HOW TO BE A BETTER ONE.

SELF-DISCOVERY

Change is intimidating, and some of us will do anything to sabotage our growth on this spiritual journey. This is never more apparent than when we face the prospect of embarking on the self-discovery phase of our journey.

Some of us create a crisis in our life in order to avoid self-examination. We decide it is time to leave our husband or take him back or move home to Indiana. We quit school or start working on our real estate license or pick a fight with our boss. Some of us can't find time to stay in touch with our support group any longer.

Some of us have a crisis of faith. Surely there's little point in playing this game of spiritual growth if we aren't even sure there's a God for us to grow toward?

Few things in life are more frightening than taking a long, hard, honest look at ourselves and our actions over the course of a lifetime. The only thing more frightening is staying the way we've been for another twenty years. Getting stuck where we are. That is true hopelessness.

The process of spiritual healing is our hope for a tomorrow that is better than our yesterdays. Let us make a commitment to hope, a commitment that our fear will no longer stand in the way of growth.

TODAY I WILL HAVE THE COURAGE TO MOVE FORWARD. I WON'T GIVE IN TO THE TEMPTATION TO DISTRACT MYSELF FROM MY JOURNEY.

MORAL SUPERIORITY

I must ask myself sometimes if I'm enjoying my moral superiority a little too much.

Being right is so seductive. Being the wronged wife allows me to ascend to a place of righteousness that I've never quite been able to attain in any other way.

I can be long-suffering. I can be holier-than-him. I can get things my way with a look or a tear or a not-so-subtle word. I can keep him in the doghouse for as long as I like. I can wring out of him every bit of guilt, shame, and remorse that a human is capable of.

If I'm doing any of those things, I must ask myself what good can possibly come of it. Is it helping restore my life to normalcy? Is it giving him incentive to change? Is it making me happy? Is it pleasing God?

Or is it simply prolonging my misery?

Is my moral superiority worth what it's costing me?

TODAY I WILL EXAMINE MYSELF FOR ANY HINT OF SELF-RIGHTEOUSNESS. I WON'T IMPROVE MY CIRCUMSTANCES WITH SUCH AN ATTITUDE. I WON'T REVIVE MY SPIRIT WITH SUCH A BELIEF. TODAY I WILL GUARD AGAINST SELF-RIGHTEOUSNESS.

LEARNING TO TRUST AGAIN

What will it take for us to risk trusting again?

Rebuilding trust is a process. And that process looks different for each of us. Here is what other women say about trust:

- "I asked others how I can tell if he's lying to me and they said, 'Are his lips moving?' That always brings a laugh when I share it, but the underlying truth is that I need to judge my husband not by what he *says* but by what he *does*. His actions are the only thing I can trust."

- "My trust is a gift I give whether he deserves it or not, because then he's in God's hands, and so am I. When I give my trust freely, and give him the freedom to respond to that however he feels he must, it lifts me to another plane spiritually."

- "Today I trust my husband to be responsible at work, to pay the bills, to be a good father. Do I trust him not to act out sexually? No. But I can figure out in what areas he is trustworthy and know that's all the trust I need today."

- "I learned that I didn't have to trust my husband. The only one I needed to trust was God, and when I did that, everything I needed would be provided, even the wisdom to know when—or if—it was safe to trust again."

We can trust one another, we can trust the higher power we turn to today, we can trust the process of rebuilding our lives. And that process will reveal to us what we need to do next about trusting our partner.

TODAY I WILL REMEMBER THAT REBUILDING TRUST TAKES TIME.
I CANNOT FORCE TRUST. I WILL DISCOVER THE RIGHT KIND OF
TRUST FOR MY CIRCUMSTANCES IN THE RIGHT TIME.

ALICE MAY

HEALTHY RESPONSES

Honesty and integrity begin with us, no matter what route the others in our life may choose. If our partner chooses dishonest and harmful responses to the difficulties in our marriage, must we respond in kind?

Of course not.

If our relationship is troubled, there are many healthy responses.

We can talk it out, with a minister, with a counselor, with one another. We can pray. We can separate while we look for answers if things are difficult or volatile enough. We can compromise and negotiate, and we can renew our commitment to showing our love even in the midst of our pain.

Those are a few of the ways a healthy, mature person responds to problems in a marriage.

Infidelity is not a healthy response.

We can leave unhealthy responses to someone else.

TODAY I WILL CHOOSE A RESPONSE THAT AFFIRMS MY HONESTY AND MY INTEGRITY, NO MATTER WHAT CHOICES SOMEONE ELSE MAKES.

NEEDING MEN

We don't need a man.

Not *this* man. Not *any* man.

We must learn to believe that before we can bring any real balance to our life.

It is true of many things, not just our belief that we need a man to be whole and happy. We don't need a new car or a cat with a pedigree or a home Martha Stewart would praise. We don't need cable TV or a notebook computer or that pair of new shoes the precise color of our new suit. Our life may seem easier or more comfortable or more fun if we have those things. We may want those things. We may believe we won't be happy or fulfilled, or that we won't survive, without some of them.

But the truth is, we don't need them.

And we don't need a man either.

Once we know that, in a soul-deep way, we may be ready to find a spot in our life that a man can fill in a healthy, balanced way. Until then, we can find all the nourishment our soul needs whether there is a man in our life or not.

I CAN BE FINANCIALLY SECURE WITHOUT A MAN. I CAN RAISE MY CHILDREN WITHOUT A MAN. I CAN BE PEACEFUL AND CONTENT WITHOUT A MAN. WOMEN DO IT EVERY DAY. I CAN, TOO.

FOCUSING ON YOUR BEHAVIOR, NOT HIS

When we first discover that our partner has been unfaithful, many of us want to know more. We read everything that has been written about infidelity. We want to know the details of his behavior. We believe that if we have enough information, if we understand, we can control. And if we can control, of course, it will never happen again.

People who get to the other side of this crisis tell us this: *His* actions, behaviors, feelings, motivations don't matter right now. His emotional makeup does not hold the key to healing us.

What matters now is accepting and understanding how we have been damaged. Otherwise, we will wake up one morning and realize that, even though he is no longer straying, we still can't get on with our lives.

If we are ready to examine *our* actions, behaviors, feelings, and motivations, we can ask ourselves a few questions that provide insight into how we've been affected by someone else's sexual conduct.

Has our partner's sexual conduct hurt or shamed us on more than one occasion? Have we gone through his desk, his dresser drawers, his closet, his briefcase, his glove compartment, or his wallet looking for evidence of his sexual activities? Has his behavior driven us to thoughts of suicide? Have we thrown away sexually graphic material? Have we ever been sexual when we didn't want to because we thought it would keep him faithful?

As these questions reveal, the clues to our problems are in our own behavior. The solutions lie there as well.

TODAY I WILL FOCUS ON MY BEHAVIOR, MY FEELINGS, MY HEAL-
ING. THEN I WILL BE READY TO GET ON WITH MY LIFE, REGARD-
LESS OF WHAT HAPPENS IN THIS RELATIONSHIP.

DETACHMENT VERSUS INDIFFERENCE

The fine line between detachment and indifference is hard to define, harder even to land on. As we try to move from enmeshment or obsession to detachment, it is far easier to swing all the way to indifference.

We detach with love. We arrive at indifference via a complete lack of emotion, including compassion or understanding or warmth.

When we detach, we may hate what our partner has done but we refuse to hate him. We hold out the possibility of our support, our forgiveness, our understanding, while still acknowledging that the behavior isn't something we excuse or condone. When we detach, we may offer aid, but we never agree to rescue.

When we detach with love, we remain aware that we are still vulnerable. Our hearts are still involved.

When we are indifferent, we have shut down and shut out. We have closed our hearts. We deny the possibility of second chances or the power of forgiveness.

Detachment is healthy. It gives us room to heal while providing protection in a painful situation. Indifference is unhealthy, although it is an extreme most of us swing to in the process of seeking to detach. But if we allow ourselves to stay there instead of continuing our progress toward detachment, indifference will stall the healing process by separating us from our emotions.

Once we have learned to detach with love, we will always have an ally when any of our relationships become difficult.

TODAY I WILL TRY DETACHMENT. I CAN LEARN IT LITTLE BY LITTLE. I WILL DETACH WITH LOVE, NOT INDIFFERENCE.

BOUNDARIES, NOT ULTIMATUMS

When we first hear about setting boundaries regarding the behavior of another person, it's often hard to see how that differs from the same old ultimatum that got us nowhere in the past.

You do this or else.

If that ever happens again, you'll be sorry.

What sets boundaries apart from ultimatums is that when we set a boundary, we are asking only one person to respect our boundaries: ourselves.

When we issue an ultimatum, we expect someone else to change.

When we set a boundary, we challenge ourselves to change.

When we set a boundary, we decide what we can live with in the future and how we will respond if confronted with that behavior again. When we set a boundary, we don't do it to punish someone else. We do it to protect ourselves. In setting a boundary, we may say: *One more deception, one more affair, and I must get out of this relationship to save myself and my sanity.*

Notice that a healthy boundary can be set without ever saying the word *you.* Sometimes we don't even have to express our boundaries aloud to another person, although to be fair we may want to tell others what the consequences of their actions may be. But we don't have to do that. Because when we set a boundary we're not demanding that another person change.

TODAY I AM READY TO MAKE MY OWN CHANGES. I WILL SEEK THE COURAGE TO SET HEALTHY BOUNDARIES AND TO DEMAND CHANGE ONLY OF MYSELF.

CONFLICT MADE SIMPLE

The women who are guiding me to healing have shared a simple plan for dealing with conflict or confrontation: Be calm, be brief, and be gone.

Be calm. We don't confront when we are angry, distraught, hysterical. We talk with someone else first, waiting for our hearts to stop pounding and our fists to unclench.

Be brief. We state how we feel, what we perceive, what we need, simply and concisely. We don't have to make accusations; we don't even have to listen to excuses or angry tirades. If we choose to, we can be ready with a calm response. *Thank you for sharing how you feel. I'm sorry you feel that way. I never thought of it that way.* This isn't a debate. We state our feelings briefly. Calmly. We listen to our partner's feelings, unless he grows abusive. If that happens, we can walk away.

Be gone. Once we have said what we need to say, once we have heard a response from the other person, we can say, *Thank you for listening.* Then we leave. We walk away before the debate begins, because the debate, the justifications, the explanations—his or our own—can easily become an argument if we remain too long.

Be calm. Be brief. Be gone. We don't have to attack anyone or be attacked just because there is a disagreement. We don't have to do anything we'll need to apologize for later.

TODAY I CAN APPROACH A CONFLICT WITHOUT BEING SHRILL OR ANGRY OR HARANGUING. I CAN SPEAK UP WITH COURAGE AND REMAIN PEACEFUL. I DON'T HAVE TO PARTICIPATE IF A CONFLICT IS ESCALATING INTO AN ARGUMENT.

FIXING OTHER PEOPLE

A friend came for the weekend. When he and his wife left on Monday, he had repaired my car radio and oiled both my squeaking front door and my squeaking bathroom door. He didn't ask whether I needed the help; he simply saw the problems and set about to fix them while his wife and I were out for a few hours.

So after he left, I had a car radio I didn't want because I had grown accustomed to quiet when I drove instead of noise. The announcers and the commercials now grated on my nerves; I turned the radio off. I also had a front door that opened silently, disconcerting me at bedtime. I realized I'd taken comfort in the idea that no one could sneak in that door without my hearing them; I didn't sleep as restfully for a while. And I had to find something to prop open the bathroom door because my friend had oiled it so thoroughly that it now refused to stand open.

All three of my friend's "fixes" were minor irritations to me.

I remind myself of that whenever I think I know exactly what my loved ones need for their lives to run more smoothly. I remind myself of that when I believe I can tell my loved ones how to solve their problems and live happier lives. I am not privy to what goes on in their hearts and heads. My solutions might have a worse outcome than the problems I perceive.

If we believe our loved ones need us to fix their lives, we can remember that we may be the only one who wants things to change. We can remember that maybe we are the only one who needs this change at this time.

TODAY I WILL TURN MY ATTENTION AND ENERGY TO CHANGING MY CIRCUMSTANCES, NOT OTHER PEOPLE. DOING SO CAN TURN MY LIFE AROUND WHETHER OTHERS CHANGE OR NOT.

NO QUICK FIXES

Sometimes the shortest distance between this moment's anguish and a pain-free future looks like the best solution of all.

Kick him out. Move to another city. Get an unlisted phone number. Just walk away from the sorrow. What a relief! With a few simple, decisive actions, the cause of all our heartache will be gone. Out of sight, out of mind.

But it doesn't work. It never works. Severing a relationship before it is time, out of anger or vengeance, causes more problems than it solves. It drags out the grieving process, making it more distressing than it needs to be. Sometimes it even causes us to look in the wrong places for relief from our pain.

The person who betrayed us may indeed be out of sight. It's so easy to decide that this person was the problem and now the problem is gone. But the truth is, we also made some contribution to our problems. And if we don't find out what our contribution was, we are highly likely to repeat ourselves in the next relationship and the next and the next, until we finally get the lesson.

If we attempt a quick fix, we stunt our own healing. We stay stuck in the problem—our problem. Maybe for a very long time.

TODAY I WILL TRUST THAT THE PATH TO HEALING ONLY LOOKS LONGER AND HARDER. I WILL REMEMBER THAT THE APPEALING SHORTCUT MAY CAUSE ME THE MOST GRIEF OVER THE LONG HAUL.

ALICE MAY

TRUE SECURITY

Healing is partly the process of letting go of the long-cherished myths that have propped us up all our lives.

One of those is the myth of security.

We've spent so much time and emotional energy constructing the illusion of security in our lives. If we have the right job, we'll never be homeless or hungry or stranded far from friends and safety. If we marry the right person, we'll never lack for affection, for approval, for creature comforts.

We construct these beliefs to keep us and our loved ones safe from harm, from disease, from tragedy, from loss.

And it's all a lie.

Security is fleeting and fragile. Upheaval is frequent and certain. We get fired. Companies go belly up. Spouses leave us. Best friends move across the country. Sooner or later, everything we hold dear can be taken from us.

So we must anchor ourselves to the only thing in life that is unshakable, the only thing in life that can't be taken from us. Our only true security is in a relationship with a higher power who will guide us through life's uncertainties. We can be secure in the knowledge that a life of the spirit holds us up.

The spiritual life gets us through lack of money, through times of hunger or illness, through loss of love. Faith never fails us. Faith is where we find security.

TODAY I WILL REMEMBER THAT SECURITY DOES NOT LIE IN THE RIGHT JOB, RELATIONSHIP, OR HOUSE. I WILL REMEMBER THAT SECURITY IS A MATTER OF THE SPIRIT.

ROUTINE CAN HEAL

Pain can cloud our vision. Fear can fog our thinking. When we are in a place of pain or fear, when our life is disrupted by chaos, we don't need to make life-changing decisions.

When our thinking is clouded by negative emotions, we are better served by turning to the soothing routines that can restore us to peace. Daily prayer, said in the same place, at the same time. Spirit-affirming readings. A morning walk or an afternoon nap. Even the sameness of a breakfast routine can ground us in the solid reality of our life. We can shower at the same time each day and regain our equilibrium. We can drive the same route to work and find solace in a routine that demands nothing more from us than showing up.

When our hearts and minds are in turmoil, we can simplify our outer world with routine. We can postpone hard decisions until we are stronger. We can avoid conflict for the moment.

ROUTINE CAN CONTRIBUTE TO MY HEALING. WHEN MY SPIRIT IS CALM AGAIN, I CAN TAKE ON MORE OF LIFE'S CHALLENGES.

NO JOB IS TOO BIG

The house was built around the turn of the last century, three stories and four thousand square feet of classic Georgian architecture. Still beautiful, it was now in the way of progress. It had to go.

Instead of tearing it down, someone decided to move it to a nearby lot where the historic home could shelter another generation.

Neighbors watched skeptically. *The job is too big. It can't be done.* Awed, they watched as the foundation was dug out, as the massive home was lovingly, inch by inch, moved to its new site. Some weeks passed with no apparent progress. Rain delayed the work. The house looked ragged and precarious on its makeshift wooden framework. Each inch of forward movement took hours and much loving labor.

As the house sat in the mud for endless weeks, neighbors gave up. *It can't be done. The job is too big.*

Then one morning they looked out to discover that the house was on the opposite side of the street, halfway home to its new location. All the intense groundwork had paid off. The months of painstaking details. The labor few understood.

People cheered.

The house now sits on a quiet corner, surrounded by trees and a garden wall. The task that couldn't be done is completed, successful.

Moving ourselves from misery and dysfunction to self-worth and contentment may seem impossible. We may seem stalled at times, making no discernible progress. But one morning we will awaken and discover that the final leg of our journey was completed while we weren't paying attention. We will have reached our quiet corner.

THE TASK IS NOT TOO BIG AT ALL. INCH BY INCH, I WILL MAKE PROGRESS, UNTIL I HAVE MOVED FROM MISERY TO PEACE.

Surviving Betrayal

WHY ME?

How many of us have asked that as our lives unraveled around us?

A cancer survivor was asked whether he sometimes said, "Why me?" His reply gives a new perspective on accepting our problems.

He said that during the course of his life he'd been blessed with a wonderful, loving family; a steadfast partner; work that fulfilled him and enabled him to live in comfort; friends he could count on. In short, he had many blessings.

"But as I look at those things, I never ask, 'Why me?' I never question why God chose me for those gifts," he said. "So why ask it when something difficult or painful comes along?"

His outlook reminds us that life owes us no explanations. It brings both good and bad into our world, and the gifts far outweigh any of the difficulties.

TODAY I WILL BE GRATEFUL I HAVE BEEN GIVEN SO MANY BLESS-INGS. I WILL CONCENTRATE ON THOSE GIFTS INSTEAD OF ON MY PRESENT DIFFICULTIES.

LOVING A MAN WITH DEMONS

She had reached peace with the effects of her husband's sexual behavior more than a decade earlier. She was speaking to a roomful of women who had learned in recent months of their husband's sexual compulsions. Their pain was raw, and their certainty about the future shaken.

"Never be ashamed of loving a man like this," she told them. "You have nothing to be ashamed of in loving him or sticking by him or hoping that his life will turn around."

Some of the women wept, because it had never occurred to them that they bore no shame for loving a man who was less than perfect, a man who struggled with his demons. Society has attached the shame, and most often not to the person who acts out but to the partner who is trapped in the wreckage.

How can you put up with it? Don't be a doormat! If you stay, you'll get what you deserve.

We wouldn't feel that kind of shame if we decided to stand by a partner who was struggling with severe depression or paralysis or cancer. Society would support our commitment in those circumstances. Men who cheat also are often driven by addictions, by mental or emotional illness, by chronic dysfunctions that take time to heal. These are not excuses, but reasons. And although society may not understand our decision, we don't need to feel shame for loving this man.

I CAN LOVE AND HOPE AND TAKE CARE OF MYSELF, ALL AT THE SAME TIME. THE SPIRITUAL LIFE CAN TEACH ME HOW.

WILLINGNESS

What are we unwilling to surrender today?

Is it something small—a fondness for chocolate, irritation with a neighbor's child, the dissatisfaction we feel when we face our reflection in the mirror and see our mother's image looking back at us? Something so small we can tell ourselves it's not the kind of thing we'd want to waste God's time with?

Is it something big? So big we can't imagine surrendering it, even to a higher power that we trust completely? Our health, our children, our financial future? Because the universe might not realize how important it is to us, how essential to our happiness.

What are we unwilling to surrender today?

Are we ready to have it go wrong? Ready to lose it? Do we really imagine that we can work things out by ourselves, or have we already seen how impossible it can be to achieve exactly what we want in life?

We can seek the willingness to be willing to surrender whatever it is that we hang on to today. We can remember that, large or small, it will be in better hands if we surrender and ask for help.

WHEN I SURRENDER SOMETHING THAT TROUBLES ME, I CREATE A CLIMATE FOR CHANGE. I OPEN MYSELF AND MY CIRCUMSTANCES TO NEW ALTERNATIVES. WHATEVER POWERS FOR GOOD EXIST IN THIS WORLD, I MAKE ROOM FOR THEM TO ACT ON MY PROBLEMS.

ALICE MAY

GEOGRAPHIC CURES

Making a new start is a good plan, as long as we remember that the new start begins within.

Moving to a new town is not making a new start. Buying a new house, getting a new job, casting aside all our old friends for new ones are not new starts. We call those actions geographic cures, attempts to fix our lives by changing external things. Geographic cures never work for long.

Because we always take the problem with us.

The problem is within us. Within our partners. Within the dynamics of our relationship. That is where the fresh start must begin.

Otherwise, we will find ourselves in new surroundings, choosing the same old dysfunctional behaviors, surrounded by the same old misery.

I WON'T TRY TO ESCAPE MY PROBLEMS BY CHANGING MY JOB, MY HOUSE, MY TOWN, MY FRIENDS. I WILL LOOK INWARD, WHERE THE PROBLEMS REALLY LIE.

UNBURDENING YOURSELF

We've made so much progress.

We have learned that we can't control our partner, and that our happiness is dependent not on our partner but on what lies in our own hearts and souls. We have found the courage to look at ourselves honestly and unflinchingly, confronting our old self-defeating behaviors.

Some of us are growing more confident in our relationship with God. Or if not God, at least with the idea that there is a loving force in the world that can bring good into our lives.

We've made much progress. And it is time to move on to the next stage of our process. Our healing journey continues.

It is time to unburden ourselves. It is time to let go of the things we've learned about ourselves. It is time to take one more look at the past so we can leave it behind.

At this stage of our journey, we share what we have learned with another person. This action strengthens our connection with others. It creates a final resting place for the past, and for all the parts of ourselves that hold us back. It is an action that both requires courage and endows us with courage.

TODAY I WILL FIND SOMEONE I TRUST AND PREPARE TO LEAVE BEHIND ALL MY OLD EMOTIONAL BAGGAGE. I AM READY TO MOVE ON.

EXCUSES FOR KEEPING QUIET

We can invent so many apparently good reasons for not talking openly and honestly with our partner about the problems in our relationship.

He's in such a bad mood. There's no point in even trying to have a rational discussion.

He's in such a good mood. I hate to rock the boat.

He's so overworked . . . so remorseful . . . so distracted . . .

Some of our reasons are valid. Maybe he's been drinking, and rational conversation is not possible. Or he's used our honesty against us so often we're afraid of being vulnerable again. He's sick, or we are.

The problem even with good excuses is that they block communication. And no relationship can heal without open, honest communication. Perhaps today we can find as many reasons to work up our courage for a long-overdue discussion as we've found in the past to avoid one.

We can bring these things up today because we owe it to ourselves and to our partner to clear the air. Because we can act as if we have courage today, even if we don't yet. Because we love ourselves enough to stop hiding behind our fear. Because we want honest healing more than we want the same old facade. Because if we don't, the relationship is over anyway.

TODAY I WILL STOP FINDING EXCUSES THAT ALLOW ME TO KEEP QUIET WHEN MY HEART AND SOUL NEED FOR ME TO SPEAK UP. I WON'T SILENCE MYSELF FOR THE SAKE OF KEEPING PEACE ANY LONGER. TODAY I WILL FIND REASONS TO SAY WHAT I NEED TO SAY.

SEX FOR THE RIGHT REASONS

Wholesome sensuality is about giving and receiving love; it is about creating joy.

It is not about feeling obligated. It is not about being nagged or coerced or guilt-tripped into compliance. It isn't about having power over another person, or that person having power over us.

Wholesome sensuality is not about escaping our own feelings or covering up problems within ourselves or within our relationship. It isn't about paybacks. It isn't even about performance or end results like orgasm.

We are sexual as a way to open our hearts, to let someone in, to free ourselves for more and deeper love. We are sexual to create moments of joy with another person. We are sexual because it is our nature to express our emotions physically with both our senses and our spirits.

IF I AM BEING SEXUAL FOR THE WRONG REASONS, TODAY I WILL BECOME WILLING TO LEARN OTHER REASONS.

CUTTING THE WORK IN HALF

I am not alone in this. You are not alone. We are not alone.

I have you, and you have me. We have a family of other women who have been where we are. Who are this moment learning that they are our sisters in pain and disillusionment. The journey asks us to join hands on the path. When we do, the work is cut in half.

When I moved from one house to another, I could not move the couch alone. It was too awkward and too heavy. I tried, because I like to believe I can do it all myself.

But I couldn't.

I had to call for help. When a friend joined me, when we shared the load, we were able to get the job done with half the energy and half the effort. Asking for help cut the job in half.

If we isolate with our problem, if we pull into ourselves, our problem multiplies. If we reach out to others, share the burden, seek help, the problem is cut in half.

TODAY I WILL BE THERE FOR YOU, AND I WILL FIND SOMEONE WHO CAN BE THERE FOR ME.

THE LOVING VOICE OF GOD

My unhealthy mind still speaks to me, even after years of healing.
It tells me I am unloved and unlovable.
It tells me everything that goes wrong in my world is my fault.
It tells me there is no hope.

Today, when I hear that voice, I recognize it as the voice of my disease, my insanity, my victimhood. And today I can choose not to listen
to that voice.

That voice cannot harm me unless I choose to let it.

Today I can listen instead to the voice of God. The voice that says:

I created you with love, to be loved.

*I created you to be responsible for yourself only, and not for the problems of the other
adults in your life.*

I created you in the certainty that, with my help, nothing is hopeless.

TODAY THE VOICE OF MY SICK SPIRIT GROWS QUIET WHEN I LIS-
TEN TO THE LOVING VOICE OF MY HIGHER POWER.

ADMITTING YOUR MISTAKES

Once we have completed our self-discovery process, we are ready to unburden ourselves of the human failings that have complicated our lives and blocked us from peace of mind.

We do that first by sharing what we have learned with someone else. We tell another person all the petty, cowardly, inexcusable things we've done in this lifetime.

This stops a lot of us cold.

I worried that someone would say to me, "No wonder you've had such a rotten marriage; you brought it all on yourself!" I worried that the person I chose to confide in would reject me, reinforcing my husband's rejection.

I've learned since that this is a core belief of people who have been affected by compulsive sexual behavior: we are intrinsically unlovable and if we are ever to be loved we must hide who we really are.

The problem with this belief is that it keeps us isolated, locked away in our pain and our misery and our sick thinking. Locked away forever from any possibility of real love, real joy.

When we find the courage to follow through and share ourselves completely with another person, we learn something amazing. We learn that we will be loved no matter what. We learn that we are not unique in our sins. We learn that we are sisters in spirit.

AFTER HEARING ALL THERE IS TO KNOW ABOUT ME, YOU LOVE ME EVEN MORE THAN YOU LOVED ME WHEN I WORKED SO HARD TO HIDE MY TRUE SELF. JUST AS I LOVE YOU MORE.

LEARN HUMILITY

When we find the courage to bare our souls to someone else as part of the unburdening stage of our healing journey, one of the payoffs is humility. Not humiliation, a matter some of us know intimately. *Humility.*

My dictionary tells me there is a subtle difference between the two. When I have been humiliated, I've been made to seem foolish or contemptible. When I am humbled, however, I have simply become conscious of my shortcomings; I am no longer kidding myself.

In confiding the details of our life, good and bad, we learn that we are neither better nor worse than the next person. We learn that all the unhealthy coping mechanisms we have developed over a lifetime may have once served to keep us feeling safe but now get in the way of a healthy, happy life.

We can see the patterns in our life that have contributed to our misery, just as our listener's patterns once held her back.

I NOW KNOW THAT I AM JUST LIKE OTHER WOMEN IN SO MANY OF MY EMOTIONS AND MY LIMITATIONS. I ALSO KNOW I CAN RECOVER, JUST AS THEY HAVE.

SERENITY IN THE FACE OF PROBLEMS

During some of the most painful or disruptive times in my life, I've reassured myself with the notion that things would soon be back to normal. Soon things would be okay again.

A wise friend likes to remind me that *things* may never be okay. But *I* can be okay.

We desperately want to believe that the painful parts of our life will soon be over and we'll be happy. Our partner will never act out sexually again. Never tell another lie. Never again break our heart.

Maybe all those things will come to pass.

Or maybe they won't. If we're waiting for them all to come true, if we're waiting for *things* to be okay again before *we* can be okay, we're setting ourselves up to be a victim. We're giving someone else power over our happiness, our wholeness, our ability to live life fully.

Our partner may have another affair. A dozen other things may happen that will cause us pain, because that's the way life happens. But no matter what is going on outside us, our insides can be okay.

We are okay because we accept what is and have faith that a divine source will help us get through it. We can be okay because we know to call someone who's been through a similar crisis and she'll share her experience, strength, and hope with us. We can be okay because we remember getting through the last crisis. We can be okay because we are gaining emotional health. And nothing outside us is worth giving that up for.

TODAY I HAVE ALL THE SUPPORT I NEED TO BE OKAY INSIDE NO MATTER WHAT THE CIRCUMSTANCES ARE OUTSIDE. SERENITY IS ALWAYS AVAILABLE TO ME, EVEN IN TIMES OF PAIN AND TURMOIL. TODAY I CAN BE OKAY EVEN IF THINGS AREN'T OKAY.

HEALTHY BOUNDARIES

If our neighbor throws her trash over the fence and into our yard, we know immediately that she's invaded our territory and violated our boundaries. If we nudge our grocery cart in front of someone else in the checkout line, we know without being told that we've trampled another shopper's rights and are not respecting her boundaries.

Seeing clearly when we've overstepped someone else's emotional and personal boundaries—or when he or she has overstepped ours—isn't always so simple.

Living in an unhealthy or emotionally unsafe situation for too long, we become enmeshed in someone else's life. We can no longer understand where our life leaves off and someone else's life begins.

We think we can't survive without the object of our enmeshment. We think that we can read that person's mind, or that he should be able to read ours. We think we have the right to tell him how to run his life. Or that we have the right to dump all responsibility for our happiness in his lap.

If we want to be healthy, we must relearn the concept of healthy boundaries. We must learn that our happiness is up to us and us alone. We must learn that even the people we love the most have their own journey and that we have no right to expect them to join us on our path. We must learn that we don't have to follow anyone into misery or degradation.

TODAY I WILL RESPECT OTHERS' BOUNDARIES. I WILL ESPECIALLY RESPECT MY OWN.

ALICE MAY

ACCOUNTABILITY

Are you accountable to someone in your life?

Have you made a commitment to someone you trust to be honest and forthcoming about your choices? Someone you can't hold out on even when you've done something you'd rather not admit out loud? Someone to whom you tell everything? Not out of guilt, not because that person demands it, but because your own growth and integrity demand it?

During that time in my life when bad ideas spun out of control in my head, I needed someone I could trust. Someone who wasn't directly involved in my life, someone who could tell me the truth about myself without being judgmental. I made a commitment to share with that person any time I walked along the slippery slopes of vengeful thinking, checking up, controlling someone else, or justifying my little dishonesties. Because only by getting honest could I pull myself out of the morass.

I chose a woman who had lived the problems I was living. I chose a woman who had sought spiritual solutions to her problems. I chose a woman willing to listen and share rather than advise.

For me, it wasn't enough to admit my indiscretions to myself when they cropped up. I needed to keep myself humble by stating them out loud, by looking another woman squarely in the eye and sharing honestly.

Knowing I am accountable many times keeps me from going down a path I would be ashamed to admit following. Being accountable saves me regrets and helps me view my own acts through the eyes of someone who loves me enough to be honest.

TODAY I WILL SEEK SOMEONE DEPENDABLE AND TRUSTWORTHY TO WHOM I CAN BE ACCOUNTABLE. THIS IS NOT A JOURNEY TO TAKE ALONE. I WILL SHARE THE PATH.

CHANGING OTHERS

Any relationship, I've been told by people who are working on their codependency issues, is only as healthy as the sickest person in it.

What that means to me is that an unhealthy person can easily drag another person down. An unhealthy person is all too often the one who determines the atmosphere in a relationship.

For those of us who persist in believing that we can fix our dysfunctional loved ones, this idea is a rude awakening. It says not only that we cannot fix our loved ones, but that any attempt to do so is likely to result in losing our own emotional health along the way. It doesn't mean that working on our emotional healing is a wasted effort but does warn of the danger inherent in unhealthy relationships. And it cautions us not to expect our own spiritual growth to work miracles in anyone else's life.

If our spiritual work benefits someone else, we can be grateful. But the only one we can expect to improve is ourselves—not our spouse, our children, our co-workers, or our best friend.

I WORK ON MY SOUL FOR MYSELF. TODAY I WON'T TAKE A SINGLE ACTION DESIGNED TO FIX OR CONTROL OR MANIPULATE ANOTHER PERSON.

DO YOU HOLD A GRUDGE?

For almost two months, the church next door to my home carried this message on the sign out front: *Love keeps no record of wrongs.*

I am often slow to get the message. But I was forced, from daily exposure to the words, to question the damage I may have done to my marriage by keeping a mental list of the wrongs my spouse committed. Had I carved his misdeeds on my heart? And if the answer was yes, was I guilty of hurting our relationship, too?

The answer, for me, was yes.

Love keeps no record of wrongs. But we fallible humans can't love perfectly any more than we can do anything perfectly. Today, however, we are better able to see our foibles when they are pointed out to us. Eventually, we may become more aware of how we are contributing to the problems in our life.

Then we can begin to change. We can work to erase our mental list of our partner's wrongs. We can seek to fill our hearts with forgiveness instead of blame. And we can stop blaming ourselves for the ways in which we've fallen short of expressing perfect love.

TODAY I WILL REMEMBER THAT LOVE KEEPS NO RECORD OF WRONGS. INCLUDING MINE.

HONESTY

Friends who strive for a spirit-filled life tell me that three characteristics are essential if our spirit is to thrive: honesty, open-mindedness, and willingness.

Many of us assume that honesty won't be a problem. Not for us. We aren't the one who's had a problem with lying, cheating, and conniving. Right?

What we sometimes learn as we seek to make room for our spirits to grow is that we may have been as guilty of dishonesty as our partners. We've just been more subtle in our dishonesty.

Have we concealed from our friends, our neighbors, our children what is going on in our homes? Have we whitewashed the state of our marriage?

Do we cover up our feelings? Have we covered up so often that we aren't even sure of our feelings anymore?

Do we lie to our spouse by faking enjoyment of sex, by pretending we aren't hurt by his behavior, by saying we love him when we'd like to wring his neck?

Spirituality asks us to be honest. Not brutally honest. Not honest without boundaries, blabbing everything to everyone. But honest when it counts. Compassionately honest. Honest with ourselves. Honest before God.

TODAY I WILL SEEK TO BE HONEST, REMEMBERING THAT LEARNING TO MAKE THIS CHANGE WILL TAKE PRACTICE. I WILL SEEK WILLINGNESS TODAY, AND I WILL WELCOME THE OPPORTUNITIES TO LEARN.

ENDING A RELATIONSHIP

Ending a cherished relationship sometimes becomes the only way out of the insanity.

If that becomes true, it isn't the worst thing that can happen. It may feel so at the time, but it isn't.

Continuing to stifle our genuine emotions is worse. Lying to ourselves about reality is worse. Allowing our children to grow up in unrelieved turmoil, learning bitterness and fear instead of love and security, is worse. Robbing ourselves of the gift of a healthy, happy future is worse. All those things, and more, are worse than ending even the most valued relationship.

Ending a relationship is sometimes necessary to begin the next stage of our journey. It is necessary in order to grow our spirits, to learn to love, to follow dreams we haven't been able to pursue as we struggled with heartbreak and dysfunction.

There are worse things than ending a relationship.

For those of us who know it's time to end a relationship, we can do so with hope and with confidence that there will be many good things on the path ahead of us.

TODAY I WON'T TURN AWAY FROM THE ABUNDANCE LIFE OFFERS.
IF IT IS TIME TO END A RELATIONSHIP, I WILL TRUST THAT THE
NEXT STAGE OF MY JOURNEY LEADS TO GOOD THINGS.

REJECT SHAME

Shame cripples us emotionally.

We feel shamed by another's actions, especially when his actions have to do with sex, an area of life about which so many of us are already conflicted. We feel shamed by our own years of denial or fear. We feel shamed by our inability to act on our own behalf.

We've felt shamed by abuse or betrayal or our own participation in our misery.

Today we can begin to let go of the debilitating effects of shame.

We can let go of shame that isn't ours. Others' deeds are not our responsibility. Society's inability to deal with sexuality in a healthy way is not our shame either.

We can let go of shame that we believe is ours and check those beliefs against what we learned during our process of self-discovery. Are we guilty of real wrongs against ourselves or others? That is something we can deal with through the cleansing actions of confiding in someone else and seeking forgiveness if necessary.

Guilt says, *My actions were a mistake.* Guilt encourages us to accept responsibility and make changes. Guilt says we made a bad situation worse by some of our actions, but we don't have to repeat those actions.

Shame says, *I am a mistake.* Shame is about feeling unworthy and irredeemable. And it has no basis in reality. Shame is a part of our sick thinking. We have the choice of rejecting it today.

I WILL REMEMBER THAT EVEN IF I MAKE A MISTAKE, I AM NOT A MISTAKE. I WILL ESPECIALLY REMEMBER THAT OTHERS' ACTIONS DO NOT REFLECT ON ME. SHAME IS NOT A HEALTHY EMOTION, AND TODAY I DON'T HAVE TO TAKE IT ON.

A SAFE PLACE FOR YOUR SPIRITS

Repeated adultery is abusive.

It damages the soul. It destroys the spirit. It inflicts wounds that scar people and relationships. It can even kill.

We don't have to endure the abuse. We don't have to make up our minds to live with it day in and day out, until we have no more soul left to damage.

We can find refuge from the psychic pain caused by chronic adultery. We can find refuge in the company of other women who have also been damaged. We can seek help and hope with those women. We can learn that our happiness does not depend on another but is a matter of the spirit.

We can take shelter in activities that feed our souls: doing volunteer projects, reading a good book, visiting a quiet spot by the lake, tending our gardens on a spring morning, pursuing our spiritual practices.

Once we've found those safe places for our souls, we can stay there long enough to find safe ways to protect ourselves and our spirits.

TODAY I AM STRONG ENOUGH TO CREATE A SAFE ENVIRONMENT, BOTH PHYSICALLY AND EMOTIONALLY. TODAY I WILL FREE MYSELF IN WHATEVER WAY SEEMS APPROPRIATE FROM ANY CIRCUMSTANCES THAT ARE ABUSIVE OR DEMEANING.

SELF-PITY

Our self-pity is justifiable. Ask anyone. When we describe our circumstances, we see the look that comes into our listener's eyes. If it isn't pity, it's pity's close kin.

Under similar circumstances, almost anyone would feel sorry for herself. Why shouldn't we?

Because it doesn't gain us a thing.

What good can possibly come from dwelling in self-pity? Can it motivate us to positive, healthy action? Can it guide us to appropriate changes in our lives? Can it bolster our self-confidence or surround us with encouragement and support?

No, most of the time self-pity merely feeds on itself. It breeds lethargy and impotence. It invites self-loathing to set up shop. Self-pity is self-defeating.

We can evict self-pity by making a commitment to our healing journey. We can focus on the changed attitudes that will take us out of self-pity and into growth. We can seek people who will be understanding of our self-pity but who will encourage us to choose healing actions instead. We can practice gratitude and acceptance even when we can't see any reason for either. We can offer service to others whose problems help us grow in compassion.

If we refuse to grant self-pity space in our spirits, we will soon find there is more space within us for serenity, for joy, for faith.

TODAY I WILL RECOGNIZE SELF-PITY WHEN IT ARISES, ACKNOWLEDGING THAT IT MAY BE A NATURAL REACTION UNDER THE CIRCUMSTANCES. BUT I WILL ALSO RECOGNIZE THAT I DON'T HAVE TO GIVE IN TO IT. I CAN TAKE OTHER ACTIONS, INVITE OTHER EMOTIONS. SELF-PITY IS SELF-DEFEATING. I WON'T LET IT TAKE ROOT.

CUTTING YOURSELF OFF
FROM HELP

One of the most damaging tricks we play on ourselves is to isolate. We tell ourselves that our secrets are so shameful we must hide them. We tell ourselves that we're just not up to company. We tell ourselves that no one will understand.

These reactions are natural at first. But if our isolation goes on, we harm ourselves. Because in isolating we cut ourselves off from all the sources of help that life places before us. We create a breeding ground for more fear and less self-worth. We enable ourselves to sink deeper into self-pity and helplessness and hopelessness, and we enable our unhealthy loved ones to keep practicing their unhealthy behaviors by creating an atmosphere where secrets thrive. We shut out love, and we shut out healing, and we shut out the voice of our inner wisdom.

We must stop hiding with our pain and our shame.

We must ease ourselves back into the world. We can go to our book club or our professional network meetings or our monthly lunches with the old gang. We can pick up the phone to call the best friend we've allowed to slip away. If the best we can do today is speak to our neighbor over the back fence, it will be a start. A good start.

We must come out of isolation.

We have a full, rich, rewarding life. We can come out of our isolation and reclaim that life.

TODAY I WILL TAKE ONE SMALL STEP TO COME OUT OF ISOLATION AND RECLAIM MY LIFE. ON MY JOURNEY, I HAVE STORED ENOUGH EMOTIONAL RESERVES TO TAKE ONE SMALL STEP OUT OF MY SELF-IMPOSED DARKNESS. I DON'T WANT TO BE ALONE ANY LONGER, AND TODAY I CAN DO SOMETHING ABOUT THAT.

OBSESSIVE THINKING

One of the forms of insanity with which many of us become intimately acquainted is obsessive thinking. We can circle around the same thought for hours, for days, examining it from every angle, and never reaching a conclusion or making a decision or taking an action.

Does he love me? What does it mean that he was late again tonight? Should we divorce? What am I doing wrong?

Obsessive thinking is a clue that we've lost our serenity. It's a clue that we're focusing on someone else instead of on our own lives, feelings, and healing.

Obsessive thinking is too powerful for us to tackle alone. Our best defense is to put an end to it before it gets started—to recognize the kind of thought that can destroy our serenity and refuse it attention as soon as it comes calling. If we don't pick it up, we won't have to put it down.

But if obsessive thinking has already taken root and we have finally reached the point of wanting to be rid of it, we might want to consider the difficulty of letting it go, of detaching from it, until we attach our thoughts to something else.

When obsessive thinking has us by the throat, we can try attaching instead to prayer or work or exercise. We can make a phone call to someone who supports us or meditate or read something inspiring. We can do something creative or be of service to someone who needs and wants our help.

We can find the courage to do the footwork that destroys the hold that obsessive thinking has on us by attaching to a healthy activity.

As I starve my obsessive thinking with lack of attention, it will diminish. As I feed my healthy thinking, it will grow.

ALICE MAY

THE SERENITY PRAYER

God, grant me the serenity to accept the things I cannot change, courage to change the things I can, and wisdom to know the difference.

The Serenity Prayer is used by millions of people to survive life's dark moments, and even its petty irritations. It is the essence of healthy thinking, of detachment, of humbly recognizing our limitations.

God, grant me the serenity to accept the things I cannot change . . .

A higher spirit grants the serenity; acceptance is our footwork. What are the things we cannot change? Other people, their actions, their feelings. Most external situations in our lives.

. . . courage to change the things I can . . .

Courage can be one of the first things to go when we've lived with difficulties long enough. We're afraid. We're immobilized by indecision. But we will be granted the courage to do our footwork anytime we ask.

. . . and wisdom to know the difference.

Recognizing the difference between the things we can change and the things we cannot is not easy when our perceptions have been distorted by daily living amid deception and betrayal. But the healing journey helps us understand the difference between the things we cannot change—the behavior of our loved ones, for example—and the things we can change—our own thoughts, our spiritual practice, our ability to cope.

The Serenity Prayer is a simple plan for bringing our lives into perspective, whether we are in crisis or if today is simply business as usual.

TODAY I WILL RECOGNIZE HOW SERENITY, COURAGE, AND WISDOM CAN CHANGE MY PERSPECTIVE ON MY LIFE. I WILL SEEK TO USE THOSE TOOLS WHENEVER I AM UNSURE WHAT TO DO NEXT.

Surviving Betrayal

BE WILLING TO ACCEPT
SPIRITUAL HELP

We're never more ready to give up our flaws than when we've just finished talking with a trusted friend about our process of self-discovery. We've seen all the unhealthy thinking and how it's led to all the unhealthy actions that have contributed to all our unhealthy relationships. And we don't want it to be that way anymore.

We want change. We want a clean slate. This is the next step in the process of unburdening ourselves.

Today we can act on that willingness. Today we can entrust ourselves—good and bad—to the higher power we are comfortable with. This is all the process asks of us at this time. A willingness to allow God or a higher spirit to work on us, improve us, and use us for good.

TODAY I HAVE MORE CONFIDENCE THAT SEEKING SPIRITUAL SUPPORT IN IMPROVING MYSELF WILL HAVE FAR BETTER RESULTS THAN TAKING IT ALL INTO MY OWN HANDS, AS I'VE ALWAYS DONE IN THE PAST.

LOVE HEALS

Are we guilty of looking for love—and expressing it ourselves—in all the wrong ways?

If someone desires us, does that make it love?

If we reciprocate, does that make it love?

If someone gives in to our every whim, is that love? Or if we give up our every wish in the face of someone else's plans, is that love?

If someone approves when we do something his way, is that love?

We've measured love in many faulty ways in the past. We now have an opportunity to learn better ways of seeing love in others' actions—and better ways of expressing it ourselves.

Today we can open our hearts to our loved ones, even when they don't cater to our every need, even when they don't behave the way we'd like them to. Today we can open our hearts to loving others just as they are, even if they still place conditions on their love for us. Today we can have the openness of spirit to be kind, to be gentle, to be giving to others around us.

We can also try to love ourselves enough to be at peace even if others don't love us back in the ways we hope for.

Love is the great healer of the universe. When we give it to others, we are healed, even if others don't accept healing for themselves. And the universe will send us love in return, even though it may be from a source we never expected.

TODAY I WILL ALLOW LOVE TO HEAL ME.

TAKE IT EASY

Relax.

We don't have all the answers today, and that's okay. We can't complete all our footwork today, and that's as it should be.

Today one of the contributions we can make to our own serenity and our own recovery is to relax.

We can nap. We can sit on our porch and soak up the first stirrings of spring or the last hurrahs of summer. We can read a book just for fun. We can get a massage or buy bubble gum or drive in the country or walk over to the neighborhood park and simply sit still until we feel peace fill our hearts.

I DON'T HAVE TO WORK HARD EVERY MOMENT TO SET MY LIFE STRAIGHT. I CAN GO WITH THIS DAY'S FLOW AND KNOW THAT I AM SAFE AND THAT SOLUTIONS ARE UNFOLDING. I CAN RELAX.

DIFFICULT DECISIONS

The need to resolve things, to know how this drama plays out, is often so urgent within me that I'm tempted to manipulate the situation, to say something or do something that I know will drive my husband out of the house. Just to have a resolution.

When I feel that sense of urgency, I try to remember what others who have been here before me share about the decision to stay or go:

- "If making the decision to stay or go is driving me crazy, that is a sign that I'm not ready to know how to handle the rest of my life. I let it go until I can reach a decision calmly."

- "This stage of my life isn't about my decision, but about the process of growth that I find myself in. This process, if I stick with it, will find me stronger, happier, healthier, more spiritually connected—as long as I trust the process and don't try to leap ahead to the resolution before its time."

- "Each morning I get up and ask myself if this is the day I am going to leave. If it isn't, I remember that today is all I have to worry about, and I let it go for the rest of the day. Tomorrow I can do it all over again. I tell myself I'm married one day at a time."

We may not know exactly what to do about our relationship today. But we can prepare ourselves for the right answers. We can practice patience. We can trust that this place of uncertainty is exactly where we're supposed to be today.

TODAY I WILL USE MY NEW TOOLS TO DEAL WITH THE UNCERTAINTY IN MY LIFE. I WON'T TRY TO FORCE A SOLUTION. I WILL TRY PATIENCE INSTEAD.

Surviving Betrayal

THE CHALLENGE TO GROW

A friend reminds me not to cheat myself out of a chance to grow.

We can turn our backs on opportunities to grow by refusing the call to take a difficult action or practice a new behavior. We can accept the challenge by stepping up and doing whatever we most resist today.

We can call someone and ask for help.

We can make an amends as soon as we realize we were in the wrong.

We can express our love even if we're afraid of rejection.

We can open our hearts to the people who pass before us today.

We can laugh like a kid.

We can share our pain.

We can take time for ourselves.

We can give, expecting nothing in return.

And when the day is over, we can feel good about what we've done. We can feel good about ourselves.

TODAY I ACCEPT THE CHALLENGE OF DOING ONE OR TWO THINGS THAT SEEM CONTRARY TO MY NATURE. I ACCEPT THE CHALLENGE TO GROW.

SUPPRESSED ANGER

Anger can be a destructive force, and never more so than when we attempt to suppress it.

Suppressed anger does not go away, does not diminish, does not convert itself into forgiveness or healing or joy. Suppressed anger buries itself deep within us, becoming a part of our spirit. There it grows and becomes toxic.

Anger that has festered most often expresses itself in two ways.

Sometimes it comes out sideways as a burst of ill will sharply directed at an unintended target—the bank teller who is too slow to suit us, the co-worker who doesn't conduct herself according to our rules, even our own children as they go about the business of simply being children.

Other times the anger we thought to ignore turns inward. We learn to despise ourselves, to diminish our worth, to become our own worst enemy. Or we become ill, responding physically to the poison in our souls with headaches, ulcers, chronic aches and pains.

We can release our anger. We *must* release our anger. We can do it in ways that do not cause damage to others. And we can do it in ways that won't cause damage to us.

TODAY I WILL LISTEN TO MY HEART AND TO MY BODY FOR HIDDEN ANGER. IF I FIND ANY, I WILL SEEK A HEALTHY WAY TO RELEASE IT. I WILL NO LONGER SUPPRESS MY ANGER.

FORGIVENESS AND BOUNDARIES

We may forgive our partner seventy times seven times, as the Bible suggests.

We may, if we are fortunate and filled with grace, need to forgive him only once.

But all the forgiveness in the world does not mean there are no consequences for his behavior. And it doesn't mean we are obliged to continue to accept unacceptable behavior.

We can forgive and still set clear boundaries. Our boundaries may include the concrete changes in behavior we hope to see, whether it is joint counseling or group therapy for men who cheat or giving up his old playmates and playgrounds. Our boundaries may include actions that foster trust in a relationship, such as curtailing late nights at work. Our boundaries may certainly include the actions *we* will take if unacceptable behavior comes up again.

Boundaries help us take care of ourselves and ensure that we're not permitting ourselves to fall into the role of victim. But healthy boundaries don't prohibit us from forgiving or giving second chances. Forgiving is an act of grace that touches us and the person we forgive. Forgiveness is a way to say that we remember that we all fall short of perfection. Forgiveness is a way to say that we can hold love in our heart even when it is broken.

I CAN FORGIVE WITHOUT EXCUSING HIM. I CAN FORGIVE WHILE STILL INSISTING ON CONSEQUENCES FOR UNACCEPTABLE BEHAVIOR. TODAY I CAN FORGIVE AND SET HEALTHY BOUNDARIES.

PAINFUL ANNIVERSARIES

Anniversaries are typically cause for celebration. But when our lives are disrupted by betrayal, our pain gives birth to a new set of anniversaries.

We remember the day we learned the truth. The day he moved out. The day life dealt us another critical blow.

It does little good to try to ignore those dates, especially in the early days of rebuilding our lives. Any negative feelings we try to bury out of sight will merely take root, sending out shoots to spring forth at the most unlikely time and place to cause us more pain. Unnecessary pain.

As an anniversary approaches, we can take action to deal with it positively. We can alert someone we trust to be at our side. We can seek courage. We can plan a ritual for releasing our pain when the day arrives—to write the reason for the anniversary down, place it in a balloon, and release it, for example. We can spend a finite, agreed-on amount of time—ten minutes, or an hour—journaling about our feelings, then move on. We can plan a rewarding day with people who nurture us.

We can honor ourselves on this anniversary, for our courage and our willingness to change.

TODAY I CAN MARK ANNIVERSARIES WITH MOMENTS OF HEALING AND FORGIVENESS. I CAN CELEBRATE MY FREEDOM FROM THE OLD PAIN.

WHEN YOU'RE STUCK

Sometimes we get stuck.

We've been moving through life's muck, making a little progress, catching glimpses of a time and place when life won't feel so hard. Then we look up one day and realize we haven't moved in weeks. Our feet are still bogged down in the same anger, pain, or shame that gripped us last month.

We are stuck.

When we are stuck, it may be because we are focused on all our negative feelings and the negative events in our lives.

It may be because we refuse to forgive, either ourselves or someone else.

We may be clinging to our old ways of coping, doing the same things over and over, expecting different results. Or we may have stopped doing the things that do work—prayer, journaling, daily contact with our support network.

There is also another possibility. We may be exactly where we're supposed to be. We may be sitting here for a rest between growth spurts or to absorb life's lessons more deeply.

We can look at all those possibilities and ask our inner wisdom to show us where we're stuck and to give us what we need to move forward. Then we can continue our footwork and ask for patience, even when we can't see the outcome unfolding.

WHEN I AM STUCK, I CAN TRUST THAT CHANGE WILL HAPPEN IN THE RIGHT TIME, IN THE RIGHT WAY, IF I AM WILLING TO WORK FOR IT.

ALICE MAY

GROWTH THROUGH ABSTINENCE

Many of us feel deep in our souls that being sexual without being intimate is a hollow experience.

So we choose abstinence. Celibacy. We may be working on our marriages still. Or we may have realized that the time is right to move on. For whatever reason, we know we will not be sexually active for the foreseeable future.

Some of us have found abstinence to be freeing. We let go of our images of our physical self. We quit thinking of ourselves in terms of how someone else will react to our breasts or our stretch marks or thighs that are giving in to gravity. We are able to save our sexual energy for other forms of creativity or productivity or giving.

We find joy in reserving our bodies and our spirits just for ourselves for once in our lives.

We even gain new confidence in our sexuality when we don't give it away cheaply, simply because a certain relationship leaves us feeling obligated.

Abstinence is not a bad word. It is not to be feared. It does not shrivel us up or dry us out. We are not wasting our prime. Abstinence can be, if we approach it as a time to find something new within ourselves, a time of expansion. A time to grow into real-life sexuality, once we are no longer trapped in society's myths about sexuality.

TODAY I WILL NOT WORRY THAT ABSTINENCE IS HARMING ME OR MY RELATIONSHIP. I WILL TRUST THAT ABSTINENCE OFFERS ME A TIME TO CHANGE, A TIME FOR PROBLEMS TO BE WORKED OUT.

TRUE CHANGE IS GOD'S WORK

Some of us have spent our entire lives wishing we were different. Trying desperately to make ourselves funnier, more demonstrative, less anxious, more artistic or sensuous or intellectual.

All our desperate attempts at perfection have convinced many of us that true change is impossible. We've tried everything we can think of, and we're still the same old person we've been dissatisfied with all our lives.

So how do we change ourselves now?

The answer is, we don't.

Up to this point on our path to spiritual awareness, we've seen how little control we have over most of the external problems in our lives. We've been introduced to hope for a better way, we've examined ourselves, and we've pinpointed the things that hold us back—our imperfections.

Now it is time to learn something that should be a great relief. Ridding ourselves of our flaws isn't *our* job.

It's God's job.

As with so much else in our lives, we must relinquish any idea that we're in charge. If we sincerely place ourselves in God's hands, we will find ourselves changing in ways we never imagined.

The personal liabilities that get in the way of a healthy, happy life—our obsessive thinking, our selfishness, our dishonesty, our judgmental nature—will begin to fall away.

Through grace, we will make progress in becoming the person we were created to be. We can't do that for ourselves. But if we are humble and willing, our higher spirit can. And will.

TODAY I WILL REMEMBER THAT I DON'T HAVE TO CHANGE MYSELF. FOR THAT JOB, I CAN SEEK THE HELP OF A POWER GREATER THAN MYSELF.

ALICE MAY

LISTEN TO THE QUIET

The clamoring in our minds is often so loud and so unpleasant that we'll do anything to avoid being alone with it.

I fill my moments of silence with books. When I read, I can avoid being alone with my thoughts and my feelings. A friend turns on the TV anytime she's home alone, cleaning house to the hum of TV voices. Some of us play the radio. Talk on the phone. Anything but get alone with the voices in our heads.

The voices in our heads feed our fear and discomfort. They tell us we're not good enough, that we don't fit in, that life is nothing but a series of hard knocks. Those inner committees shut out any chance of hearing what the silence has to teach us.

The external noise we create only appears to silence the inner voices that cause us uneasiness. In reality, outer noise simply gives our inner noise room to grow, to multiply, as a virus spreads.

We must learn that we have nothing to fear from the silence. We are not alone in that place of silence. Unlike our noisy minds, the silence doesn't spout messages that hurt us. The silence is where we connect with our spirit. The silence is where we begin to heal, where serenity is born and spirituality grows.

TODAY I WILL TAKE A FEW MOMENTS TO BANISH THE OUTER NOISE AND EXPOSE MY INNER NOISE. THEN I WILL INVITE SEREN-ITY TO REPLACE IT.

ASK AND ACT

Our new principles of living won't take root overnight. No matter how determinedly we tell ourselves to detach and forgive and love unconditionally, the journey from our head to our heart is an uncharted path. We can't force it to happen.

But we can be sure that our new way of viewing life will grow if we continue doing our footwork. If we act as if we are able to surrender our fears and disappointments, eventually we will be able to. If we pray for the strength to forgive and then treat people as if our hearts had already been filled with forgiveness, that transformation will take place. Whatever miraculous changes we want to occur within our hearts and souls will happen, if we ask and act.

One day, if we ask and act consistently, we will wake up to realize that the changes we hoped for have taken place. Without realizing it, our ability to live a spiritual life will have moved from our heads to our hearts. We will be different, we will be better, we will be renewed.

IF I WORK TOWARD GOOD EVEN IN MY MOST LIMITED CAPACITY,
I WILL BECOME ANOTHER OF LIFE'S MIRACLES.

HYPERVIGILANCE

Hypervigilance will not save us one moment of pain. It will not circumvent one hurtful event in our life. It will not change a single action of a person who is determined to deceive us.

Hypervigilance is not the same as taking care of ourselves. It is not the same as healthy boundaries. It is not the same as making wise choices about the people we surround ourselves with.

Hypervigilance is a way we betray ourselves. It is forcing ourselves to live in constant tension, ever alert to subtle hints or waving red flags, thus making us more susceptible to physical and emotional breakdown. It is sacrificing this moment to our fears about tomorrow. It is wasting all our spiritual, emotional, and physical energy in an attempt to control something that is out of our hands.

Today we can recognize the fallacy in believing that being on continuous red alert will save us from pain. For a few minutes, we won't worry about what someone else is doing or how we could catch him at it. We can ease up. We can give up our efforts to read someone else's mind or change it. We can pay attention to how it feels when we release our grip on things—the way our shoulders release, the way a deep breath fills us up. We can absorb every pleasant feeling we have in those moments when we let go of our hypervigilance.

Then we can ask ourselves which way we feel better. We can try to remember that feeling of ease the next time we respond to the alarms ringing in our heads.

TODAY I WILL RECOGNIZE HOW I ABUSE MYSELF WHEN I REMAIN ON A CONSTANT VIGIL AGAINST PAIN. TODAY I WILL FIND HEALTHIER WAYS TO PROTECT MYSELF.

NOT YOUR TIMETABLE

When spring comes, the grass grows by itself.

A friend passed along that quote from the Tao at a time when I desperately wanted things in my marriage to change. Immediately.

I wanted to stop hurting. I wanted to know with certainty that I could trust my spouse. I wanted him to look at me with welcome and love in his eyes, the way he once did. I wanted the storm to be over. I was ready for the rainbow. Immediately.

Whenever my life is unsettled, I grow impatient with God's timetable for change, for healing, for the good to overtake the bad. I become certain that if I figure out just the right action to take, I will set in motion the chain of events that will swiftly transform my life. I forget that things happen as they do, when they do, for a reason. I forget that I do not set the timetable and that life is under no obligation to reveal its timetable to me.

When spring comes, the grass grows by itself.

We needn't coax the grass. We needn't tug on the new shoots, urging them out of the earth faster than nature has in mind. Indeed, if we do, we'll probably kill the new growth. We can only feed and water the grass, when the time is right.

TODAY I WILL LEAVE THE GRASS ALONE AND TRUST THAT IT WILL GROW WITHOUT MY HELP, WHEN IT IS TIME.

A HUNGER FOR SPIRIT

If he loved us, surely he wouldn't do these things. If he loved us, surely he would change. If he loved us, surely he would be the perfect partner, lover, friend, spouse.

If he loved us enough, maybe that would fill the hole in his soul.

More likely, however, one person is not enough to fill that vacuum in his spirit. Not a wife. Not even a mistress, a one-night stand, a temporary bit of physical pleasure.

That hole in the soul is too large to be filled by love or even sex. He may not understand that, so he keeps trying. His actions are not about us, they are not aimed at us, they are not attempts to hurt us. That is important for us to recognize and accept.

It is also important for us to recognize and accept that each of us has this same hunger, a gaping need that the most wonderful of transitory pleasures won't fulfill. So we are learning to connect with a higher spirit at a time when the hole in our soul is too large to fill with anything this world has to offer.

Our partner's love will not be enough to make our lives whole; ours is not enough to do the same for him.

I AM HUNGRY FOR PEACE. I AM HUNGRY FOR A LIFE OF THE SPIRIT. TODAY I CAN TAKE THE ACTIONS THAT FEED ME.

REBUILDING TRUST

The first time we catch ourselves trusting a man who has betrayed us, we may be struck with fear or shame or both.

How can we believe he is where he says when we remember so vividly all the times he wasn't? How can we trust this excuse when he's proven in the past that he'll say anything to cover his tracks?

Before we give in to our self-recriminations, let us ask for the wisdom to view our circumstances and our actions realistically. Have we been seeking guidance in this relationship? Have we been honest with ourselves regarding our role in this partnership? Are we doing the difficult footwork of learning how to set healthy boundaries and how to speak up honestly about our needs and our emotions? Are we nurturing our connection to the other women who can help us admit our true motives?

If we lapse into trust too soon, too easily, perhaps we owe it to ourselves to second-guess our reactions. But if this moment of trust comes after a period in which we and our partner have both worked on healing, on rebuilding, then perhaps it is time to accept this moment as a next natural step in mending the relationship. Perhaps it is time to show a little trust in ourselves and our instincts.

If his actions continue to support that trust, such moments will come more often. It will take time, but the day may come when the moment that startles us is the moment of mistrust.

As we continue on our journey, we can be open to whatever truth comes from the voices of wisdom in our lives. We can trust that truth when it comes.

TODAY I WILL REMEMBER THE HARD WORK I'VE DONE TO REGAIN MY ABILITY TO SEE LIFE AS IT IS. I WILL ALLOW MYSELF TO TRUST MY INSTINCTS A LITTLE MORE TODAY.

ALICE MAY

POSITIVE CONTRIBUTIONS

What positive things do we bring to our families?

Are we creative? Enthusiastic? Do we bake cookies from scratch? Take our children to the library once a week? Can we laugh at our mistakes? Are we friendly or generous or quick to see good in others? Are we loving without being controlling or smothering?

Each of us brings something good to our families. Sometimes we overlook the good we contribute, especially when circumstances are gloomy.

Our self-discovery process will help us see ourselves in a true light, good and bad, neither outweighing the other. Seeing ourselves more clearly gives us the opportunity to act out of our strengths more often than we act out of our shortcomings. And when we do that, the balance begins to shift. We like ourselves more and need our negative traits less.

What we focus on dominates our lives. Today we can focus on all the good things we bring to our family. We can try to focus on the positive when we look at others, too. Not in an effort to deny the truth about anything, but merely to do our part to shift the balance in our family from negative to positive. Even if we are the only one in our family making such a shift in point of view, it will help. It will benefit the family. It will make it more pleasant to live in our own skin.

TODAY I WILL BE HONEST ENOUGH WITH MYSELF TO SEE HOW MANY POSITIVE THINGS I BRING TO MY FAMILY. I WILL WORK AT EXPANDING ON THOSE THINGS.

WRITE DOWN YOUR TRUTH

How do you measure your progress? How do you arrive at clarity when your head is spinning with contradictory thoughts? How do you capture the truth about your circumstances so that you aren't blinded by euphoric recall later? How do you get gut honest? How do you connect with the higher spirit you are learning to trust?

Some of us do any or all of those things with a daily journal.

Our journals take many forms. Some of us write about our feelings. Some of us commit to paper the apparently insignificant details of our day. Some of us write in spiral-bound notebooks or attractive blank books designed especially for journaling. Others journal on computers.

It was suggested to me that I write my journal entries in the form of letters to God. Nothing is too trivial to set down in those letters. Nothing is too important to weep or rage or rejoice over in them. And no matter where my spirits are when I begin my letters, I find that by the time I close I am ready to surrender all my problems again. In gratitude. In humility.

However we approach journaling, it can be a powerful tool for healing. The writing doesn't have to be grammatical or literary. What we write doesn't have to be fit for anyone's eyes but our own.

What we write only needs to be as honest as we can make it. Like everything else on our journey, our journal will lift us and teach us and free us. All we have to contribute is as much willingness and as much honesty as we are capable of today.

TODAY I WILL JOURNAL. I WILL OPEN MY HEART ON A BLANK PAGE AND LEARN SOMETHING NEW ABOUT MY EMOTIONS, MY CIRCUMSTANCES, MY PROGRESS.

ALICE MAY

ACCEPTANCE, NOT ACQUIESCENCE

A friend reminds me, "Half my problems are solved by practicing acceptance and gratitude. The other half, by gratitude and acceptance."

Acceptance. We may resist the idea because it reminds us of times when we've allowed ourselves to be walked on in the name of keeping peace. We've accepted unacceptable behavior. We've accepted whatever someone else dished out because we didn't know that we didn't deserve it or because we didn't know how to stand up for ourselves.

As we grow stronger and healthier and closer to our true spirit, acceptance takes on a new meaning.

Today we accept the reality of our circumstances. We accept our inability to change others, their actions, or their feelings. We accept the past as past. We accept that true change for the better comes only when we act as nearly as possible in concert with a higher spirit.

TODAY I CAN RECOGNIZE THE DIFFERENCE BETWEEN ACCEPTANCE AND ACQUIESCENCE. TODAY I WILL PRACTICE HEALTHY ACCEPTANCE.

ATTITUDE OF GRATITUDE

Gratitude is another indispensable tool for gaining serenity, hope, and healing.

Can we find something to be grateful for today? Are we healthy? Do we have loyal friends, a roof over our heads, food on the table? Is the sun shining? Does our dog still love us?

Whatever pain we are in, life always holds countless good things for which we can be grateful. If we are prone to forget those things when life deals us a blow, we can take time today to make a written list of all that is good in our lives.

Some of us use the alphabet to get us started when we're feeling particularly ungrateful. A is for the affection of others. B is for the neighborhood bakery. C is for our children. Things both simple and profound make life a joy. It works for me to review my day, paying attention to all the positive things that have touched my life that day—a call from a friend, a productive workday, the chickadee at the bird feeder.

We can put our list in our purse or our briefcase or our jeans pocket, where we will have easy access to it at times when our grief and pain overwhelm us. Those days will come, and we can be prepared for them. We can have at least one of our tools at our fingertips.

When we practice gratitude, we remember that the source of our misery is not at the center of our universe.

I WILL VIEW THE WORLD TODAY WITH GRATITUDE AND ALLOW MYSELF TO BE REMINDED THAT I HAVE ALL THAT I NEED, AND MORE.

ACTING ON IMPULSE

The Serenity Prayer becomes a bridge to sanity that many of us use in times of stress or pain or anger. A variation on the prayer also serves as a reminder that our reactions often contribute to our problems with others.

God, grant me the grace to find the space between impulse and action.

What is our first impulse when we feel anger? When we feel threatened or discounted? Do we rage? Belittle? Wound with sarcasm? Do we rush to apologize, to smooth over, to make peace? Bottle up our emotions?

Do our impulses sometimes make our problems worse instead of better? Do we mistake hasty reaction for standing up for ourselves? Anger and aggression for asserting ourselves? Retaliation for justice? How often have we jumped to react only to do or say things that made us end up looking and feeling like the culprit when the original wrong wasn't ours?

At these times, this simple variation on the Serenity Prayer reminds us that our first impulse may be born out of our own soul-sickness. Our first impulse may keep us unhealthy; it may come between us and spiritual growth. This prayer tells us that we needn't raise our voices, run and hide, inflict pain. Before we launch into a course of action, we can talk to someone else first, vent to someone who can be objective. We can journal until we're calm or walk two miles until we've cooled off or bolstered our courage.

By taking a moment to reflect, we can find that space between rash impulse and harmful action, a space where we can find serenity, sanity, and good judgment. We can remember that we have choices about our actions.

TODAY I CAN PAUSE BEFORE I REACT AND CHOOSE AN ACTION THAT PROMOTES MY HEALING, AS WELL AS HEALING IN MY RELATIONSHIPS WITH OTHERS.

Surviving Betrayal

EXPECT LESS OF YOURSELF

When we are in crisis, when stress rules our lives, we owe ourselves the kindness of expecting less of ourselves.

Our minds don't work as efficiently. Our memory slips. Decisions are harder. Our bodies wear out more quickly. We need more rest.

At times like this, let us grant ourselves the luxury of taking it easy. Doing less. Resting more. Eating well, or even indulging ourselves in a treat once in a while.

For the truth is, these things aren't luxuries at all. In times of crisis, they are necessities. Loving care—in the form of an afternoon break to sit in the park or a morning to sleep in—can make the difference in whether we make it through this crisis sane and healthy or break down physically or emotionally.

TODAY I WILL DEMAND LESS OF MYSELF AT A TIME WHEN LIFE IS ALREADY STRETCHING ME TO THE LIMIT.

REPAIRING THE ENERGY LEAK

Are you exhausted? I was. After months and years of dealing with one crisis after another, I was completely worn out. It was all I could do to drag myself out of bed in the morning, all I could do to accomplish a bare minimum of work.

In fact, I was bone-tired for an entire year after I embarked on my healing journey.

But most of us don't have time to be exhausted. We have children to care for, homes to run, jobs or carpools or volunteer activities to manage. Where do we find the energy to keep going when this crisis has taken so much out of us?

Over time, most of us figure out that what was robbing us of our energy was our reaction to the problem, not the problem itself. We were expending huge amounts of emotional energy on worry, on manipulation, on attempts to control or keep track of him. Minutes, hours, days of our lives were being poured into our problem.

Today we can retrieve that energy. We can shut off the valve to worry and control. We can save all that energy for the real concerns of our day. It may still take time and a lot of intensive self care for us to refill our emotional reserves, but we can stop the energy leak today.

TODAY I WILL CONSERVE MY ENERGY FOR THE TRULY IMPORTANT AREAS OF MY LIFE. I WILL SPEND MY ENERGY WHERE IT COUNTS, ON THINGS THAT I AM RESPONSIBLE FOR. I WILL NOT WASTE ONE OUNCE OF IT ON WORRY OR FEAR OR TRYING TO CONTROL SOMEONE ELSE.

RELEASE YOUR REGRETS

Some of us will commit to rebuilding our damaged relationships. Some of us will separate and accept the uncertainty. Some of us will end the relationship and rebuild alone. Some of us will change our minds a few weeks or months down the road.

Whatever path we take today, we can't afford to hang on to old regrets. We can't cling to those bitter feelings that things should have been different, could have been different, if only . . .

We cannot be tied to the past by our regrets. We cannot block the path to healing by continuing to relive and mentally rewrite the parts of our lives that didn't turn out as we wanted. We must try to give up our regrets and begin to recognize that everything that happens to us can be turned around to achieve good things in our lives.

Our worst choices, our greatest sorrows, become the source of our joy, our growth, our faith. So how can we regret? To regret is to deny abundance. To regret is to refuse our gifts. Our new way of life has no place for regrets.

INSTEAD OF NURSING MY REGRETS, TODAY I WILL STRIVE TO OPEN MY HEART TO WHATEVER GOOD LIFE HAS IN STORE FOR ME. I WILL REACH THE GOOD THINGS SOONER, MORE EASILY, IF I'M NOT WEIGHED DOWN BY REGRET.

STAYING PUT

Some of us plan to leave when we learn about our partner's infidelity because we think we should. We think it's the only answer that will keep our self-respect intact. How can we look our friends, or ourselves, in the eye if we stay?

But as one woman who weathered the storms to rebuild a strong marriage said to me, "Be careful that you don't divorce the wrong man."

In other words, this crisis can change us, can make us better, stronger people. Sometimes it can do the same for our partner.

We stay because it seems right for us as individuals. That's the only measure that is meaningful at this point. *Does it seem right for me, at this moment in my life? Do I have some particle of faith that this relationship can be not just restored to what it was before but made stronger than I ever imagined? Can I look at my partner and see the good as well as the bad? Do I see evidence of a real commitment to change on his part—a willingness to seek counseling or other forms of healing, a commitment to concrete actions that will restore my trust and rebuild intimacy?*

If we see any of those things, and it feels right to us, we may decide to stay. And we can do so with the knowledge that this decision may change, that we can reevaluate later.

Then we can make a different decision. But today all we have to know is what feels right for this moment.

TODAY I WILL DECIDE TO REMAIN IN THIS RELATIONSHIP OR END IT FOR CONCRETE REASONS, AND NOT SIMPLY BECAUSE I THINK ONE CHOICE OR ANOTHER IS WHAT OTHERS EXPECT OF ME.

WHAT ARE YOU TEACHING YOUR CHILDREN?

What are we doing in this crisis that we would like our children to learn?

Do we want a son or daughter to learn that it's okay to be a doormat, to lie down and accept any kind of unacceptable behavior?

Do we want a child of ours to learn that forgiveness isn't an option? Or that taking action to relieve our own misery is too hard to even attempt?

The children in our lives learn from us. And they learn most readily not from our lectures or tirades, but by watching what we do. We teach them how to be men and women by modeling behavior. They learn how to conduct their lives with honesty, with integrity, with goodness of spirit and openness of heart, from what we do, not what we say.

MY CHILDREN ARE LEARNING FROM MY BEHAVIOR TODAY. IF I AM NOT TEACHING THEM WHAT I REALLY WANT THEM TO KNOW, I WILL MAKE A CHANGE. I WILL MODEL GOOD THINGS FOR MY CHILDREN.

ALICE MAY

UNACCEPTABLE BEHAVIOR

We're being asked to let go of our expectations. We're being asked to change ourselves instead of him. We're being asked to accept the harsh realities in our relationship and to give up the dream of the perfect partner.

As we work on surrendering our need to control our partner's behavior, some of us worry that we're being asked to settle. That we're being set up for a life of accommodation and compromise. We feel as if we're being asked to give up our most deeply held values simply to hold our lives together.

It is true that we are being asked to give up all the illusions and delusions we brought to our relationship. But we are not being asked to give up our values. *We are not being asked to accept unacceptable behavior.*

We are learning to accommodate and compromise with a partner who is willing to do the same. We are learning to join hands with a partner who seeks, as we do, to heal our relationship and to participate actively in that healing. But we do not have to accept unacceptable behavior.

TODAY I WILL DETERMINE WHAT MY BOTTOM LINE IS, AND I WILL PRESERVE MY VALUES.

SLEEP WELL

Sleep can be elusive when our minds and hearts are troubled. We may lie awake for hours, unable to quiet our minds. Or we may startle awake in the middle of the night, hounded out of a restless sleep by the worries that consume us.

Rest is essential, especially during times of emotional stress. If we don't rest, we're increasingly less capable of handling what the days dish out.

Others who have been through what we are now experiencing share a variety of methods for getting the rest we need.

To interrupt the cycle of negative thinking that makes sleeping difficult, some sit up and make a list of all the things they are grateful for. Others pray to stop their obsessive thinking. Some journal. Some listen to soothing music. They rock. They do yoga. They recite the Serenity Prayer until sleep comes.

Sometimes all we can do is take a nap the next day.

Sleep is a comfort and a necessity. It will come. The less we fret over it, the more easily it will come.

TODAY I WON'T OBSESS IF I AM NOT SLEEPING WELL. I WILL REMEMBER THAT ALL MY DIFFICULTIES WILL EVENTUALLY IMPROVE, EVEN THIS ONE. UNTIL IT DOES, I WILL BE GENTLE WITH MYSELF.

ALICE MAY

CLEAR COMMUNICATION

What we believe we are saying is not always what other people hear. We are speaking from our experience, and they are listening from theirs. We are speaking in code, and they are listening with filters.

How can we do our part to further the cause of clear communication, especially in our intimate relationships?

We can make a commitment to listen carefully.

We can resist the urge to judge what we hear, so that we may hear with compassion and understanding.

We can repeat what we believe we've heard and ask whether we got it right.

We can talk honestly, without subterfuge or sugarcoating. We can leave out loaded words and phrases. *You always . . . You never . . .* We can talk without blame.

We can curb our reactions until we've had a chance to calm down and run the discussion past someone we trust.

We can pause, before the conversation begins, and review our commitment to being fair and courteous. We can be aware of our motives and our biases. We can remember that we can keep only our own side of the conversation on track. And that will be enough.

TODAY I WILL WORK ON COMMUNICATING CLEARLY, HONESTLY, AND WITHOUT ILL INTENT. I WILL NOT BE DRAWN INTO UNHEALTHY COMMUNICATION AGAINST MY WILL.

FAMILY DRAMA

"The thing I am most grateful for," she said, "is that I am no longer attracted to the chaos that comes with infidelity."

She had grown so accustomed to the constant turmoil, to the adrenaline rush, to the high that accompanies various stages of crisis and rescue and disaster, that she had forgotten how to live normally. Calm made her uneasy. Serenity felt like the death of emotion.

Many of us become very attracted—addicted almost—to the by-products of dysfunction. Yes, the family drama may result in ulcers, migraines, depression, addiction. It may disrupt our work or cause a breakdown in other areas of our lives. But we stay and stay, long after we are exhausted and ill.

Why? What is the payoff?

We may love the chaos. We may relish the shouting or throwing things. We may find our calling in life in rushing up on our white horse to set the world right following the latest crisis. Maybe we find satisfaction in playing the martyr or take pride in coping with difficulties that break others. Do we revel in the sainthood role sometimes attributed to people who endure others' destructive behavior?

Whatever boost we receive to our battered self-image, we must recognize that by continuing to participate we make ourselves sick. The longer we play the role, the sicker we become. And the longer we refuse to do our part to bring down the curtain on the family drama, the sicker the entire family becomes.

TODAY I WILL TRY TO SEE WHERE MY PAYOFF IS IN MY FAMILY DRAMA. I AM READY TO RECLAIM SANITY, READY ONCE AGAIN TO FIND PLEASURE AND COMFORT AND SATISFACTION IN THE EVERY-DAY, THE NORMAL.

ALICE MAY

DIFFICULT DAYS

Some days fear still rules our lives.

Some days uncertainty still paralyzes us. Prayer comes hard. Sadness is overwhelming. And faith is beyond our grasp.

On those days, we can talk to a higher power anyway. Maybe we can't pray, but we can pour out our anger and our frustration to whatever spiritual source we trust.

On those days, we can find a way to serve others.

We can rest. We can sit in the park.

We can use whatever talents we were created with—we can paint or bake bread or teach a child or take over the car pool for someone else.

We can be quiet, or we can rage until our anger is spent.

We can listen to music. We can run until our legs won't pump any longer and our lungs can't gasp another breath.

We can talk to someone else, then invite them to talk. We can listen, and let their lives occupy our hearts and minds for just this moment.

Then we can talk to our higher power again. We can feel the peace that comes from knowing that God never minds our doubt, never expects perfection from us.

And sometime during that day, we can find the grace to move beyond our fear, our uncertainty, our sadness.

EVEN ON BAD DAYS, I WILL PRACTICE THE BEHAVIORS THAT GIVE ME PEACE. I WILL TAKE THE ACTIONS THAT CONNECT ME WITH THE SOURCE OF MY HOPE AND COURAGE.

LIVING YOUR OWN LIFE,
NOT SOMEONE ELSE'S

Only during our separation did I recognize how carefully I had structured my life around my husband.

He planned golf or lunch with his buddies when he wanted to. But I planned outings only for times when he was out of town on business. I checked *his* schedule to see whether I was free. I had to make sure I was available in case he wanted some of my time.

I didn't do this because he demanded it of me. I doubt whether he even realized I did it. I did it because I had lost myself in him. I had submerged my life in his.

I did it because I felt his withdrawal and believed it was something I could change. I did it because I believed in my heart that I had to be able to do something to make him happy, to make him love me the way he once had. I had lost myself in my attempts to reverse his rejection.

Today I understand that I am not responsible for any shortfall in his life or for the gaps in his spirit. Today I understand that his life is his to heal.

And my life is mine to heal. It is a big enough job to keep me busy.

Now I can carry out my day based on what I want to do. I can and do make plans around activities that nurture me. And in doing so, I bring more richness to our relationship.

TODAY I WILL LIVE MY LIFE AND NOT SOMEONE ELSE'S. I WILL BE
A VALUABLE PART OF THE RELATIONSHIP, NOT JUST SOMEONE
WHO CLINGS.

GIFTS, NOT ENEMIES

My husband is not the enemy.

The other woman is not the enemy.

Change is not the enemy, although I fight it with all the tenacity of the squirrels looking for acorns in my yard.

All the painful things that occur, all the people who wound us, all of them are merely mileposts marking our progress on this journey. They mark the spots where we advanced, or took a wrong turn that ultimately led us to the next peak or plateau. They are gifts along the way.

So we can stop fighting them.

The only enemy is our fear, and then only when we allow it to dictate our choices along the path. Instead of giving in to our fear, we can name it and discuss it with someone else. We can examine our fear for a finite period of time—ten minutes, say—and carry it as far as we can take it, to the worst-case scenario. Then we can focus on the ways we would handle that fear if it came true. We can see that our new tools will enable us to handle even our worst fear. And when our time is up for worry, we can turn our attention back to the day at hand. We can seek courage in meditation or affirmations.

And we can use our fear to keep us focused on the tools of our healing journey. Then, even our fear becomes a gift that propels us forward.

TODAY I WILL REMEMBER THAT FEAR IS ONLY A FEELING. IT HAS NO CONTROL OVER ME. IT DOES NOT DICTATE MY BEHAVIOR. TODAY, WITH THE HELP OF OTHERS, I HAVE CONTROL OVER MY FEAR.

BECOMING TRUSTWORTHY

How do we learn to trust again? How do we find the proper balance between trusting too quickly and killing our souls with a refusal to trust?

One way—a healthy way—is to begin by learning what it means to be trustworthy ourselves.

We can stop gossiping.

We can start fulfilling our commitments.

We can stop telling little white lies whose only purpose is to make our lives more comfortable.

We can be as reliable as we would like our partner to be.

And we can become aware of all the little ways in which we have failed to live up to the trust and confidence placed in us by our friends, coworkers, children, neighbors, and partner.

In doing so, we further our own healing. We take our focus off someone else and accept responsibility for ourselves instead of seeking control of others. We align ourselves more surely with the spirit of love in the universe. And we begin to be more familiar with the face of trustworthiness.

I WILL LEARN TO RECOGNIZE TRUSTWORTHINESS WHEN I CULTI-VATE IT WITHIN. TODAY I WILL SEEK TO BE SOMEONE OTHERS CAN TRUST.

YOU ARE NOT TRAPPED

Do you feel trapped? Locked into a painful relationship with no way out because of finances, family expectations, or your own insecurities?

You may feel trapped. But here is the truth: You are free to make good choices for your own health and happiness.

You are free to make choices.

Your choices are not always easy or pleasant. They may cause pain or hardship. But pain and hardship are temporary. The benefits of unlocking your cage and throwing away the key far outlast the temporary difficulties that come with change.

You can choose to be lonely for a while. You can choose to live more frugally. You can choose to make others responsible for their own happiness by becoming responsible for your own happiness.

Temporary discomfort does not last forever. The difficulties or heartache that arise from tough but necessary choices will pass. And all of your choices can be reversed, if that is what turns out to be best for you.

Believing you are trapped is a fear, not a fact.

I DO HAVE CHOICES. I WON'T ALLOW ANYONE TO CONVINCE ME THAT I DON'T. I AM NOT TRAPPED.

EVERYONE LOSES IN
AN ARGUMENT

How often does a disagreement become an argument because we *must* convince someone that we are right? How often do we allow a conflicting point of view to escalate into a big, ugly, hurtful fight?

It doesn't have to be that way. We can do our part to create a healthier outcome.

In our present circumstances, conflict and disagreements will certainly arise. At those times, the best gift we can give ourselves is to handle ourselves with dignity and with honor. We can contribute to the solution rather than the problem.

One way to do that is to remember that a conflict does not have to be about right and wrong, win or lose. Rarely is someone entirely right or entirely wrong. Most of the time we can find a middle ground, a place to which we bring our best and he brings his. A conflict can be a way to reach agreement on the difficulties and differences that divide us.

If we seek solutions that contribute to harmony and growth, we can be sure of a better outcome than if we are out only to see our way prevail.

TODAY I WILL TRY TO WIN AN AGREEMENT, NOT AN ARGUMENT.

TAKE NOTE OF YOUR PROGRESS

When we are on a difficult part of life's journey, we tend to take notice of the bad things that occur. We can counteract the litany of negative developments with a chronicle of our triumphs.

Even if we journal at no other time, we can keep a record of those moments when our healing and our connection with our spirit shine above the misery. We can call our friends and ask them for a pat on the back for the progress we're making. We can dot our calendar with gold stars for every good decision and courageous step forward we make. We can buy a bouquet of daisies or mail ourselves a card of congratulations.

We can note the day and time we applied for our first job in twenty years. The day we made a major decision on our own. The day we painted the family room a color that was bolder or warmer or just more fun than the colors we would have chosen a year before.

We are changing. Let us note and celebrate all the positive changes in this difficult time.

TODAY I WILL CONGRATULATE MYSELF WHEN I GROW. I WILL BE OPEN TO ALL THE LITTLE SIGNS THAT MY LIFE IS IMPROVING AND I AM IMPROVING.

DON'T CONDEMN YOURSELF
FOR DIVORCE

The first thing to do, if separation or divorce becomes the best option, is to let go of the guilt.

We aren't facing divorce because we're bad people. We aren't here because we didn't do our part, because we didn't work hard enough at the marriage. We aren't on the brink of divorce because we're failures.

Sometimes divorce becomes the best choice—the only way to move forward with dignity, the only way to heal, the only way to provide a home for our children that isn't filled with strife or hostility.

When divorce is the next right thing to do, remember that you are making a choice for emotional health and let go of the guilt.

I AM NOT A BAD PERSON BECAUSE MY RELATIONSHIP IS NOT WORKING OUT. I WON'T CONDEMN MYSELF FOR A DECISION THAT MAY HAVE BEEN THRUST UPON ME BY SOMEONE ELSE. I ESPECIALLY WON'T CONDEMN MYSELF IF I'VE GIVEN THIS RELATIONSHIP MY BEST AND CAN SEE THAT IT IS NOT HEALTHY FOR ME AND IT IS TIME TO MOVE ON.

DEFINE YOUR BOUNDARIES

Standing up for ourselves can be difficult. But it is up to us to figure out what we can live with and what we cannot. It is up to us to set boundaries that help us feel safe and confident that we can heal.

We begin by determining what is unacceptable behavior. We ask ourselves what violates our values, what behavior we are unwilling to live with. For some of us, it will be another affair. Or any continuation of the behaviors that contributed to our partner's cheating—nights out with the guys, close friendships with women, surfing the Internet. It may be his reluctance to participate in counseling or tendency to tell little white lies that call his honesty into question.

Next we must decide what actions we are prepared to take if the unacceptable behavior continues. Are we prepared to separate? To see an attorney? To ask him to move into the spare room? To discontinue our sexual relations? Our consequences must be concrete, and they must be something we are ready to do.

Once we've determined these boundaries, we may want to share them with our partner, being very clear and very specific. We don't do it to motivate him to change or to be punitive. We do it because we've decided it is right for us.

And if our partner chooses unacceptable behavior, our next move is clear. We won't have to figure things out at a time of crisis. We already have a plan of action, prepared when we were calm. We will be okay. We are healthy enough today that we no longer have to accept unacceptable behavior.

TODAY I WILL DEFINE MY BOUNDARIES AND DECIDE WHAT ACTION I AM PREPARED TO TAKE IF ANOTHER PERSON DOES NOT RESPECT THOSE BOUNDARIES. THEN I CAN RELAX, KNOWING THAT I AM PREPARED IF THERE IS ANOTHER CRISIS.

GIVE YOURSELF TIME
AND ENERGY

When troubles overwhelm us, we must sometimes narrow the focus of our lives. The idea is not to concentrate solely on our problems but to gain the energy, the emotion, and the time in our day for healing behaviors.

Too much extraneous activity when our lives are falling apart robs us of the strength we need to focus on solutions. It distracts us, giving us wonderful excuses for ignoring the wreckage around us.

This can lead to denial. It can also lead to exhaustion.

For the foreseeable future, as we try to cope with the aftermath of crisis, what can we pare out of our lives? Can we forgo the elaborate dinner parties, the family get-togethers, the weekly lunch with a co-worker we can't be around without losing our patience? Can we curtail our involvement with people who exhaust us? Can we eat out more often if cooking is one more headache we hate to face at the end of the day? Can we delegate more household chores to others?

Anything that drains us is something we need to think twice about doing. Anything that leaves us with a negative feeling. Anything we're doing only because we believe we "should."

We can't do everything, and everything we do at a time like this should be something we've considered carefully and chosen to do.

TODAY I WILL DO WHAT NURTURES ME. I WILL DO WHAT ENER-GIZES ME. I WILL DO WHAT FEEDS MY SOUL. I WILL DO WHAT FEELS RIGHT FOR MY SPIRIT AND LET GO OF THE REST.

ALICE MAY

FORGIVE YOURSELF

As we practice new behaviors, we begin to heal. One of the most healing behaviors, we discover, is forgiveness. Our hearts and spirits are soothed as we let go of resentments. We feel more peace.

When that happens, some of us want to put the power of forgiveness to work in our lives again. We want to deepen the growth we've found in forgiveness by finding ways to forgive ourselves.

None of us, of course, is perfect. We see that more clearly all the time. And we no longer believe that makes us worthless or shameful or unlovable people. It simply makes us human, and being human is not a character flaw.

But some of us have held ourselves overly responsible for the problems in our lives. Others of us have flinched from taking responsibility for our mistakes because we were afraid to let others know who we really were. Either way, most of us have regrets.

As we become ready, we can let go of those old regrets. We can ask forgiveness, and we can forgive ourselves.

TODAY I LOOK FORWARD TO THE FREEDOM THAT COMES WITH A CLEAN SLATE. I WILL LOOK FOR WAYS TO SEEK FORGIVENESS, KNOWING THAT I DO IT FOR MYSELF, FOR MY OWN EMOTIONAL WELL-BEING.

FEAR OF INTIMACY

Once we've been on our journey for a while, we begin to see our own emotional secrets, the hidden truths that have held us back, blocking us from love and growth and joy.

One of those truths, for some of us, is that we cannot be emotionally intimate.

We think, at first, that our partner is the one with intimacy problems. He is the one who can't open up, who seeks out meaningless encounters because he can't give and receive love. This is what we think, and it may be true.

But his intimacy problems are not our concern.

The deeper truth may be that we have chosen him precisely for that reason. Because if he can't love us and be close to us, we don't have to risk being loving and open either. We don't have to discover that we fear love, that we have walled off our hearts.

This doesn't make us bad people. It just means we've learned about one more shortcoming that limits our lives. And by using our new tools for living, we can learn to open ourselves to intimacy.

TODAY I WILL WORK TO DISCOVER MY HEART. I AM LEARNING TO EXPERIENCE ALL MY EMOTIONS. AND AS I GROW MORE CAPABLE OF INTIMACY, I WILL NATURALLY SURROUND MYSELF WITH PEOPLE WHO CAN ALSO BE INTIMATE.

TAKE STOCK

Most of us don't have a bit of trouble reciting all the ways we'd like him to change. We know exactly what would make us happy regarding him and his behavior.

But changing him won't make us happy if there are still things wrong inside us. And even if it would make us happy, we can't change him or make him want to change.

So the best thing we can do is ask ourselves what we want to change about ourselves in this relationship.

We can begin to see the answers if we are honest and thorough in looking at our own life. And as we take stock of ourselves and share the results with someone else, the very act of speaking the words begins to shape our understanding of where we need to work on ourselves as a member of this relationship.

What is our instinctive reaction to conflict? What are our fears surrounding this relationship, and how do we keep them at bay? What actions do we take over and over again, believing they will change his behavior this time? What are our expectations of our partner and this relationship? How do we react if those expectations aren't met? How healthy and fulfilling are our activities outside this relationship?

These questions get us started when we are ready to consider changing our role in this relationship or any other. If we ask for the help of another person in assessing our behavior, we can see where we are making ourselves unhappy. And we can take the steps necessary to change them.

I CANNOT CHANGE HIM. BUT I CAN CHANGE MYSELF. I HAVE THE TOOLS. I HAVE THE HELP OF MY SPIRIT AND MY INNER WISDOM. I CAN CHANGE. AND WHEN I CHANGE, MY CIRCUMSTANCES CHANGE.

THE PROMISE OF
SPIRITUAL GROWTH

A promise will be fulfilled as we continue our journey. Sometime during the process, we will be drawn into an intimate relationship with God or our higher spirit.

Some of us hope for something more concrete. A happy marriage. A lucrative divorce settlement. A man who adores us for sticking with him through the tough times. We aren't interested in something as nebulous as an awareness of some higher power working in our lives. And we certainly aren't interested in maintaining impossible moral standards, spending half our waking hours on our knees in church.

In the experience of those who have been down this path before us, spiritual awareness at the most basic level is an ability to live at peace with others and with whatever life brings. That becomes possible when we gain a deepening sense that our life has purpose and direction, no matter who we've been before, and no matter how lacking in spirituality or meaning our lives might have been before.

We can have—*will* have—a meaningful relationship with whatever higher power we choose, one that will transform our lives. And all we have to do is begin using the principles of surrender and seeking and forgiveness and awareness.

TODAY I WILL CONTINUE MY JOURNEY, CONFIDENT IT WILL IMPROVE MY LIFE IN WAYS MORE MEANINGFUL AND FAR-REACHING THAN ANYTHING I MIGHT WISH FOR TODAY.

FLAWED HUMAN BEINGS

One sign of a healthy relationship is that we can accept his faults as well as our own. We acknowledge that we are both imperfect and that neither of us will ever be perfect. Then we affirm our commitment to give love to another flawed human being.

A tool that helps us accept his imperfect state is our own journey of self-discovery. As we look back over our life and pinpoint all the ways in which we've fallen short of perfection, we become more tolerant of others who also fall short. We recognize that we've been doing the best we could with what we had to work with. And we can see that he is doing the same.

Sometimes the mere process of accepting ourselves just as we are helps us become more accepting of others as well.

Our self-discovery process helps, too, by showing us the truth about our good qualities. It helps us see that each of us is a mix of strength and weakness, good and not-so-good, plus and minus.

TODAY I WILL FOCUS ON MY GOOD QUALITIES AND TRY TO DO THE SAME WITH ANYONE ELSE IN MY LIFE I AM INCLINED TO JUDGE. THEN I WILL WORK ON MY OWN SHORTCOMINGS, ALSO WITHOUT JUDGING.

LOVE IS ACTION

One of my spiritual heroes says that love is not emotion, love is action.

If you're like me, you've spent much of your life equating love with that swell of emotions evoked by another person. I've been full to bursting with excitement and exhilaration. That, my friend says, is hormones kicking in. That is emotion breathing life into my fantasies.

Hormones level off, and fantasies are replaced by next year's model.

But love is a decision we make to become a force for good in someone else's life without shortchanging ourselves. Love is nurturing someone's spiritual growth, and therefore our own. Love is supporting someone's goals. Love is consistent, day-by-day commitment to be there when needed. Love is accepting someone's flaws. Love is spending time instead of money. Love is kind words and behavior that matches.

Love is a decision we make to behave in a way that allows another person dignity to pursue growth and personal progress.

We can't force or coax anyone into the act of loving us. But we can make a decision to act with love toward others in our life. Including ourselves.

TODAY I WILL LOVE OTHERS THROUGH MY ACTIONS. ALTHOUGH THERE IS NOTHING WRONG WITH MY EMOTIONS, IT IS WITH MY ACTIONS THAT I TRULY EXPRESS MY LOVE FOR OTHERS AND FOR MYSELF.

THE URGE FOR RETRIBUTION

Her husband had been unfaithful, and she looked at it this way. His behavior had given her free rein to be the worst partner imaginable, with no consequences whatsoever. She could eat and drink too much, work too little, be irresponsible and ill-tempered.

After all, what right did he have to complain?

A half-dozen years later, her husband filed for divorce. He'd done his best to turn things around, but she never let go of the past and her assumed right to make him pay indefinitely. Finally, he'd had enough.

Revenge, retribution, payback. All are deadly to any relationship, but especially a partnership. They continue poisoning the relationship. If we find that payback is our goal, we could save ourselves a lot of pain and simply walk away now. If we are not working toward the goal of healing the relationship—even if that means bringing it to an end when the time is right—we are contributing to its eventual death.

TODAY I WILL MAKE A CLEAR DECISION ABOUT WHETHER I AM WORKING ON A POSITIVE OUTCOME OR A NEGATIVE ONE.

HONOR YOUR NEED TO ABSTAIN

Sometimes we need to be sexually abstinent, and he is not happy about it.

He may pout like a thwarted toddler. He may rage or threaten. He may be so good and so appeasing that we are tempted to believe we've made a mistake.

His reaction to our need to take care of ourselves is not our problem or our concern. We don't have to react to his reaction. We don't have to capitulate. We don't have to bargain or soothe his wounded ego or promise to make it up to him later, or in other ways.

We have made a decision that is right for us. We aren't doing this to rebuke or discipline him. We are doing it because our emotions are too tumultuous or too deadened at the moment for us to be sexual. We are doing it because there are too many questions in our relationship.

We can do what is right for us whether it makes him happy or not. We don't have to explain our decision again and again. We don't have to engage in a debate. We can be calm in our decision and allow him to obsess over sex if he chooses to.

ABSTAINING FROM SEX IS SOMETIMES A GOOD CHOICE. BEING INFLUENCED BY SOMEONE ELSE'S WANTS IS NOT.

BRINGING CLOSURE

Geographic cures—changing houses, cities, jobs, friends, spouses—seldom work. We always pack up our pain, our despair, our anger, our difficulties, then unpack them at the new location.

To achieve true healing, we must walk through the problem. As Emerson said, "The last way out is through."

But after a measure of healing has taken place, after the bitterness has softened, changing some of our external circumstances can be a way of bringing physical closure to emotional and spiritual journeys.

Three years after the crisis in our home, my husband and I realized it was time to move. There had been times in the middle of the healing process when I suspect both of us would have paid good money to wake up somewhere else, miles away from our problems. But that wasn't the immediate solution, and we knew it. So we stayed and prayed and waited. We did the best we could with our footwork, as we understood it, and waited for the solution to unfold.

When we did at last move, it was a way to say good-bye to the place where we'd experienced so much pain. It was a way to take our new selves, our new lives, to a place where there were no ugly memories, no painful connotations. We felt fresh, and a fresh start seemed appropriate.

But if we had made that move too soon, we would have simply taken our baggage with us and gone about the business of creating more ugly memories in our fresh new location.

TODAY I KNOW THAT CHANGING MY EXTERNAL CIRCUMSTANCES WON'T HEAL WHAT IS GOING ON INSIDE ME. I WILL WORK ON MY INNER SELF FIRST AND CHANGE MY EXTERNAL CIRCUMSTANCES LATER, IF AT ALL.

TIMES OF STRESS

My friend pulled into her driveway, up the steep incline toward her back door. Halfway up the hill, she noticed a baby bird huddled in the middle of the drive. My friend didn't want to hurt the baby bird, but she didn't want to park on the hill either.

She stopped short of the bird, which then hopped a few feet farther along the drive. My friend eased forward in her vehicle and waited again. Again, the bird hopped and my friend eased up. Eventually, my friend made it to the flat parking area behind her house, one baby-bird hop at a time.

When she parked and got out of her vehicle, the baby bird finally flew off into the woods.

"At first I thought, 'Why didn't you do that a few minutes ago?'" my friend said. "Then it occurred to me that even though the baby bird could fly, flying was still very new behavior. In its panic, faced with a stressful situation, it could only revert to its old, comfortable habit."

The baby bird could hop when confronted with something fearful, but it could not remember how to use its new flying skills.

TODAY IF I AM FACED WITH A STRESSFUL SITUATION, I WON'T BERATE MYSELF IF I MOMENTARILY FREEZE AND FORGET MY NEW COPING SKILLS. I MAY HAVE TO HOP OUT OF DANGER, BUT THAT'S OKAY. I'LL HAVE ANOTHER CHANCE TO PRACTICE FLYING.

ALICE MAY

HOW DO YOU TREAT YOURSELF?

How would you treat someone who came to you for comfort after being betrayed by her partner?

Would you blame her for what had happened? Would you criticize her appearance, her personality, her cooking? Would you suggest that this never would have happened if she'd been a better lover, a smarter homemaker, a more talented woman?

Would you tell her she has nothing more to live for?

No? The very idea of treating a hurting friend so callously offends you, doesn't it?

Then why do we think it's okay to treat ourselves so shabbily? It isn't okay, and we can change that way of thinking and behaving.

TODAY I WILL REFUSE TO SAY ANYTHING TO MYSELF THAT I WOULDN'T SAY TO MY BEST FRIEND. TODAY I WILL BE GENTLE WITH MYSELF. I WILL PRACTICE BASIC SELF-CARE AND SELF-LOVE. TODAY I WILL BEHAVE AS IF I WERE IN EMOTIONAL INTENSIVE CARE.

MAKING MYSELF CRAZY

When I am dwelling in the problem, I believe that I can hang on to my sanity only if I know whether or not he's remaining faithful.

Deep in my soul, I must learn that I can remain sane only if I let go of the need to know what he is doing.

What makes me crazy and keeps me unhealthy is the wondering and worrying. Finagling the conversation in an attempt to trip him up. Keeping an eye on him at all times.

And he is doing none of that to me. I am doing it to myself.

I am making myself crazy with my suspicion, my fears, my constant focus on someone else.

He is going about his business, his life, his everyday pursuits. They may be harmless, or they may be destructive to me and others. For the moment at least, that may not be for me to know. But regardless of his actions, I am choosing to immerse myself in doubt and fear. In insanity.

Instead, I can concentrate on enjoying this moment when there is no fire to put out. It may be only the calm between the storms. Or it may be a long stretch of smooth sailing, which I am wrecking with my obsessive thinking.

TODAY I WILL CONCENTRATE ON MY LIFE. IF THERE IS NOTHING BAD GOING ON IN PLAIN SIGHT, I WILL ACCEPT THE RESPITE FROM MY WORRIES. I WILL NOT SPOIL IT WITH SPECULATION AND SUSPICION.

ALICE MAY

LISTEN TO YOUR INNER WISDOM, NOT OTHERS

Don't end this relationship because your mother says a leopard never changes its spots. Or because your sister tells you she never liked him anyway. Or because you can't take the reproachful look in your best friend's eyes one more day.

Don't end this relationship because of any other person's convictions—not your father's, your daughter's, your counselor's, your boss's, or your priest's.

End this relationship, or continue working on it, because of the calm certainty that doing so is best for you. And you will know when that calm moment arrives. It arrives without fear or urgency or anguish. If you pray and meditate and watch and listen, the answers always come.

TODAY I WILL NOT LISTEN TO ALL THOSE AROUND ME WHO HAVE OPINIONS ABOUT MY LIFE. TODAY I WILL LISTEN FOR THE CALM WHISPER OF MY INNER WISDOM.

HOLIDAY STRESS

The ways in which our society celebrates holidays often heap stress on the happiest and healthiest of us. The burden can seem unbearable when we are in crisis.

Whether at Passover or Christmas or Thanksgiving, we feel the weight of our imperfect family.

We shoulder the burden of hiding our misery from those we want to protect from grief.

The effort to smile one more time, to experience one more moment of someone else's holiday cheer robs us of the energy to care for ourselves.

There are solutions.

We can simplify, just this once. We can opt out of some of the more poignant traditions or festive occasions. We can turn to the financially needy and, in helping them, feed our wounded spirits. We can rest more. We can eat and drink less and pray and meditate more.

And we can ignore the holidays anytime doing otherwise is too much for us to handle.

THIS YEAR'S HOLIDAY SEASONS MAY BE MORE DIFFICULT THAN OTHERS HAVE BEEN. I GIVE MYSELF PERMISSION NOT TO BE THE PERFECT FAMILY THIS YEAR. THIS IS ONE BURDEN I CAN LAY ASIDE.

A REFUSAL TO SURRENDER

The squirrels in my yard are relentless. They insist that I feed them, and they are willing to go to any lengths to make it happen.

They dig up my flower pots looking for acorns. They plunder my bird feeders. At different times, they have destroyed the wooden roof on one and chewed through the perches on another. Where there is birdseed, they will find a way.

I finally purchased a squirrel-proof feeder and a brightly painted metal canister in which to store birdseed on my porch. I had found a way to win the war.

For more than a week, the squirrels did not give up. They were convinced they could change these unpleasant new circumstances. Their determination had always paid off before. The extent to which they would go became apparent one morning when I discovered hundreds of tiny scratches left by their little claws on the metal canister.

The top of the canister was spotted with blood.

The next time I am determined to change someone else's behavior, I will remember the squirrels in my yard. I will remember how they injured only themselves, drew their own blood, because they refused to surrender and accept reality.

TODAY I WILL REMEMBER THAT THE ONE I HURT THE MOST WITH MY REFUSAL TO ACCEPT REALITY IS MYSELF.

INSTANT RESULTS

There are no quick fixes.

There are bandages, but they only cover the wound to give healing a chance to take place. Sometimes we need bandages.

The world promises us quick fixes, from magazine covers to television ads. Ten days to a flatter stomach. Seven ways to divorce-proof your marriage. Herbs that melt away fat.

We all want to believe in the quick fix. But the truth is, life doesn't offer cosmetic surgery for spiritual ills. And an ailing relationship is a spiritual disease. The only solutions are spiritual, and the spiritual requires commitment, willingness, time for transformation.

Be willing to wait out this time of healing and transformation in your life. Be patient if the fix isn't quick. Instead, it will be profound.

TODAY I WILL TRUST THAT I AM WORKING TOWARD A DEEPER HEALING THAN I CAN ACHIEVE QUICKLY. I WILL BE PATIENT AS MY LIFE IS TRANSFORMED.

GETTING IN TOUCH WITH
YOUR SPIRIT

Meditation is a powerful tool for bringing us into closer contact with God, with our own spirit, with whatever higher source we trust today. But many of us have avoided meditation because we believe it is practiced only by certain religions or has no application to our lives.

Meditation can be practiced by anyone of any faith, or even by those of us who are still only seeking faith.

To meditate is to quiet our minds, and the world around us, so that we can hear the voice of wisdom. Meditation can take many forms. Each of us can keep seeking until we find the one that works best for us. We can sit quietly and observe nature. We can focus our thoughts and energy on a single phrase that calms and centers us. *Love heals,* or, *All things work for good in my life,* for example. We can meditate on a passage from some literature central to our own religious beliefs. I play classical music to eliminate distractions. Some people pay attention to their breath while they do yoga or walk or swim.

Or we can simply observe the chaos in our heads, letting it flow through us without attempting to still it or control it. Then, in its own time, it will grow weary and leave us in peace.

The benefits of meditation rarely happen right away. Meditation is a discipline; it requires practice.

When we practice, we eventually grow quiet. Then we know inner peace. Perhaps only for a moment. But if we keep inviting the silence, in whatever way works best for us, the moments will grow into minutes.

TODAY I WILL TRY SOME FORM OF MEDITATION. I WILL MAKE IT A DAILY DISCIPLINE, KNOWING THAT MEDITATION CAN CONNECT ME WITH MY SPIRIT, WITH THE GOOD IN MY WORLD.

REJECT THE VICTIM LABEL

We are not victims.

Whatever else we must do to reach the other side of this painful part of our lives, let us reject the label of victim.

Victims have no power because they have given it away to those they depend on for their happiness. Victims are at the mercy of those who do them harm because they expect those people to change so the pain will go away. Victims depend on others to save them because they won't take action to save themselves.

We are not victims as long as we make up our minds to move forward as best we can; as long as we forgive; as long as we live in this moment; as long as we take responsibility for finding and doing the things that will help us heal.

We are not victims. We have been hurt, perhaps even damaged or scarred. But we turn to others we can trust for the courage to make positive changes in our lives. We have the power, with help, to reclaim our lives.

I AM NOT A VICTIM. I AM NOT AT THE MERCY OF ANOTHER PERSON'S BELIEFS OR BEHAVIOR. I HAVE RECLAIMED MY LIFE BY SEEKING TO LIVE IT WITH HOPE AND COURAGE AND SPIRIT.

SHARE YOURSELF WITH
THOSE YOU LOVE

My cat developed an irritating habit of running into the kitchen whenever I was there, meowing incessantly and pacing back and forth to her bowl. The bowl was rarely empty or even low on food. But in an effort to appease her, I would sprinkle fresh food into the bowl anyway.

She continued to pace and meow, pace and meow.

What more did she want?

One day I took a few minutes to sit beside her bowl, pour in the fresh food, and talk to her while I did so. She immediately grew quiet and walked over to her bowl. Purring loudly, she ate.

All she wanted was my company. Some attention. An indication that I cared enough to slow down and spend a few moments with her.

Are there others in my life who hunger for some sign that I care? Others whom I can't be bothered to slow down long enough to acknowledge? Other ways in which I am too busy to take part in the lives of those around me?

Today I take time to visit with my cat while she eats. And I look for simple but rewarding ways to share my time and my attention with others I've made a commitment to love.

LIFE IS ABOUT MORE THAN CHORES, ERRANDS, AND RESPONSIBILITIES. LIFE IS ALSO ABOUT LOVE AND ATTENTION AND SHARING SMALL, EVERYDAY PLEASURES. TODAY I WILL SHARE MYSELF WITH THOSE I LOVE.

NEW PRIORITIES

I would never have believed the day would come, but at times I don't care whether my husband is faithful or not. Some days his fidelity isn't high on my list of priorities.

Today my relationship with God is a priority. Living my own life well and honorably is a priority. Other priorities are being emotionally available for friends and family, my own program of personal growth, and learning to find the joy in this day.

And if my husband is not faithful, it doesn't have to upset any of those priorities in my life. If I need to stop and deal with my husband's weaknesses and their impact on my life, I will know it when it is time for me to know it.

Until then, I can focus on my real priorities.

TODAY I WILL KNOW WHAT REALLY MATTERS TO ME, AND I WILL CONCENTRATE MY EFFORTS ON THOSE PARTS OF MY LIFE. I WON'T DIVERT MY ATTENTION FROM THEM BY WORRYING ABOUT SOMEONE ELSE'S BEHAVIOR.

SEEKING GOD

My peace of mind shatters so easily when I distance myself from God.

I distance myself from God when I don't pray; when I don't take care to contact someone each day who shares my commitment to a spiritual life; when I indulge in thoughts or actions that make me feel worse about myself and block me from my own spirit.

When I am in touch with my spirit and with all the actions that feed my spirit, I know peace. I move through my days effortlessly, making decisions easily, interacting with others even in difficult circumstances without losing my calm. I attract others who also know peace; the good in my life expands when I am in touch with my spirit and with a higher power.

Staying in touch with my spirit is simple. Getting back in touch once I have sacrificed my serenity is harder.

TODAY I WILL PRAY, MEDITATE, CONNECT WITH SOMEONE ELSE WHO IS ON A SPIRITUAL JOURNEY. TODAY I WILL WEIGH MY THOUGHTS AND ACTIONS CAREFULLY. THIS IS A SIMPLE PRESCRIPTION FOR STAYING IN TOUCH WITH GOD TODAY.

BACKSLIDING

Some days the best we can do is backslide.

We cry all day. Or stay in bed and stare at the ceiling. We engage in a shouting match with our boss or children. We snoop into things we're better off staying out of because we want to believe one more time that it will help us decide how to put our lives back together.

When we temporarily lose ground, the greatest gift we can give ourselves is forgiveness.

Slipping back into behavior that isn't good for us doesn't mean we haven't made progress. It doesn't mean we're in for another long stretch of misery. It doesn't mean we will never feel good about our lives again, or that we don't deserve to.

That kind of condemnation comes from the voice of emotional and spiritual disease in our heads.

Our slips simply mean we're human. We aren't designed to be perfect. Others don't expect it of us, and we shouldn't expect it of ourselves.

I AM HUMAN. SOME DAYS I WILL TAKE TWO STEPS FORWARD AND ONE STEP BACK. ON THOSE DAYS, I CAN PRAY, I CAN TALK TO SOMEONE ELSE ABOUT MY BEHAVIOR, I CAN MAKE AMENDS IF NECESSARY. THEN I CAN LOVE MYSELF ENOUGH TO LET GO OF MY MISTAKES AND MOVE ON.

THE HEALING PROCESS

A friend who recently had surgery complained that he didn't want to *get* well, he wanted to *be* well.

He didn't want to deal with a catheter or stitches or IV tubes. He didn't want to bother with bed rest or the right doses of medication. Bored after a few days of being an invalid, he wanted to bounce out of bed and get on with life, back at the top of his game.

Don't we want the same? Don't we want to be finished with this period of healing and uncertainty? The painful discussions, the marriage counseling, the tension, the grieving, the appointments with attorneys? Don't we simply want to *be* well instead of going through the painstaking process that helps us *get* well?

And isn't it as unlikely that we can bounce back from infidelity without a healing process as it is that my friend will wake up the day after surgery and be ready for a walk in the park?

TODAY I WILL ACCEPT THAT HEALING IS A PROCESS, NOT AN EVENT. IT HAPPENS OVER TIME, NOT OVERNIGHT.

FALLING INTO DEPRESSION

How long have you felt so exhausted and hopeless that you can barely drag yourself out of bed in the morning? How long ago did you lose interest in dressing well, reading the morning paper, meeting a friend for lunch?

And what about difficulty making decisions? Inability to concentrate? Having so little energy that you sometimes spend entire afternoons staring at the wall? No appetite? No interest in the things you once enjoyed?

How long have these things gone on?

Any of these are natural reactions to the trauma you've been through, of course. You may experience any of them for a time, or even off and on for a day here and there.

But if they go on continuously for more than a few weeks, you may need help. You may be falling into severe depression. And severe depression is something we cannot always come out of alone; this is especially true the longer it goes on, or for those who have had previous episodes of depression.

If you have felt any of these things for more than a few weeks, talk to someone you trust. Talk to your doctor or your therapist. Chronic depression is not a weakness. It is more than sadness or grief. It is an illness. And it can be deadly.

Do not let shame or apathy allow you to pull the covers up over your depression. Seek help. Ask a friend to help you find effective help if you don't feel up to the task yourself.

Sadness is normal. But prolonged depression is not something you must endure. It can be treated.

IF I AM DEPRESSED TODAY, I WILL SEEK HELP. I WILL REMEMBER THAT THERE IS HOPE EVEN IF I CAN'T IMAGINE IT AT THE MOMENT.

ALICE MAY

YOUR PARTNER HAS A GOD, TOO

Does our partner have a God or higher power who is willing to watch over him, lead him away from temptation, and give him courage for this day's difficulties?

Can our partner tap into spiritual strength and wisdom and protection with a simple prayer, at any time?

Can our partner rely on inner wisdom to guide him, to help him make wiser and more loving choices?

Does God have a plan for our partner?

The answer, of course, is yes. Spiritual healing is available to our partner, just as it is available to us. A higher source will guide and protect our partner in all life's difficulties, just as it will protect us.

And just as we are free to reject God's plan for us, God's fondest hopes for us, God's guidance for us, so is our partner.

Our interference won't help our partner accept guidance. Our horning in won't make him more likely to turn to spiritual help. But our meddling can wedge us in between our partner and his spirit, making things more difficult for both of us and making it harder for him to see or hear God's plan.

TODAY I WILL ALLOW MY PARTNER TO DEFINE HIS OWN RELA-
TIONSHIP WITH GOD. AND I WILL REMEMBER THAT, ALTHOUGH
MY PARTNER HAS A GOD, IT ISN'T ME.

BE OPEN TO THE GIFTS

There is a gift for each of us in this unhappiness that life has brought us. Something good—even miraculous—can grow out of our worst crises, if we are open to it.

We see it happen all around us. Parents talk about how they've learned more about love from their children with disabilities than from any other source. Alcoholics hit bottom, lose everything they value, and find grace, a gift more precious than anything material that was lost. Accident victims face death and have their eyes opened to the preciousness of life.

If we don't close our hearts, we will be led to some gift even in the midst of pain and betrayal. We may be shown the depth of our children's love for us. We may find a renewed commitment to a marriage that was foundering. We may find new friends who value us and thereby teach us to value ourselves. We may find a new way of life that surpasses the best hopes we've ever had.

YES, THIS MOMENT HURTS. BUT IT WON'T LAST FOREVER. AND AT THE END OF THIS MOMENT IS ANOTHER MOMENT WHEN I WILL BE GIVEN SOME TREASURE THAT WILL LAST FOREVER.

ALICE MAY

SEEK PATIENCE

Is it time to confront him? Or is this the time to let it go and keep quiet?

Like so much else in a damaged relationship, these questions have no certain and easy answers that hold true every time, in every case. To confront or not. To separate or not. To be intimate or not. To trust or not.

It is times like these when I know that the best answer for me lies in prayer, especially the prayer that I will have the courage not to obsess but to trust that I will be shown what I need to know when I need to know it. I ask for guidance and courage and patience. I seek the wisdom to see whatever I am supposed to learn in my present circumstances.

Mostly I trust that I will know what to do at the exact moment of decision.

I SELDOM FIND ANSWERS OR SOLUTIONS SIMPLY BECAUSE I WANT TO STOP FEELING MY DISCOMFORT. BUT IF I DO MY FOOTWORK AND CARRY OUT SOME HEALING ACTIONS, I ALWAYS FIND MY SOLUTIONS AT EXACTLY THE RIGHT TIME.

GOD HAS PACKED FOR TOMORROW

We can't see the end of the path we're on. We can't see where it leads, what awaits us once we complete this part of the journey.

That uncertainty fills us with anxiety, immobilizes us with fear, sometimes even angers us to the point that we stubbornly refuse to move forward.

What is happening to us? When will we be happy? What can we do to ensure that we end up where we want to be?

There are no answers to those questions in this present moment. We are not intended to hold the key to tomorrow in our hands today. We can only trust that a higher power has looked ahead and has a better destination in mind for us than the one we would choose for ourselves. We need only be sure that this same power knows precisely what tools we will need for tomorrow's journey and will place them in our hands as soon as they are needed. Not today, when they would only weigh us down, but tomorrow, when we will need them. Tomorrow will be soon enough.

When the time comes, God equips us for the journey.

TODAY I WILL PUT ONE FOOT IN FRONT OF THE OTHER AND TRUST THAT THE PATH LEADS TO MY NEXT DESTINATION. FOR NOW, I WILL REMEMBER THAT GOD HAS ALREADY PACKED MY BAGS FOR TOMORROW.

ALICE MAY

YOUR GREATEST FEAR

A friend asked recently, "What is your greatest fear?"

I was speechless when I realized that I didn't have a single fear I could label great.

That wasn't always true. I once had great fears, many of them, so great they overwhelmed me and often ruled my life. I was afraid of being abandoned. Afraid of failing in my marriage. Afraid of growing old and unattractive. Afraid of making a mistake and looking foolish or pathetic to others. Afraid I wouldn't be able to pay the bills. The list went on and on.

Today I still have the occasional fear, a niggling concern that crops up from time to time and causes momentary discomfort. But I can't think of a single fear that rules me or causes problems in my life.

Yet I've done nothing aimed specifically at banishing my overwhelming fears. I haven't analyzed or applied logic to them. I haven't gone through years of psychotherapy. I haven't gained confidence through physical challenge.

All I've done is apply a few basic spiritual principles to my life. All I've done is alter the way I view my world by changing my attitudes and beliefs. All I've done is learn to live with a little bit of faith.

A LITTLE BIT OF FAITH CAN CONQUER A LOT OF FEAR. TODAY I NO LONGER HAVE TO BE DOMINATED BY MY FEARS.

MIRACLES THROUGH ACTION

She is beautiful inside and out, the kind of person who brightens every room she enters. But when I first met her, she was struggling. Her light had gone out. Her husband had been unfaithful, and after several years she still had trouble letting it go.

That event, coupled with her mother's death when she was still a child, had left her filled with self-loathing and convinced that she couldn't trust God. She treated herself poorly. Many of her actions seemed designed to lead her along the same path to poor health and early death that her mother had followed. Or to make others think as little of her as she thought of herself.

But she was eager to change. Willing to do whatever it took. Including the painful process of self-assessment, which dredged up many unpleasant awarenesses. But she had heard others talk about the dramatic changes brought about by the process, so she dove in. She wanted a miracle.

She completed her personal inventory and asked me to listen to what she'd written. We talked and cried for hours. When she left my home, she said she felt empty, disappointed. There hadn't been a miracle after all. Maybe, she said, she was too big a reclamation project even for God.

On the way home, she stopped twice at fast-food restaurants to salve her spirits.

Three days later, I returned home from running errands to find her sitting on my front porch. She stood up and came toward me. She was crying, and smiling her wonderful smile. All she said was, "I love myself."

SEEKING MY SPIRIT WILL HEAL ME WHERE I AM BROKEN. I WILL BE TOUCHED IN MIRACULOUS, AFFIRMING WAYS. ALL I NEED IS WILLINGNESS AND PATIENCE.

ALICE MAY

SETTING THINGS RIGHT
WITH OTHERS

If we are ready to put the healing power of forgiveness to further use in our life, one of the actions we may want to take is to set right the things we've done wrong ourselves. We may want to apologize or make reparations to others. If so, we will want to check our motives first.

We don't want to apologize with any hope of changing other people. We don't do it so they will forgive us or think better of us. We do it solely to clean our side of the street.

Setting things right with others is a part of our spiritual housecleaning. It is a decision we make only because we are ready to feel better about ourselves and because we don't want to carry old baggage with us into our new way of life. As with the rest of our life these days, the focus of this process is on us.

TODAY I WILL TAKE ONE ACTION TO SET THINGS RIGHT WITH SOMEONE I'VE HURT. I WILL DO MY BEST, KNOWING THAT THE IMPORTANT THING IS MY SINCERE EFFORT. WHEN I HAVE TAKEN THIS ACTION, I WILL FEEL LIGHTER, BETTER ABOUT THE PERSON I AM BECOMING.

TREATING YOUR SYMPTOMS

How tempting it is to pretend our problems are fleeting, a minor mishap that threw us temporarily off course. The problem is over, we don't need to dwell on it, and the best way to handle it is to get on with our lives.

Recognizing that infidelity is a symptom of other problems that require attention is a heavy burden at a time when we are so wounded that just getting through the day requires superhuman effort. We don't want to learn to communicate or handle conflict effectively or examine the demons that make us shy away from intimacy.

If we ignore it, surely it will go away.

Perhaps it will. For a while. The symptoms may subside for a period of time. But if the disease in our relationship has not been treated, it will incubate. It will spread. It may grow fatal, like a cancer that could have been treated successfully if only we'd paid attention sooner.

As overwhelming as it may seem, we have been given the opportunity to get to the bottom of whatever problems plague our relationship. Through counseling, through self-examination, through renewed commitment to healthy communication and honesty and unconditional love we can make progress. We can treat the disease in our relationship before it spreads, before it grows fatal.

TODAY I WILL TURN TO THE SOURCE OF MY HEALING FOR THE COURAGE I NEED TO LOOK HONESTLY AT THE PROBLEMS IN MY LIFE AND THE STEPS I MUST TAKE TO TACKLE THEM.

WORKPLACE ANXIETY

One of us cowered at the thought of looking for work. What did she have to offer? Who would hire her after all the years she'd been a home-maker? Her, a woman with no skills and no references?

Another of us dreaded starting at the bottom, working too hard for too little. And yet another couldn't imagine how she would manage children *and* a job. For one woman, the realization that she would have to find a job that paid better than the part-time creative work she loved was another hard blow.

Some of us may have to find a job. And especially at this time, we don't feel equipped to prepare a résumé, to scour the want ads, to take on another task, to risk one more rejection.

Like everything else we face today, finding work will go more smoothly and be easier on us emotionally if we use our spiritual tools. We can ask for guidance, perhaps talking to other women about their careers and how they decided what positions to seek. We can find a class on job hunting. And we can go on interviews despite our fears, focusing on the opportunity to stretch ourselves, not on the possibility of rejection. We can do a little footwork every day.

All of us have learned that if we simply take one small action toward our goal each day, the right doors will open. We will find the job we need. We may have to start at the bottom and move up gradually. We may be asked to accept the challenge of learning new skills and moving outside our comfort zone. But we will not be alone. We will have all the support we need. And we will gain new confidence with each step we take.

IF I AM FACED WITH THE PROSPECT OF ENTERING OR RETURNING TO THE WORKFORCE, I WILL TAKE ONE SMALL ACTION TODAY TO BEGIN THE PROCESS. I WILL DO SO KNOWING THAT EVEN A SMALL STEP BUILDS MY COURAGE.

SWEARING OFF LOVE

Swearing off love makes us neither free nor safe.

Swearing off love is tempting, but it is not a solution. It is not the path to healing or to a future free of messy or painful entanglements. In fact, swearing off love is simply one more way of saying, *I can fix this myself. I have the answers. I am in charge of my life, and I know the best solution.*

Setting aside the need to be in a relationship for this moment may be an excellent choice. We may decide to avoid a relationship for six months or a year. This gives us time to focus on ourselves, our healing, our commitment to change. It gives us time for children or jobs when our energy may be limited.

But swearing off relationships for good, building a wall that says we are no longer open to the possibilities of love is not a path to full healing. Like dieters who swear off all the foods they enjoy most, swearing off relationships is an invitation, sooner or later, to binge on the very things that aren't good for us. It makes the forbidden—the kind of men who are off-limits or who invariably aren't good for us—seem very enticing.

Perhaps a better choice, after our commitment to live relationship-free for a specified period is over, would be to drop our agendas, trust our new instincts, and be open to whatever love comes into our lives.

Even those of us who have never managed to make a go of love may find ourselves in healthy relationships if we have no preordained expectations. Regardless, our open and loving hearts will enrich our lives and the lives of those around us.

TODAY I CAN DECIDE TO TAKE SOME TIME OFF FROM RELATIONSHIPS IF THAT ROUTE SEEMS SAFEST AND HEALTHIEST. AND I WILL BE OPEN TO WHATEVER LIFE OFFERS ME ONCE I HAVE FOUND HEALING AND SERENITY.

ALICE MAY

FACING THE TRUTH ABOUT LOVE

What delusions did we bring to our relationship?

Some of us believed we could change him—and some of us still believe it. Some of us believed our need for one another was the same as love. We believed he would place our needs above his own and that made it right for us to reciprocate. We believed love delivered happily-ever-after.

Even now we hate to give up these self-deceptions. And many of our efforts now sometimes are aimed at restoring those mirages, piecing them back together and returning them to the pedestal we constructed for our fairy-tale life.

Our healing is not about returning to a place where delusion reigns. Our healing is about moving to a new place where we no longer need our misconceptions. A place where we can live in the light of the truth and feel safer than we ever felt with our delusions for company and comfort.

We cannot change each other and would not find happiness if we could. Need is not the same as love—they are not even distantly related. We cannot burden anyone else with meeting our needs once we are adults. And love is more than passion and blind devotion.

Embrace reality. Acknowledge the unhealthy and unmet needs we bring to any relationship. Accept the frailties that will always pit us against the people with whom we most long to be intimate. See that love is a lifelong process of acceptance and change and support and overcoming disappointments.

I KNOW I AM SAFE IN THE PLACE WHERE I FACE TRUTH. I KNOW THIS IS WHERE I WILL FIND PEACE AND FREEDOM AND LOVE.

TRUST IN THE POSSIBILITY
OF GOOD

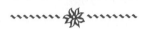

The way I give such weight to my fears and so readily dismiss the possibility of good outcomes is another example of how distorted my view of the world can become.

I am sure I will end up homeless in the event of a divorce. I am sure no one will ever love me again. I am sure my misery will drive me to compulsive overeating and I'll gain fifty pounds.

It never occurs to me to believe that I could end up in a cozy cottage at my favorite beach if I am no longer tied by my husband's job to living in a certain city. It never dawns on me that I might find a partner whose love is deep and true once I let go of one whose love is self-centered and faithless. It certainly never crosses my mind that I could take this time of change as an opportunity to work out, stop cooking to satisfy him, and lose fifteen pounds.

My fears are credible to me. But I don't dare trust my hopes and dreams.

With a tiny action, I could turn that around. I could commit myself to changing the channel when I tune in to my doomsday predictions. I could make a list of alternatives and read it to myself whenever I begin to obsess over negative outcomes. I could call a friend and recite my fears in lurid detail until we are laughing over my tendency to be melodramatic.

Life holds good and bad. When bad arises, we must deal with it. But we don't have to invite it to set up shop in our heads before it even occurs.

TODAY I WILL LIVE IN THE MOMENT AND ASSUME THAT SOME GOOD WILL COME ALONG TO BALANCE MY DIFFICULTIES. I WON'T RUIN THIS DAY BY SCRIPTING MY DOWNFALL TOMORROW.

ALICE MAY

SLOW DOWN

A friend tells me never to be in a hurry when it's important.

I used to be in a hurry all the time, and it was *all* important. *I* was important. I had meetings to run, decisions to make, deadlines to meet. And wherever I was, at least half my mind was always focused on where I had to be next.

My computerized to-do list once had meetings and deadlines and projects plugged in eighteen months ahead.

Today, when friends ask what I'm doing this afternoon, my answer is often, "I don't know yet. Let me take care of this morning and I'll let you know."

I go slower today. I don't zip in and out of traffic to save thirty seconds; instead, I catch up at traffic lights with the people who zipped in front of me. I don't push myself to cram as much as possible into this day, this month, this lifetime. I have learned to move through most days with serenity.

The last time I forgot myself and began to rush around, I ended up mistakenly shoving the Toyota key into the Volkswagen ignition switch. It wouldn't start the car, and it wouldn't come out either. In my rush to do too much, I created one more problem to deal with. I made myself late. I inconvenienced others. I tied a knot in my gut.

When we slow down and focus on this moment, we have all the time we need. And that's enough.

TODAY I WILL SLOW DOWN. I WILL RECOGNIZE HOW MUCH MORE I CAN ACCOMPLISH WHEN I'M NOT IN A HURRY. I WILL REMEMBER THAT I HAVE ALL THE TIME I NEED TODAY.

PARANOIA VERSUS GULLIBILITY

For years after my husband's first episode of infidelity came to light, anything I didn't immediately understand became a sign that he was straying. If his actions weren't indisputably innocent, they were not just suspect but guilty.

Until one day a loving friend explained, "You're so paranoid that if you came home and the jar of mayonnaise was missing, you'd be sure the sexy next-door neighbor came over to borrow it while you were gone and ended up sleeping with your husband."

She was right, of course. I had become paranoid. From having been so gullible that I allowed myself to be deceived for years, I had swung to the other extreme. I couldn't trust my instincts, and excessive doubt seemed better than being played for a fool again.

Swinging back to a healthy balance between paranoia and gullibility takes time. It takes faith that we will know everything we need to know at the best time for us to know it. It takes a willingness to turn our attention away from our suspicions when they arise. It takes an understanding that our partner's behavior demeans only him; our behavior when we give in to our suspicions demeans us.

TODAY I WILL LOOK FOR A REASONABLE EXPLANATION WHEN THE MAYONNAISE JAR TURNS UP MISSING. I WILL TRY TO ASSUME THAT EVERY LITTLE THING THAT IS OUT OF PLACE IN MY LIFE IS NOT A SIGN OF MY PARTNER'S BETRAYAL.

AMENDS, NOT APOLOGIES

The dictionary tells me that the verb *amend* means to make better, to improve; to remove the faults of; to change or revise.

I like to keep that definition in mind when I am working on unburdening myself as part of my spiritual journey. This stage of my journey offers me the opportunity to atone for my past and make reparations wherever I owe them, including to myself.

Making such reparations is much more than simply apologizing for past wrongs. In fact, as one person has said, the act of saying we're sorry is merely the announcement of our intentions to set things right.

To truly make amends, we change. We change how we feel about the other person. We change how we treat that person or talk about that person. We make a commitment to do things differently than we've done them in the past.

If we've allowed anger at our spouse to seep into our relationships with our children, we make an effort not to do it again. If we've used our suspicions to justify snooping into our partner's life, we seek the strength not to make that mistake again. If we've told our loved ones how to run their lives, we learn to hold our tongues until we can remember that their lives aren't ours to direct. If we've lied, we cultivate honesty. If we've been judgmental, we look at others with compassion in our hearts.

When we make amends to others, we are the ones who benefit most, no matter how they react. Because we are forgiven, not necessarily by the people we may have hurt, but by ourselves.

TODAY I WILL WORK ON CHANGING ONE BEHAVIOR THAT HAS CAUSED A PROBLEM WITH SOMEONE IN MY LIFE. I WILL FEEL THE RELIEF THAT COMES WITH MAKING ONE SMALL CHANGE IN MY UNHEALTHY BEHAVIOR.

NEGATIVE VOICES

Deciding to divorce often activates every negative voice in our heads. *I never was good enough. I nagged too much or weighed too much. I should've finished college. I never should have taken that job earning more than he did.*

Divorce brings up our guilt, our inadequacies, the fears that hobble us emotionally. It brings up the voice of our emotional disease.

Today, when we hear the voice of our disease, we can tune it out. We can tell it to go away and leave us alone. We can laugh at it or sing at it or call our friends and ask them to argue with it.

We can tell it that we did the best we could in a tough situation. That if others who love us don't expect us to be perfect, who are we to demand more? That we are lovable just as we are. That we're getting better every day.

We can accept responsibility for our part in our failed marriage. But we don't have to listen to the voice that insists we accept the blame for everything that ever went wrong.

THE NEGATIVE VOICES IN MY HEAD ARE WRONG. I CAN, WITH THE HELP OF SOMEONE I TRUST, DETERMINE WHO I REALLY AM AND WHAT IS REALLY TRUE. BUT I WON'T ACCEPT THE JUDGMENT OF THE NEGATIVE VOICES IN MY HEAD.

ALONE BUT NOT HELPLESS

Some of us wind up living alone, either temporarily or on a more long-term basis. But we don't have to equate being alone with being lonely. And just because we are alone, we don't have to be defenseless.

We can take care of ourselves. One way we can do that is by reaching out for help in unfamiliar or daunting situations. We can ask friends for advice or for the name of someone who can help. We can tackle unexpected problems one baby step at a time, knowing it's okay not to have all the answers ourselves.

Shortly after a separation, I realized it wouldn't be possible to ignore the calf-high grass in my yard any longer. I pulled out the lawn mower. Just cranking it was hard enough, but I also had three-fourths of an acre of overgrown grass to mow.

About fifteen minutes into the task, the mower's handle flew apart and the engine stalled. I sat in the grass beside the broken mower, too frustrated even to cry.

As I sat there, I realized I had two choices. I could give up and for the foreseeable future relinquish my ability to cope. Or I could take my broken handle to the hardware store and ask how to fix it. I decided to ask for help.

Following good advice, I fixed the lawn mower myself.

I cut the grass.

I knew I was going to be okay.

I might have been powerless at that moment to save my marriage, but I was not helpless.

TODAY I CAN EMPOWER MYSELF BY TACKLING SOMETHING DIFFICULT I NEVER BELIEVED I COULD DO. I WILL LEARN THAT I AM NOT HELPLESS.

CELEBRATE THE JOY

How can we celebrate this moment, this day, this life?

One of the first things to leave us in difficult times is our joy. We are mired in pain or anger or depression. We lose our ability to smile, to laugh, to soak up all that is good around us.

We can recapture our joy by seeking the small things that are good in this very moment. The sound of a bird outside our window. Sunlight filtering through the trees. Children's laughter. Even something as simple as slipping off our shoes and letting our bare feet breathe for a moment.

We can seek out people and activities that make us smile, that feed our spirit. And we can limit our exposure to those who drain us or feed our negativity.

We can open our hearts to the joy our world holds. It is there. It is ours to take.

THE JOY IN MY WORLD WILL GROW AS I AM ONCE AGAIN OPEN TO CELEBRATING THIS MOMENT, THIS DAY, THIS LIFE.

ALICE MAY

PLAYING DETECTIVE

A friend wanted to hire a detective the last time her partner was out of town on business.

Been there, done that. Spent hundreds of dollars, in fact, on two different occasions to hear that there was no playing around—only to learn later that the reports I'd paid for with the mortgage money were wrong.

The problem with trying to prove that my husband is acting out sexually is that I can't prove anything if he is not acting out. There is no proof of fidelity. And if nothing turns up to prove infidelity, it never reassures me. I simply figure he managed to pull it off this time, and I make up my mind to try harder to catch him the next time.

But I am never convinced of his innocence when I am focused on proving his guilt.

I have learned to leave it to some power outside myself to prove my husband's guilt or innocence. I now trust that the facts will be revealed when the time is right. And the results are always more reassuring, more reliable, and far less expensive to both my bank account and my self-esteem than my own efforts to play private investigator.

IT IS NOT MY JOB TO KEEP TABS ON MY PARTNER TODAY. I KNOW THIS BECAUSE I REMEMBER HOW AGITATED AND INSANE AND DESPERATE I HAVE FELT WHEN I'VE TAKEN ON THAT JOB IN THE PAST. I WON'T DO THAT TO MYSELF AGAIN.

WHO FEEDS YOU,
WHO DRAINS YOU

The personal coach Cheryl Richardson, in her book *Take Time for Your Life*, challenges us to differentiate between relationships that drain us and relationships that fuel us.

She identifies six types of people who drain us spiritually and emotionally. They are the Blamer, who blames us and others for his problems; the Complainer, no explanation necessary; the Drainer, a needy person who always looks to us for guidance, support, and advice; the Shamer, who may cut you off, put you down, or make fun of you or your ideas in front of others; and the Gossip.

Richardson suggests that we replace these people with people who are, instead, proactive, or on a path of personal development; appreciative of our gifts, talents, and strengths; communicative; attentive, paying attention to what we say without judgment; honest; and accountable.

Today let us care enough about ourselves to take an honest look at all our close relationships. Let us see who feeds us and who exhausts us. Let us see who is committed to his or her own emotional and spiritual growth, and thus supportive of ours as well.

TODAY I WILL ASK MYSELF WHETHER I AM MAKING THE BEST CHOICES IN SELECTING MY FRIENDS AND PARTNERS.

THE TIMETABLE FOR HEALING

Get over it.

We may hear this from him if he grows tired of our tears, our doubts, our inability to behave as if everything is quickly and effortlessly back to normal.

It's over and done with. It was months ago. Get over it.

He may say it in anger. He may use it as a threat, intimating that our clinging to the past will drive him away again.

It's important for us to remember that his reaction is his problem. His anger or impatience is merely a sign that he still has feelings to process. We can detach from his negative reactions and return our attention to our own healing. We can remember that our process of healing cannot and should not be rushed to alleviate his guilt, his shame, or even his anger. Because if we rush it, our anger and our pain will be waiting beneath the surface to sabotage our happiness further down the road. Count on it.

We can do our best to express our grief in a healthy way and not in a punitive or self-pitying way. We can take positive steps to focus on healing and not on the damage. But beyond that we cannot ask ourselves to heal on anyone else's timetable.

I WILL GET OVER IT WHEN I GET OVER IT. I WILL HANDLE MY GRIEF IN POSITIVE WAYS. BUT GETTING OVER IT WILL TAKE TIME, THE RIGHT AMOUNT OF TIME FOR ME.

THE DANGERS OF KEEPING SCORE

The problem with doing something nice for the people we love is that so often we've attached the expectation of a payback. I'll scratch your back if you scratch mine.

Say I make peanut butter cookies for my spouse on a Saturday afternoon. I know he likes them. I believe if I do this for him, maybe he'll be more inclined to go to that three-hanky movie I've been wanting to see. I deliver the warm cookies to him as he watches a football game on TV, already planning what I'm going to wear to the movie.

On a scale of one to ten, I figure home-baked cookies are a number-eight good deed.

My partner is grateful. He makes up his mind to do something nice for me later in the day. Maybe he'll take out the trash before he settles in to watch game number two. Sure, the trash. A number seven on his do-good scale. That way, he's ahead of the game because he figures the cookies are a four or a five.

And that is where the problem comes in. I think I've got an eight in my column. And since I think he's supposed to take out the trash, his payback only earns him a two. In my mind, he's six down, and in his mind he's two up. I want more. I'm feeling slighted. He feels underappreciated. Suddenly our pleasant Saturday is the scene of a cold war that neither of us fully understands.

When we do something for someone we love, we do it solely out of love. We don't do it for payback. We don't keep score of our generosity or theirs. No expectations. No resentments. Just a heart warmed by doing something nice for free and for fun.

TODAY I WON'T KEEP SCORE WHEN I GIVE FROM THE HEART.

ALICE MAY

197

WORRY VERSUS PRAYER

Worry about nothing, but pray about everything.

Or as someone else puts it: If you worry, why pray? If you pray, why worry?

Worry is a choice we make. A poor choice. A choice that wastes energy and emotion. A choice that can make us ill and rob this moment of its joy.

But we need not worry. There is an alternative. A powerful alternative.

Today, if we are tempted to worry, we can pray instead. We can pray about the big concerns in our lives. We can pray about the small details that add up to big serenity-spoilers. We can remember that all parts of our lives are in better hands when we pray about them than when we worry about them.

TODAY I WILL CHOOSE NOT TO WORRY. I WILL CHOOSE TO PRAY INSTEAD.

HAVE YOU HARMED YOURSELF?

Even as we're making restitution to others for the wrongs we've done over the course of our lives, in a not-so-small corner of our minds many of us are wondering, "So when does somebody make amends to *me*?"

And of course, we all know who we want the amends to come from first.

Whether anyone else in our lives is truly sorry for hurting us is beyond our control. If we're waiting for that to happen before we permit ourselves to heal, we may be stuck in our spiritual illness for a long time.

But there is one person who has harmed us whose actions we can control. One person from whom we can expect reparations. We have harmed ourselves, as much as or sometimes more than anyone else in our lives.

Have we held ourselves in low regard? Have we let others define us? Have we missed out on important moments in our children's lives because of our obsessions? Have we overeaten or overspent or run ourselves into the ground with overwork? We've wronged ourselves by engaging in countless demeaning and hateful behaviors that have cut us off from our own spirits.

We've damaged ourselves. And as we decide to whom we owe reparations, let's make sure we place ourselves high on the list.

TODAY I AM PREPARED TO SET THINGS RIGHT WITH MYSELF, NO MATTER WHAT SOMEONE ELSE DOES.

WHEN YOU DON'T RESPECT
YOUR BOUNDARIES

I threw my husband out three times when I first learned about his infidelity, and he never got past the end of the driveway. I always caved in and relented.

Have we ever considered the real consequences of all our threats? What happens when we vow not to put up with certain behavior any longer, then utter the same vow with increasing shrillness a week or a month later?

What we are doing is teaching our partner that there are no consequences for his behavior. We are showing him we are not as good as our word. We are showing him our weakness and our willingness to overlook his indiscretions time and time again.

Why should he change if we allow him to remain the same? Why should he behave differently today if we teach him through our actions that nothing has to change? Why should he take us seriously if we don't take ourselves seriously enough to make a decision and stand by it?

The next time we feel compelled to threaten our partner with dire consequences, we can stop. We can make sure we are ready to deliver on our promise before we make it. If we are not, we can seek courage and wisdom. We can ask to be shown the next right action and to be given whatever we need to carry it out. We can talk out our confusion with another person. We will not issue an ultimatum until we are sure we're ready to follow through.

We owe that to our relationship and to ourselves.

TODAY I WILL REMEMBER THAT I CAN'T ASK OTHERS TO RESPECT MY BOUNDARIES IF I CAN'T EVEN RESPECT THEM MYSELF.

BITTER OR BETTER?

So many outcomes are uncertain at a time like this. But one outcome is clear. Depending on how we handle this crisis, we can either get better or we can get bitter.

We can hang on to our anger. We can resent the people who have hurt us. We can curse fate and make self-pity our favorite companion. We can let fear guide us. We can get bitter.

Or we can pray for the courage to forgive. We can seek guidance in our dealings with those who have hurt us. We can take certain actions to heal ourselves. We can welcome the good things arising out of our changed circumstances. We can mourn our losses and let them go. We can get better.

The choice is ours.

WITH THE HELP OF OTHERS WHO HAVE GONE BEFORE ME, TODAY I CHOOSE TO GET BETTER.

FACING HARSH REALITIES

Many harsh realities must be confronted as we accept the truth of our partner's infidelity.

One of those—one of the most frightening—is sexually transmitted diseases. STDs are a part of today's world, a reality each of us must deal with in a healthy and self-preserving way.

Some of us want to hide from the possibility of STD. We don't want to be tested. We don't want to practice safe sex with the man we've loved and trusted because it would be a continuing reminder of his actions. We want to pretend there is no danger.

Others of us want to get at the truth and get at it now.

As with so much else in this murky land we now inhabit, there are no easy answers, and there is no single answer that is right for everyone.

We can seek guidance, asking others what they have done and why. We can try to define reasonable precautions for ourselves. And we can commit to not endangering anyone else—including possible unborn children—while we are in our own uncertainty.

If we seek the right answers, the right answers will come. If we ask for the courage to put the answers to work in our lives, we will be given that as well.

TODAY I WILL NOT IGNORE THE HARSH REALITIES THAT COME WITH MY PARTNER'S INFIDELITY. I WILL ASK FOR HELP IF I NEED IT AND WILL MAKE HEALTHY DECISIONS FOR MY OWN SAFETY.

NOTHING IS HOPELESS

Wait without hope, knowing that nothing is hopeless.

My friend passed this message on to me right after my husband and I separated. She had heard it from a friend whose body was ravaged with cancer, as our lives were ravaged by betrayal.

Wait without hope.

He meant, my friend told me, that he accepted the circumstances he was in. He meant that he could not cling to the expectation that his present circumstances would work out in a particular way, a way that would suit him. He meant that he was content simply to take the journey life had planned for him.

Wait without hope, knowing that nothing is hopeless.

He meant, also, that God does deal in miracles. He meant that God can use whatever crisis we are in to accomplish something of great beauty and joy. A miracle.

Perhaps not the miracle we would have chosen, but a miracle nonetheless.

TODAY I WILL WAIT AND TRUST THAT GOD HAS A MIRACLE IN MIND FOR ME. I WILL BE OPEN TO LETTING GOD DECIDE WHAT THAT MIRACLE WILL BE.

TAKING HIS TEMPERATURE

How often have we taken our partner's temperature to see how we are feeling?

If he felt bad, we've thought it meant that we must feel bad also. If his day was ruined, so was ours. If he was having a good day, we had permission to enjoy our day as well. Not his permission, but our own.

The truth is, we are separate persons, with moods and feelings and daily ups and downs of our own. Our emotional well-being is not tied to someone else's, unless we choose to let it be. We can have moments of joy or serenity or well-being even if our partner is drowning in his negative emotions.

Compassion and empathy do not require us to climb into the first emotional or mental pit our partner flings himself into. In fact, when we do that we render ourselves incapable of providing any real help to a loved one who is suffering.

TODAY I WILL DETACH. I WILL REMAIN IN THE FLOW OF MY DAY AND BE READY WITH ENCOURAGEMENT OR A LISTENING EAR IF IT IS NEEDED. I WILL MONITOR MY OWN MOODS AND ACTIONS, NOT SOMEONE ELSE'S.

SURRENDERING YOUR LOVE LIFE

"I was forty-eight when I realized I didn't know how to do healthy relationships," said a friend. "So I gave them up. I turned my love life over to my higher power and admitted defeat."

What happened to her was miraculous.

No, life did not place the perfect partner in front of her and launch her on a fairy-tale existence. Life instead provided her with a friend to walk with so she could keep her sanity while recovering from the relationship she had ended. When she met a few people who needed her help, her hours began to fill with productive behavior and deeply satisfying friendships. She began a new career in a healing profession to replace the job in technology that had been eating away at her spirit. Now, through her work, she connects deeply with people every day.

"When I gave my love life to God, I was given more love and support and intimacy than I had ever imagined possible," my friend said. "I was given what I needed from so many different sources that I realize now I don't ever need to lack for warmth and affection.

"And God managed all that without any sign of a sexual partner. But I'm happier and more fulfilled than I've ever been."

I WILL STOP LOOKING FOR THE PERFECT LOVE AND TRUST LIFE
TO BRING ME THE LOVE I NEED IN WHATEVER FORM IT COMES
TODAY. I NEED NEVER AGAIN BE WITHOUT ABUNDANT LOVE.

SIGNALS OF EMOTIONAL RELAPSE

Today we will watch ourselves.

We will watch ourselves for small signs that we are losing control of our emotions. Perhaps, if we can detect the first stages of an emotional lapse, we will soon be able to take the actions that head off such a lapse before it becomes full-blown.

So today we will watch ourselves. We will watch ourselves in traffic to see whether little things trigger a not-so-little reaction. We will observe the way we react in stores if the line moves too slowly or the clerk is not as efficient as we would like. We will watch ourselves at work, with our children, when things don't go as planned.

By observing without judging, we can learn to recognize telltale signals that we are about to erupt emotionally. Perhaps we can learn to stop every time we bang a palm on the steering wheel and, instead of swearing, remind ourselves: *This is not about that driver who just caused me to miss a light. What is it about? What positive action can I take before this turns into a full-scale inner war I'm bound to lose?*

Feeling all our emotions fully is not a bad thing. But allowing our emotions to rule us, allowing them to determine our actions or lead us into a downward spiral of depression or obsessive thinking, is not good. And it is avoidable.

EMOTIONAL RELAPSE CAN TAKE ME BY SURPRISE. BUT SOMETIMES I AM FOREWARNED. I WILL BECOME AWARE OF THE WARNING SIGNALS AND REMEMBER THAT I CAN DEAL WITH MY EMOTIONS CONSTRUCTIVELY AND CHANGE DIRECTION AT ANY TIME.

PERFECTIONISM

I don't have to be perfect today.

I've lived so long with an undercurrent of disapproval that I told myself the only way to buy approval was through perfection.

I've told myself for so long that all the problems in my marriage were my fault that I learned to kick myself whenever I wasn't perfect.

I've criticized myself and blamed myself when others abandoned or betrayed me. I've taken it on my own shoulders when others weren't capable of giving me the love I needed.

I've spent a lifetime striving for perfection, certain that if I could only attain perfection my problems would disappear. Because my problems, in my eyes, were all about my shortcomings.

There is no question that I've made mistakes and have my share of personal limitations. But my need to be perfect is one more lie I've told myself. One more way of denying the realities of my life. My perfectionism has been one more way of squeezing the life out of my soul.

My lack of perfection is not a defect of character. It is not the reason my life is not perfect. It is not the reason the people in my life can't give me the love I need and deserve. My lack of perfection is simply a sign of my humanity.

Today I will make a list of all the things I love about myself, all the things I do well as this day goes on. I can make a list of every nice thing someone says about me for the next week. And I can make note of the fact that the world does not come to an end on those occasions when I don't conduct myself perfectly. Today I will burn the toast and stumble on the sidewalk and smear my mascara.

TODAY I WILL REMEMBER THAT I NO LONGER NEED TO BE BURDENED BY MY PERFECTIONISM.

ALICE MAY

TENSION IN YOUR BODY

My massage therapist tells me that our bodies are like rope. Some of us are a length of rope tossed into the yard, looping and coiling effortlessly. If one end of such a length of rope is tweaked, the rest of the rope is unaffected by the tweaking. The rope remains loose.

If, however, that same rope is stretched taut, a pluck on one end of the rope will reverberate down the length of it.

Are we loose, effortlessly coiled pieces of rope, able to flick off irritations in our life? Or have crises left us pulled so tight that we feel every minute shift in our life throughout our bodies? When the latter is true, each disturbance spreads.

Today we can seek help in releasing our tension. We can remember that our bodies are made up of connective tissue and that with enough unrelieved tension, our entire body can soon be affected in negative ways.

So we can read a book, watch a movie, sit in a rocker. We can write in our journal, walk with a friend, go sailing or skiing or swimming. We can release our tension in whatever way works for us.

TODAY I WILL LEARN TO LISTEN TO MY BODY, PAYING ATTENTION TO THE PLACES WHERE I STORE MY TENSION. I WILL NOTICE WHEN I AM TIGHTLY STRUNG AND TAKE SOME ACTION TO LOOSEN UP.

STAYING CLOSE TO GOD

How well I cope in my intimate relationships is tied to how close I am to God.

If I am close to a higher power, I have the tools I need to contribute to the health of a relationship. I have some measure of compassion, tolerance, honesty, and unconditional love. I can communicate without fear or manipulation or control.

If I am close to my spirit, my needs are already being met and I won't burden others with the expectation that they will complete my life.

If I am living spiritually, I am able to distinguish between being of service and being a doormat. I can be a partner, neither calling all the shots nor allowing someone else to stage-direct my life.

If I am close to my higher power, every relationship I have will be touched by that spirit. And staying close to God is as simple as remembering that I am not in charge of the world.

TODAY I WILL REMEMBER THAT EVERY PART OF MY LIFE IS AFFECTED BY MY SPIRITUAL WELL-BEING. AS MY SPIRITUAL STATE CHANGES, SO DO OTHER THINGS IN MY LIFE, ESPECIALLY MY RELATIONSHIPS. I WILL SAFEGUARD MY SPIRITUAL STATE AND TAKE CARE OF MY RELATIONSHIPS AT THE SAME TIME.

UNCONDITIONAL LOVE

Unconditional love—love with no strings attached—is never easy. Loving someone in spite of flaws, in spite of hurtful behaviors, goes against our natural emotions.

Love without price tags is scary. And that is part of what we're being asked to learn right now.

While we heal, our greatest challenge is learning to practice unconditional love. We can do that by making a choice to commit no acts that we'll regret later, doing our best to cause no further damage. We can measure all our actions against the behaviors of a kind and loving partner.

Can we be civil, even if we feel like raging? We can if we have a healthy outlet for our rage and have learned when, how, and to whom we can express it appropriately.

Can we set aside our need to accuse, to chastise, to condemn? We can if we remember that we, too, have made mistakes we've wished we could undo.

Can we focus on the ways in which this person has been a good partner just long enough to see whether the long-term good outweighs what may be the temporary bad?

Can we love our partner just for today, and see whether that gives us strength to get through one more day of healing?

TODAY I WILL TRY TO PRACTICE UNCONDITIONAL LOVE FOR THE PEOPLE IN MY LIFE. I WILL REMEMBER THAT LOVE DOES NOT COME WITH A PRICE TAG.

LOSING GROUND

Spiritual healing is never a straight line.

As we do our footwork to recover from the effects of someone else's sexual acting out, we make progress. And we lose ground. We gain a measure of serenity and self-confidence one day, then fall back into the pit of self-pity and despair the next. We focus on ourselves today and open his mail in a desperate bid to control him tomorrow.

That doesn't mean we're weak. It doesn't mean we're worthless. It doesn't mean that all the negative things we've believed about ourselves for years are true after all.

It simply means we're human.

It simply means that the emotional damage we're trying to get over is both extensive and potent. We won't recover overnight.

What we do is make peace with today's lesson the best we can, knowing that we may have to learn it at a deeper level next week or next year. And when that happens, we may backslide again. What we do is focus on today's progress toward forgiveness, healing, and self-love, knowing that when those things slip away, it's okay and it's temporary. We'll be given another chance tomorrow.

HEALING IS NEVER A STRAIGHT LINE. I ALWAYS CIRCLE BACK TO MY LESSONS. AND THEN, A LITTLE STRONGER, A LITTLE WISER, I MOVE FORWARD AGAIN.

TREATING YOURSELF DIFFERENTLY

This process of personal growth tells me that one of the people to whom I owe restitution is myself. I've wronged myself as surely as have the people I blame for all my pain. But I can do something about the pain I've caused myself.

How do we make things up to ourselves? The same way we make redress to others, of course. By changing the ways we treat ourselves.

We respect ourselves by being gentle with ourselves when necessary and firm with ourselves when it is called for.

We watch the messages we feed ourselves and tune out when we're inclined to belittle or berate ourselves.

We gather around us those people who love and support us, people who feed our spirit, and excuse ourselves from the company of those who are negative, degrading, or toxic.

We learn to listen to our heart.

We stop judging ourselves and others so harshly. We can love ourselves and others unconditionally.

We can live in this moment and let go of the past, including the unhealthy ways we've treated ourselves in the past.

TODAY I WILL BEGIN TO TAKE CARE OF MYSELF AS LOVINGLY AS I WOULD TAKE CARE OF A VULNERABLE CHILD. I WILL TRUST THAT, WITH SUCH CARE, I WILL BLOSSOM.

WHEN LOVED ONES REACT

When our previous cat needed a change of diet in her later years, she was not happy with the new food. Her response was first to refuse to acknowledge it. If she ignored it, perhaps it would go away. When that didn't work, she decided to be more vocal about her protests. She complained, ever more loudly.

The people we love are often like that when we switch to healthier behaviors. We would like them to react by graciously adopting healthier behaviors of their own. But the truth is, they are often likely to make their unhappiness known the way my cat did—by stepping up their efforts to gain our attention with their protests. Maybe, if they protest loudly and irritatingly enough, they can hook us into returning to our old behavior.

We can wish our loved ones would react the way we want them to, but past experience has taught us that isn't likely. Chances are that, when we get healthier and they realize they are losing their enabler or their scapegoat or the one they control, they will redouble the behaviors that have always hooked us before. Now we can choose not to react to them by reverting to our old behaviors.

I WILL SEEK WHATEVER HELP AND SUPPORT I NEED IN PRACTIC-
ING MY NEW LIFE SKILLS. I WILL REMAIN CONFIDENT I AM DOING
THE RIGHT THING TO RESTORE MYSELF TO EMOTIONAL HEALTH,
NO MATTER HOW OTHERS REACT.

HEALTHY SEXUALITY

As I looked at the unhealthy behavior I engaged in and endured in the name of love and for the sake of sex, I learned that I was incapable of recognizing healthy sexuality.

It was a sobering discovery, one of the hardest parts of my journey. Sex had been such a big part of my life. How could I have gotten everything so wrong?

I learned that my decisions regarding sex had been made either from a need to control and manipulate or from a place of fear and insecurity. I had allowed myself to be used, and I had used others in a doomed search for intimacy. I had come to view sex as the most important sign of love.

I grieved over the discovery that my beliefs surrounding sexuality might be as unhealthy as my husband's.

What is healthy sexuality? And how do we find it?

Maybe it's a lot like finding our own personal relationship with a higher power. My answer may not be yours, and yours may not be mine.

Healthy sexuality is based on healthy boundaries. Anything that makes us feel uneasy is our bottom line. Moreover, we learn our partner's bottom line and respect that as well. We recognize when something doesn't feel right to us and know that it's okay to speak up about those feelings. We don't expect anyone to read our mind. Our sexuality is not at the mercy of anyone else's expectations, or the answer to anyone's fantasies.

When we are healthy, we don't use sex as a reward or a punishment. And we don't *give* ourselves *to* another person, we *share* ourselves *with* another person.

TODAY I SEE HEALTHY SEXUALITY AS A GIFT. WHEN BOTH MY PARTNER AND I ARE PRESENT EMOTIONALLY, IT IS A SPIRITUAL EXPERIENCE EXPRESSED AS A PHYSICAL ACT.

A BREAK TO REGROUP

We can take five minutes to regroup and redirect ourselves any time we need to.

After an argument or a disappointment or a close call on the freeway—anytime life throws us for a loop—we can take five minutes to collect ourselves.

We can sit in silence and close our eyes. We can turn off the phone or refuse to respond to a knock on the door. We can take a deep breath and release it slowly, feeling our heartbeat grow calmer, following the pace of our breath. We can repeat the Serenity Prayer or a personal affirmation that soothes our emotions.

Whatever is going on around us, we do not have to relinquish control to negative circumstances or negative emotions. We do not have to spiral downward to a place where even more is likely to go wrong with our day.

We can take five minutes to remind ourselves that the present situation is only a few moments in this day or this week. In those five minutes, we can find the quiet place in our heart where wisdom resides. We can let go of our tumultuous emotions and our distressing situation by remembering that in the larger picture this moment is less important than we believe it is. We can invite peace. And we will receive an answer.

WHEN MY DAY GETS OFF TRACK AND I LOSE MY SERENITY, I CAN TAKE FIVE MINUTES TO RESTORE MY PEACE OF MIND. THEN I CAN MOVE FORWARD, ASSURED THAT THE NEGATIVE DIRECTION IN MY DAY HAS BEEN REVERSED.

ALICE MAY

TIME TO MOVE ON

Some of us reach that moment when our most pressing issue is how to get out of this mess. Leaving a relationship that has caused us nothing but pain for longer than we care to remember finally seems like the best, the only, solution.

When that is the right answer, we know it in our hearts. We know it with calm certainty, without the mind-swirling turmoil that comes when we're simply trying to force a solution. We decide to leave, and we become peaceful, even in the midst of our grief.

When that happens, we can move on with kindness and with compassion. We can do it without feeling the need for paybacks, without vindictiveness. We can look at the partner who has caused us such pain and know that he wouldn't have done the things he did if he were a whole, happy, emotionally healthy person.

And sooner than we think, we can feel gratitude for his part in helping us grow spiritually, in helping us learn our own lessons of wholeness, happiness, and emotional health.

WHEN I CAN LEAVE WITHOUT DOING ANYTHING I'LL NEED TO SEEK FORGIVENESS FOR LATER, THE TIME IS RIGHT. I CAN MOVE ON. MY JOURNEY IS CHANGING, AND THE CHANGE WILL BE GOOD.

DO YOUR FOOTWORK

A passerby paused to congratulate Saint Francis of Assisi on the beauty of his garden. Such lushness, the passerby said, had to mean that Saint Francis prayed a lot. To which Saint Francis reportedly replied, "Yes, then I start digging."

This story reminds us that God will do for us what we can't do for ourselves, but God will not do for us those things we're capable of accomplishing ourselves.

Life does hold miracles, but we must do our footwork.

Nature will bless the earth with glorious tulips in the spring, but only if we plant bulbs the previous autumn. Our inner spirit guides us to the right decision, but our part in the process includes not second-guessing every move we make. A higher power can remove our fears and ease our emotional pain, but only if we participate in the process. If we pray. If we talk to people who are living in the solution. If we turn our attention to this day's work, which gives God room to act on our hearts and our souls.

Our footwork is seldom complicated. A telephone call. Reaching out to someone else in pain. Eating a healthy meal when we think we can't swallow a bite. Crying when we hurt instead of stuffing the pain. Treating others, and ourselves, gently. These are manageable tasks, doable even when our life is in turmoil.

TODAY I WILL DO WHATEVER FOOTWORK IS NEEDED TO KEEP ME ON THE PATH TOWARD HEALING AND GROWTH.

NO ONE IS PERFECT

Everyone else can get it right. Why can't we?

That is one of the pitfalls in comparing our insides with other people's outsides.

When we perceive that others are perfectly content and gloriously happy, we must remember that we can't see behind their facades or into their hearts. We don't know what sorrows, fears, or ugliness they live with. We must remember the times when our friends, family, and neighbors believed that our lives looked pretty perfect, too.

How wrong they were. How wrong we may be, too.

At this stage in our journey, we are better able to trust that our imperfections don't brand us as failures, unworthy of respect or love. Our imperfections merely say we are human. We can learn to accept those imperfections and stop wishing to replace them with our unrealistic views of others. Others are no more likely than we are to have a perfect existence, so we can stop envying what we believe we know about them.

IF SOMEONE ELSE EXHIBITS BEHAVIORS THAT I ADMIRE, I CAN WORK ON ADOPTING THOSE BEHAVIORS WITHOUT BELIEVING THAT I AM LACKING. I AM HUMAN AND I AM GROWING, AND THAT IS SOMETHING I CAN ADMIRE IN MYSELF. I NO LONGER NEED TO ENVY WHAT OTHERS SEEM TO HAVE THAT I DON'T.

FILL YOURSELF WITH HOPE

If no one else speaks the language of hope to you today, speak it to yourself.

If no one else tells you that you can survive this, tell yourself.

If no one else tells you that once this is over you will be stronger and happier and emotionally healthier, look yourself in the mirror and say the words yourself.

All of it is true. Even a situation that hurts this much and feels this despairing has room for hope. No matter how bleak it looks at this moment, you will do more than survive. You will thrive. You will grow. You will look back at this moment and recognize it as the catalyst for the best changes you've ever made in your life, whether your external circumstances change or not.

And that isn't just hope speaking. That is experience.

TODAY I WILL HEAR THE MESSAGE OF HOPE. I WILL HEAR IT FROM THE WOMEN WHO HAVE GONE BEFORE ME ON THIS PATH. I WILL HEAR IT IN MY HEART, FROM THE WISE VOICE OF MY SPIRIT.

YOU CANNOT GO BACK

I did not want to hear what my friend had to say. "Nothing between you will ever be the same again." It echoed in my heart like a curse, one I desperately wanted to ward off.

Many of us cling to the hope that our partnership can be restored to what it was before betrayal.

It can't happen. We cannot erase what has happened and go back to that place of innocent faith without damaging ourselves with denial.

So where does that leave us?

The only place to move is forward. The only courses open to us are either to acknowledge irreparable damage or to find a way to turn that damage into strength. Declaring irreparable damage may be the best path for some of us, and the one some of us choose despite the pain and anguish of starting over.

Rebuilding is equally hard, and attempts to do it may ultimately fail. But if we succeed, we will be stronger personally for our struggles, and the relationship may be also.

The process of rebuilding can teach us to communicate on deeper levels than were possible before.

We may find ourselves giving and receiving unconditional love.

We may find ourselves living spiritually.

We may also find real gifts in a sexuality based on intimacy and connection rather than mere pleasure.

The gifts of a spiritually aware partnership can be limitless. They aren't achieved easily or painlessly. But they are far better than paying the price of trying to go back to a place that no longer exists and can't be restored.

BACK THERE IS WHERE THE PAIN BEGAN. AHEAD OF ME IS WHERE IT ENDS. TODAY I WILL KEEP MOVING AHEAD.

Surviving Betrayal

RITUALS OF SURRENDER

I can't, but God can.

Whatever troubles us, the answer lies in surrendering the problem to God. But sometimes the only surrender we can manage is mental. We tell ourselves it's the right thing, and our heads comprehend the logic of it, but our hearts are not getting the message.

For some of us, rituals are concrete ways to signal our hearts that it is time to let go.

We can write our problems down and burn them, one by one, saying an affirmation or prayer as we do so. We can assign each problem to a stone and toss our pile of stones into a stream. We can write our problems down and stuff them into a can we've labeled our God Can.

Some people use old coffee cans. Or decorative tin boxes found in antique stores. Some people decorate their God Cans. Some don't. Whatever works for each of us is fine.

Get a God Can. Use it to tuck away your problems whenever you need a symbolic reminder that this is a problem only God can handle.

I can't, but God can.

I think I'll let him.

TODAY I WILL IDENTIFY RITUALS THAT CAN HELP ME LET GO OF MY WORRIES. I WILL FIND CONCRETE WAYS TO SURRENDER MY PROBLEMS.

THE BATTLE TO CONTROL YOUR FLAWS

A nearby theme park has a game called Whack-a-Mole. Each player is given a foam mallet to whack away at mechanical moles when they raise their heads out of holes in a platform. As the game progresses, the moles pop up more quickly. As soon as the player knocks one back into the ground, two more pop up.

It sometimes feels as if I'm engaged in a game of Whack-a-Mole when it comes to beating back my weaknesses of character.

If I work on my fears for a while, I'll look up to find that selfishness has cropped up. If I get that under control, suddenly I'm facing dishonesty or arrogance.

The first lesson for me is that I'm incapable of controlling my character flaws on my own. They're too clever for me, too numerous for me. And if I'm counting on my limited powers, I am doomed to lose the battle. In my case, only God has the power to keep my failings under control.

The other lesson for me is to remember that I am only human. I was never intended to beat back all my flaws and emerge perfect, although the worst of them may someday disappear if I persevere. But even that is not a condition of my being a worthwhile and lovable person.

I AM FAR FROM PERFECT. BUT I CAN CONTINUE TAKING A SWIPE AT MY FLAWS WHEN THEY POP UP, REMEMBERING THAT I AM LOVABLE JUST AS I AM TODAY.

HEALTHY CONFLICT MANAGEMENT

Where there is as much tension as we find in a home affected by infidelity, there are plenty of opportunities for arguments.

Some disagreements can be healthy and productive, if we are listening well and keeping our emotions in check. Others are only additional wreckage. Those arguments can be avoided, and we don't even need our partner's cooperation in order to stop a fight before it begins.

If we don't catch the ball, there's no game.

Especially during tough times, our partner may bait us into fighting. It eases his guilt. It gives him permission to continue his behavior. *Who wouldn't look for a little outside companionship, married to an ill-tempered person like this?*

So our best bet is to refuse to fall into the role he wants us to play.

If we don't catch the ball, there's no game.

An argument requires at least two participants. We don't have to be one of them. We can walk away. We can keep quiet. We can offer to discuss the matter later, when everyone is calm. We can refuse to catch the ball. And we can keep practicing this nonconfrontational behavior until we are adept at it.

If there is an issue that really needs resolution, it will surface when everyone is able to discuss it calmly. Certainly the most important issues deserve better than an ugly argument. And so do we.

WHEN EMOTIONS ARE RUNNING HIGH AND A RATIONAL DISCUSSION ISN'T POSSIBLE, I CAN REFUSE TO ENGAGE IN AN ARGUMENT. NO ONE HAS THE POWER TO DRAG ME INTO A CONFRONTATION AGAINST MY WILL.

THE JOURNEY TO GOD

The journey to a spiritual way of life is simpler than we think.

The trip may sometimes be a difficult one. It may take longer than we would wish. But it is a simple trip for one simple reason.

God meets us where we are.

The spiritual life doesn't require us to be at a certain place at a certain time on our journey. It doesn't ask us to dress a certain way or speak a certain language. There is no code, no secret handshake. God meets us where we are.

Whenever we cry out for help, God is at our side.

Whenever we are hungry for a deeper spiritual life, our inner spirit is ready.

Whenever we can't go one more step, God takes us in his arms as soon as we ask.

If we have doubts and seek answers, a higher wisdom will come to us. If we're cursing life for all our problems, a higher power stays by our side until our anger is spent.

The God we depend on today is more patient than we are. More tolerant of the messes we create and the detours we take on our spiritual journey. The only demand this higher spirit makes of us is willingness. Willingness to listen, to seek, to change.

TODAY I WILL GIVE GOD A CHANCE TO MEET ME WHERE I AM.

GOSSIP DAMAGES

One of my oldest friends is someone I no longer confide in; we rarely get together today because I can't share with her what's going on in my life. We grow further apart with every day that passes.

The reason is that I know she gossips.

I don't judge her for this. I can't afford to, since I was once her gossip buddy. We hashed out everyone's life and went on at length about our opinion of the mess they were making.

And when my life fell apart, I discovered that my friendship with her didn't make me off-limits as a subject. With no malicious intent, she betrayed my confidences to others. It was my life she hashed out.

I don't hold it against her today. But gossip has driven a wedge between us.

Since my life has been touched by infidelity, I have a very different view of gossip. Once, I thought it was harmless. Today I recognize how damaging and hurtful gossip can be. Today I see how it alienates me from others because no real intimacy is possible between people who gossip.

Today, if I feel the urge to talk about someone else, I remember how much I was hurt by gossip at a time when I already had enough pain in my life. I remember that passing on stories about others can destroy friendships. And I remember that telling too much even hurts the one who passes on the news, by damaging her in the eyes of those she talks to and those she talks about.

TODAY I WON'T TELL WHAT I KNOW ABOUT OTHERS. I WON'T PARTICIPATE IF OTHERS TRY TO TELL ME WHAT THEY KNOW. I WILL WORK TO RID MY LIFE OF GOSSIP AND BECOME SOMEONE OTHERS KNOW THEY CAN TRUST. I WILL REMOVE ONE MORE BARRIER TO INTIMACY BETWEEN US.

ALICE MAY

WISDOM VERSUS KNOWLEDGE

We can work to enlighten ourselves, gathering information to the point of obsession.

Women's magazines on how to affair-proof our marriage. Books by authorities on why he does it. Chat rooms on intimacy or sexuality. The world is drowning in information, some of it valuable.

But all the knowledge in the world won't make us happy again. And it won't guarantee that we can save this relationship. It can, however, confuse us with so many theories and opinions that we don't know which way to turn.

Today we can seek wisdom instead of knowledge, an intuitive thought instead of mountains of information. Today we can seek guidance, then trust that it will come in some simple, straightforward way. We can talk with others about their journey through this dark valley, and we can learn from their experiences. We can absorb information in small doses, being discriminating about whose information we trust and careful not to inundate ourselves. We can listen for our own quiet insights. That will guide us more than all the opinions of experts.

TODAY I WILL SEEK WISDOM INSTEAD OF INFORMATION.

EUPHORIC RECALL

When the path becomes clear and we can see that it is time to leave a difficult relationship, our mind may begin to play tricks on us.

It reminds us how happy we were when we first moved into our new house. How close we were after our second child was born. All the endearing ways he's shown his love for us over the years.

After tallying all that was once so good, we may question whether we've made the right decision. In spite of everything, should we really leave?

That's where our mind can take us. It's called euphoric recall. And it is the voice of our diseased thinking, the voice of our emotional dependency, calling to us. It is prompted by fear. Aided and abetted by denial.

All those good things may have been true. But they may no longer reflect today's reality.

Euphoric recall asks us to abandon our hard-won progress, to turn our backs on all the truths we've faced so courageously, at such great cost. It asks us to go backward.

We can ignore the lure of euphoric recall. We can trust our decisions if they were reached with the help of loving friends who are objective about our problems. We can even trust that, if it is right to reverse a decision at some point in the future, we will be guided to that as well.

But that bend in the path will not be lit by the false light of euphoric recall. It will be lit by wisdom, and it will promise continued change, growth, and faith rather than a return ticket to our own personal never-never land.

EUPHORIC RECALL IS A TRICK. I WILL BE CAREFUL NOT TO QUESTION MY HARD-WON DECISIONS SIMPLY BECAUSE OF EUPHORIC RECALL.

EASING THE PAIN OF DIVORCE

Divorce is hard.

It is hard when it is someone else's decision, being forced on us. It is hard even when we made the choice and we know it's the right one for us.

But sometimes all we can do is accept the inevitability of divorce and move through the process. At those times, there are things we can do to ease the pain of divorce.

We can stay close to people who comfort us with their love and understanding.

We can be gentle with ourselves when we are tired or rundown.

We can choose activities that feed our positive nature rather than those that point us in a negative direction.

We can decorate our office with a poster that makes us smile.

We can indulge a small whimsy.

We can say thanks each day for the people we've been given to love and to be loved by.

We can ask for some small healing in our spirits today.

MY CIRCUMSTANCES MAY BE PAINFUL, BUT THERE ARE COUNTLESS WAYS I CAN FIND COMFORT TODAY. I WILL BE OPEN TO COMFORT AND ACCEPT IT FROM ALL THE HEALTHY SOURCES IN MY WORLD.

RESPONDING TO HUMILIATION

We can't always manage to keep our circumstances secret. We sometimes find ourselves humiliated by our partner's behavior.

Our children know. So do our parents, our co-workers, half the town. We have been betrayed, and we feel humiliated.

First, we can remember that this will pass. In a week or a month, some other gossip will move to the top of the list.

Second, we can remember that what others say or think about us behind our backs reflects more about them than it does about us. We don't have to be brought down by anything they whisper after we leave the room.

Third, let us never forget that we are in charge of our reaction to this humiliation. We can behave with dignity. We can resist the urge to defend ourselves or to salvage our dignity by badmouthing someone else. We can refuse to engage in the gossip, and we can refuse to react to the gossips.

TODAY I CAN WEATHER A HUMILIATING SITUATION WITHOUT HUMILIATING MYSELF. I CAN RESPECT MYSELF.

PATTERNS OF BETRAYAL

When we do our written self-assessment, many of us are stunned to recognize the pattern of betrayal that runs through our lives. We haven't been betrayed just once, we've allowed it to happen again and again.

Often, if we look closely, we can discover other times when we have aligned ourselves with people who could not be honest and loyal. Perhaps our parents were the first, setting us up for an inability to recognize dishonesty and walk away from it.

Once we've examined each of our close relationships—parents, siblings, friends, partners, co-workers—and determined whether betrayal or dishonesty were significant components of any of those relationships, we are ready to examine the part we played.

Did we gravitate to them? Did we ignore instinctive reactions that something wasn't right? Did we excuse their behavior or repay them in kind? Did we use their behavior as an excuse to hold ourselves above them, or to set ourselves up as a martyr? We can't always see these things on our own, but if we are open to self-examination we will seek help from someone who can be lovingly honest in helping us recognize the truths we need to see.

If we can recognize the part we play in attracting betrayal or in any other destructive pattern in our lives, we can begin to change.

TODAY I CAN BEHAVE DIFFERENTLY. I CAN THINK DIFFERENTLY. I CAN MAKE DIFFERENT CHOICES AND BRING DIFFERENT PEOPLE INTO MY LIFE. FROM THE INSIDE OUT, MY LIFE CAN GRADUALLY IMPROVE.

NOTHING IS WASTED

The wasted years haunt us at times. The years invested in this relationship. The years we put a career or family on hold for this person. The years we poured into the effort to salvage a relationship that now seems doomed.

The years are not wasted.

We have grown during those years. We have learned lessons, gained wisdom, deepened our spiritual awareness. We have developed a side of ourselves that might have gone lacking without the challenges of this relationship. We have matured. We have prepared ourselves for the next stage of our journey.

No time is wasted if we embrace what life has brought us through these circumstances, during this time. All our experiences can contribute to our greater good. All our experiences lead us back to our spirits so we can become the best person we can be.

TODAY I WILL BE OPEN TO LEARNING WHY I NEEDED TO SPEND THESE YEARS IN THIS RELATIONSHIP. AND I WILL BE CONTENT WITH KNOWING THERE IS A REASON EVEN IF IT ISN'T TIME FOR ME TO UNDERSTAND THAT REASON.

IS HE A KEEPER?

Is he worth hanging on to? Is he worth the struggle to repair this damaged relationship?

We sometimes wrestle with that question to the point of obsession. If only there were a clear-cut answer. The answer is rarely easy to arrive at. Here are some thoughts to help us through the process.

- Is this a onetime misstep, or one in a long line of betrayals?

- Has he demonstrated a willingness to be honest about his behavior? A willingness to work on his part of the problem?

- Can he be trusted in other areas of our life?

- Is this part of a larger pattern of dysfunction or disease, such as alcohol or drug addiction, depression or bipolar disorder? If so, is he willing to seek help with his other problem?

- Has there been physical or mental abuse?

- Is he a good father, or is he as neglectful and careless of the children's emotions as he has been of mine?

- Does he accept responsibility for his behavior, or does he blame me or something outside his control?

We can consider our responses carefully, weigh them, seek guidance and courage. We will know what to do at the right time.

TODAY I WON'T OBSESS OVER WHETHER OR NOT I SHOULD STAY IN THIS RELATIONSHIP, GOING BACK AND FORTH UNTIL I MAKE MYSELF CRAZY. TODAY I CAN ANSWER A FEW QUESTIONS FOR MYSELF AND TRUST THE INNER GUIDANCE I RECEIVE.

FUN HEALS

Sometimes the most important thing for us to do is stop and play with the puppy. Put together a puzzle with our son or daughter. Pretend we never grew up and give in to the urge to write our names in the wet cement.

Fun heals. And in the throes of crisis and pain, we lose our ability to have fun. We can't laugh. We no longer know how to have fun, and we can't see why it is important to have fun anyway.

Fun is important because it reminds us that not all of life is bleak. It brings us hope. It teaches us balance.

It gives us back our hearts.

Laughter heals. Play enriches us. Delight in small pleasures points the way out of our darkness.

Today we can stop long enough to paint our toenails or dance with the doorknob or eat an ice cream cone so slowly it drips down our chin. Today we can do one small thing that is not productive or gainful or results-oriented.

TODAY I WILL PLAY. I WILL HAVE FUN. I WILL FIND SOMETHING IN MY LIFE THAT MAKES ME LAUGH. AND I WILL FEEL THE HEALING THAT COMES WHEN I GIVE MYSELF THE GIFT OF BEING PLAYFUL.

SEEING YOURSELF CLEARLY

She insisted that she had not been deeply affected by her husband's chronic infidelity. Pretty and sweet and married twenty-plus years, she was very clear that she had not contributed to the problem either.

But as we talked, a story began to unfold. She laughed about the time they argued over another couple, longtime friends. Her husband defended the man, who was having an affair. She sided with the betrayed wife and was outraged that he could defend the cheating husband. Although the argument wasn't about them at all, she found herself losing control, in the grip of an uncontrollable rage.

She struck her husband and broke his nose.

The truth about that argument emerged for her as we talked. Her outrage wasn't about her friend. It was about her own impotence and buried rage over her husband's hidden betrayals, which she had felt in her soul but had been too afraid to acknowledge for years.

It came out in violence.

It also came out in other ways that were destructive to her. In an unhealthy urge to please, to comply, to become invisible in the relationship.

If we think we are not affected by infidelity, we are wrong. And the longer we deny it, the more damage it does.

TODAY I WON'T MINIMIZE HOW HARD THIS HAS BEEN ON ME. I WON'T IGNORE OR DISCOUNT THE WAYS IN WHICH MY SPIRIT HAS BEEN ERODED. I WILL ACCEPT THE TRUTH AND COMMIT TO HEALING.

RELEASING YOUR GRIP

The unexpected blizzard caught us on the interstate, too close to home to stop. I was terrified as the snow swirled wildly, sticking to our windshield, turning to slush on the road.

Driving in snow and ice has always frightened me, and I did what I always did. I tensed. Although my husband was driving and nothing I did contributed to our safety, I still gripped the sides of my seat, grasping control. I became one huge clenched muscle for the next twenty minutes.

As we exited the freeway and turned down the slower street toward home, I relaxed. I was safe. I was going to make it.

But I was exhausted. Whipped physically and emotionally by twenty minutes of stress, tension, and the compulsion to control.

I recognized, as we pulled into our drive, how rarely I had to feel that way any longer. And I saw with clarity what a toll it exacts when I live in fear and the perceived need to protect myself from danger.

TODAY I AM GRATEFUL THAT MOST OF THE TIME I REMEMBER I AM SAFE AND THERE IS NO NEED TO GRIP ANYTHING TOO TIGHTLY.

ALICE MAY

LEARN FROM GIVING

Shortly after finding out about my husband's affair, I was committed to beginning weekly volunteer work. I would spend an hour each week delivering meals to the homebound. I had agreed to volunteer some months before our crisis. But now, faced with this personal trauma, I didn't see how I could honor my commitment.

What might happen in that hour I was out of the house? What might he get away with? How might the situation further deteriorate if I wasn't there to hold it all together?

I did not want to deliver meals to shut-ins. My heart was not in it. I embarked each week in a near panic.

But something strange happened. I discovered, as I delivered meals and forced myself to smile at people who had problems of their own, that for a minute or two at a time I forgot my problems. I turned my attention to the person in front of me and found that I could not hold in my mind at the same time both concern for them and obsession over my marriage.

For an hour a week, I forgot my problem. I released my obsession. Even in my reluctance to be of service to someone else, I was given the grace of comfort for myself.

TODAY I KNOW THAT HEALTHY GIVING TO OTHERS GIVES BACK MORE TO ME THAN I CAN EVER REPAY. I WILL REMEMBER THAT, IF I GIVE MY FULL ATTENTION TO WHAT IS RIGHT IN FRONT OF ME, I DON'T HAVE ROOM IN MY MIND AND HEART FOR OBSESSING OVER MY PAINFUL CIRCUMSTANCES.

HIDING YOUR FEELINGS

We had made an offer on a house that was under construction. We were working with a woman at the construction company on choices about paint colors and floor coverings. Because our offer was contingent on the sale of our house, we were trying to make choices that would both please us and be neutral enough to please others in case the house had to go back on the market.

We were all willing to compromise, but it soon became clear that the woman who worked with the builder had trouble expressing her real opinion when she didn't like our choices.

At one point, we selected a color for the exterior of the house, a color she apparently didn't like. Instead of saying so and working with us to reach a compromise, she selected another color herself and had the house painted without our knowledge. We hated the color. The builder had to bear the cost of repainting a three-story house.

Her inability to speak up about her true feelings put her job in jeopardy and cost someone a lot of money.

What are the consequences for us if we can't speak up about our true feelings? We may have to pay in ways that are far more costly than dollars and cents. We may have to pay with our health, our serenity, our emotional well-being.

WHEN I HIDE MY TRUE FEELINGS, THE PRICE IS ALWAYS TOO HIGH. TODAY I WILL RECOGNIZE MY FEELINGS AND SHARE THEM AT TIMES AND IN WAYS THAT ARE APPROPRIATE.

START OVER AT ANY TIME

She had given herself the gift of riding lessons, something she had long wanted. Part of each lesson was to saddle up properly. A few minutes into her fourth lesson, she realized she hadn't followed all the procedures for saddling up.

The oversight bothered her. She wasn't able to concentrate on her lesson. She wasn't enjoying the experience. In her mind, she was back in the barn, going over and over the shortcut she'd taken.

She mentioned her mistake to her instructor, who assured her it was no big deal. It was only her fourth lesson, and she didn't have to get every detail perfect. She could understand that, but she also knew she needed to backtrack now that she was aware of where she'd gone wrong.

Her instructor agreed. She stopped, resaddled, and continued with her lesson, head and heart now on the business at hand.

We can start over anytime we realize we've done something that needs correcting. We can begin again without blame or putdowns. This is true of a project at work, a craft or hobby we're engaging in, even our marriage. We can recognize where we went wrong and begin again.

WHEN I GIVE MYSELF PERMISSION TO START OVER AT ANY TIME, I AM FREE TO GET ON WITH THIS MOMENT'S CONCERNS AND PLEASURES WITH NO DISTRACTIONS AND NO MISGIVINGS.

GIVING AND RECEIVING LOVE

Do we know how to receive love? Do we allow ourselves to receive love? What do we do to shut ourselves off from the abundance of love in our world?

Perhaps we feel unworthy of love if we are less than perfect. Perhaps we feel love is a payback we receive only if we give and give and give.

Perhaps we reject the love people try to give us by deflecting it. We may automatically act as if their expressions of love are empty gestures or counterfeit displays.

Or we may look for expressions of love that have nothing to do with genuine love, thus settling for less than we deserve.

And we may ignore heartfelt, everyday expressions of love—an offer to wash the dishes while we put our feet up, a phone call to lift our spirits, unfaltering support when life crashes around our shoulders. We may hold out instead for puffed-up expressions of love—the expensive gift, the grand gesture, the pretty words that may or may not have any real emotion behind them.

Today we can examine the ways in which we interact with people we are close to. We will try to see how they express their love and how we react to those expressions. We will at least consider the possibility that we don't receive the love we want because we sabotage others' attempts to love us.

TODAY I WILL BE OPEN TO GIVING AND RECEIVING LOVE IN A HEALTHY WAY. I MAY HAVE TO CHANGE MYSELF OR MY CIRCUM-STANCES. TODAY I HAVE THE COURAGE TO DO EITHER.

DAILY AWARENESS

When we began our healing journey, it stretched out before us, a mysterious and uncharted territory. Some of us didn't understand what we were being asked to do or where we were headed.

Today the stages of our journey make more sense to us. During the surrender stage, we learned to let go of our problems. We learned to accept our lives, pain and all. Some of us began to pray. During the second stage, self-assessment, we looked at ourselves for the clues to our problems and learned that our solutions are found there as well. We sought help from others, and our hearts began to open. In stage three, we unburdened ourselves. We became more honest and forgiving and humble. We worked on changing our self-defeating behaviors.

Our healing has brought us to the next stage in our journey, daily awareness.

Daily awareness is about making our spiritual connection a daily practice. We may use prayer or meditation. We may also review each day honestly to see where we need to make corrections in our path.

This stage of the journey is about continued growth. We have most of the tools we need to deal with whatever life brings, and we are now being challenged to use them to the best of our ability on a daily basis.

TODAY I WILL BE AWARE OF THE PATH I AM ON. I WILL DO THINGS THAT ENHANCE MY PROGRESS. I WILL RECOGNIZE THAT THE HEALING JOURNEY IS NOT A ONETIME EVENT, BUT A LIFE-LONG PROCESS.

ARE YOU ENABLING?

Do we enable our unfaithful partner?

The very question may enrage us. But like the loved ones of alcoholics or addicts, we may do things that make it easy for our partner to continue cheating.

Do we expect him to be accountable for his behavior, accepting both responsibility and consequences? Or do we allow him to blame his weak behavior on something or someone else—the other woman, his lousy upbringing, all the other guys who do it, too?

Do we overlook his unacceptable behavior, ignoring signs such as excessive spending or broken promises or increased time away from home?

Do we lie for him so that parents, co-workers, or neighbors don't think badly of him?

Do we let him off the hook by accepting his apologies and his remorse as substitutes for changed behavior?

If we are doing any of these things, we may be giving permission to our partner to deceive us. We are making it easier for him.

We can stop enabling. We can stop letting him off the hook. With the support of other women, we can protect ourselves instead of him. We can stop making excuses for him, stop listening when he places the blame elsewhere. We can start asking how he plans to change. We can make it clear that we need more than one more promise that it will never happen again.

TODAY I WILL ASK FOR THE HELP I NEED TO STOP MY CONTRIBUTION TO OUR UNHEALTHY FAMILY CIRCUMSTANCES. TODAY I WILL HOLD HIM ACCOUNTABLE.

DANGER SIGNALS

One of the terrifying thoughts about getting out of a bad relationship is the realization that we could walk right into another one just as bad. Do we really trust ourselves to recognize a good man?

There is no foolproof formula for spotting emotionally healthy partners. But there are signals that something is wrong even early on.

- Do I feel uneasy letting him see me just as I am? Do I make a concerted effort to hide certain things about myself, or do I even create a New Me to replace the Real Me?

- Do I go along with things that make me uneasy because I don't want to rock the boat?

- Do I make excuses for his behavior, his beliefs, his past?

- Do I spend less time with my old friends or family because he doesn't fit in, or doesn't like them?

- Was our attraction instant and overwhelming? Or was I attracted to him only because he was attracted to me?

Any of these are possible danger signals. They are signs that we should slow down, back off, think again. They are clues that this person triggers our unhealthy responses. Instead of roaring full steam ahead, we can trust the uneasy whispers of our soul. They will not lead us astray.

MY CIRCUMSTANCES AND THE GROWTH THAT HAS COME AS A RESULT OF IT GIVE ME NEW TOOLS TO USE IN ESTABLISHING NEW RELATIONSHIPS. INSTEAD OF STICKING TO MY OLD PATTERNS, I WILL TRUST MY NEW TOOLS.

WHEN HE CHANGES

We've worked hard to learn that the only person we can change is ourselves. We cannot fix, heal, or rearrange the hearts and minds of other people, even those we love the most.

Now that this truth is beginning to sink in, we can consider the man who said, "The longer I work on myself, the more others change."

They change, of course, because we see them differently. They change because we no longer view all their actions as direct assaults on us. Because we now understand that their behavior is about their inner difficulties and not about us.

They change because we treat them differently. We're not constantly on their backs or down their throats. We give them dignity and space. They react to that change in us by behaving differently themselves.

Or is the change all in our reaction to them, all in how we view them? Sometimes it's hard to tell. Most of the time, it doesn't really matter.

If we react differently, if we feel different inside, does it really matter whether they are different or not? If we are content and at peace, does it matter whether they are more like we want them to be or we are simply more accepting of who they are?

As we change, they change. How and why are not important when dealing with miracles.

TODAY I WILL ACCEPT THE MIRACLE THAT MY WHOLE WORLD CAN CHANGE THROUGH NOTHING MORE THAN A CHANGE IN ME.

ALICE MAY

YOUR WEAKNESSES ARE PART
OF THE JOURNEY

The first hint I had that my husband was being unfaithful came two weeks before Christmas. My mother was dying of cancer, and I had more to deal with than I could manage.

When I overheard a conversation that revealed he was hiding something, I confronted him. He'd always been so trustworthy that I knew there must be a simple explanation. And I was prepared to believe him.

His explanation was so implausible that I immediately knew the truth.

I was devastated, overwhelmed, and disconnected from God. I didn't have the emotional energy to turn my life upside down. I told myself that if my husband was straying, I would deal with it later, after my mother died.

I spent the next ten months slipping in and out of denial, losing all sense of reality and every ounce of confidence I had in myself and my ability to cope with life. I lost myself in deceit and denial. I was dying inch by inch, day by day.

It was the best I could do at the time.

And it prepared me for complete surrender. By the time my mother died and I once again had the problem thrust in my face, I was so whipped that I had no reserves left. The gift in that complete brokenness was that I couldn't see any way out. I had to have help.

And that, of course, was the beginning of my healing.

For all those months, denial had been the best I could do. Had I not stayed in denial so long, I might have had enough strength left to keep trying to solve my own problems. My denial had been a critical part of my preparation for the spiritual journey.

TODAY I WON'T BERATE MYSELF WHEN I'M WEAK. I WILL ASSUME THAT WHEN THE TIME IS RIGHT MY LIMITATIONS WILL SERVE A USEFUL PURPOSE ON MY JOURNEY TO HEALING.

Surviving Betrayal

A DAY OF HEALING

Today can be a day of healing.

Today we can hand every negative thought or emotion that enters our heads or hearts over to our personal source of inspiration, for transformation.

Today we can smile.

Today we can call someone we know is in pain and listen—only listen—to whatever she needs to share.

Today we can view everyone we encounter with compassion.

Today we can slow down and breathe deeply. We can seek to be of service in every situation we are in, rather than wondering how we can benefit.

Today we can heal.

TODAY I WILL MAKE HEALING CHOICES. I WILL BE GUIDED BY THE INNER WISDOM THAT IS BECOMING EASIER TO HEAR AND UNDERSTAND WITH EACH DAY I AM ON MY JOURNEY.

FILLING YOUR EMPTINESS

When we are in crisis, in pain, we are encouraged to detach, to find an emotionally neutral zone where we can get through the day, or the moment, without losing ourselves in the behavior of another person.

But when we reach the emotionally neutral zone of detachment, some of us feel empty. We wonder whether the price we pay for peace of mind is no longer loving our partner.

That empty feeling is natural when we step back from the turmoil. For so long, we've filled ourselves with an excess of chaos, with an overload of intense emotion—rage or fear or despair or the enmeshment we've come to call love.

When we clear out those things, the emptiness alarms us. What is left?

Don't rush to fill the empty spaces.

Wait for those empty places to refill themselves—with calm, with compassion, with energy for life. With real love. With the gift of serenity.

It may have been so long since we've experienced normalcy that our first impulse is to rush back to the insanity we know and feel comfortable with. Wait. Pray. See how life fills the emptiness.

TODAY I WILL BE PATIENT WHILE MY SPIRIT IS FILLED. I WILL TRUST THAT GOOD THINGS WILL COME INTO THE EMPTY SPACES IN MY SOUL AS A RESULT OF MY HEALING JOURNEY.

GOING TO EXTREMES

We contribute to our emotional nightmares in two ways. Some of us stay in relationships long after most people would have left, sometimes after we've been betrayed time and again. At the other extreme are those of us who sever relationships for one mistake, unwilling to even consider forgiving and forgetting.

Living in either extreme may be a sign that we are either unwilling or unable to risk a healthy relationship.

In one extreme, we punish ourselves unduly. In the other, we punish a loved one for the sin of imperfection and bad judgment without waiting to see whether he is willing to change. Our role in a relationship is not self-sacrifice; neither is it to assign and uphold rigid standards for others.

If we sincerely want a relationship that is good for everyone in it, we will seek balance. We will seek to be both responsible for our own happiness and forgiving of another's shortcomings. We will look for a partner who can provide the same for us.

TODAY I WILL SEEK THE MIDWAY POINT BETWEEN THE EXTREMES IN ALL AREAS OF MY LIFE, RECOGNIZING THAT THE SEARCH FOR BALANCE SOMETIMES INVOLVES A SWING FROM ONE EXTREME TO THE OTHER. THAT IS OKAY TODAY. I WILL FIND BALANCE IF I AM COMMITTED TO SEEKING IT.

SEX DOES NOT EQUAL LOVE

It was a day set aside to celebrate their love. It began sweetly, with gifts and togetherness. And although they had each committed to a period of celibacy following her husband's sexual acting out, she found herself anticipating something a bit more romantic than hearts and flowers as the day went on.

As the day drew to a close and it became apparent there would be no sexual overtures, she grew resentful. Clearly, he didn't love her enough. Clearly, this marriage was in big trouble if he could so easily stick to his agreement of abstinence.

By bedtime, she was ready to lash out. Ready to call in the attorneys.

Then she was given the grace of a moment of clarity in which she could see the core of her faulty thinking. She had been equating sex with love.

All day her husband had been delivering messages of love—a special present, the gift of time spent together in activities they both enjoyed, hand-holding and warm conversation. And perhaps most important of all, he had demonstrated his willingness to honor a vow they had both entered into in the hope of strengthening their troubled marriage.

But when he stuck to their agreement to abstain from sex, she couldn't see those signs of love for what they were. All she could see was that the physical act of love—which sometimes has little to do with love at all—was missing.

Sex may be a beautiful component of love when other components such as compassion and communication are also present. But sex does not equal love.

TODAY I WILL ATTEMPT TO PLACE SEX IN ITS PROPER PERSPEC-
TIVE. I WILL REMEMBER THAT SEX IS ONE PART OF INTIMACY. I
WILL REMEMBER THAT SEX DOES NOT EQUAL LOVE.

CHILDREN CANNOT BE FOOLED

We may believe we can cover up our difficulties well enough that our children will not be aware of them, or will not be adversely affected by them.

We are wrong. Children cannot be fooled.

I grew up in a home where no one spoke of the problems in the family. Parental arguments were carried on quietly, late at night, long past my bedtime. Or as a silent battle of wills, a cold war that fooled no one.

One of my most vivid childhood memories is of lying awake in the dark night after night, waiting for the battle to begin. When it did, I crept out of bed and glided silently down the hall in my bare feet. I would huddle on the hardwood floor late into the night, listening to them spewing hate and hostility in hushed, bitter voices.

There was no love in my house, and I grew up without learning how to love. I grew up feeling the insecurity of knowing that my parents stayed together only because my sister and I posed an obligation. And that further taught me that I was responsible for the animosity everyone pretended did not exist, a false belief I carried into my marriage.

My parents could not fool me, and we cannot fool our children. Trying to do so causes more damage than the truth will ever cause.

TODAY I WILL NOT TRY TO SELL MY CHILDREN A BILL OF GOODS ABOUT A HAPPY HOME. TO PREVENT THEM FROM CARRYING DYSFUNCTIONAL BEHAVIORS INTO ADULTHOOD WITH THEM, I WILL DO MY BEST NOT TO PERPETUATE UNHEALTHY WAYS OF BEING A FAMILY. I WILL GIVE THEM THE SECURITY OF KNOWING THEY CAN DEPEND ON ME FOR OPENNESS AND HONESTY.

ALICE MAY

ALL THOSE SILLY QUESTIONS

One night recently, when my husband called from out of town, I didn't even think to ask what he planned to do for the evening.

That may sound like a big "so what?" to a lot of people. For me, it's nothing short of a miracle.

For years during and after his affairs, I always asked—with all the casualness I could muster—how he planned to spend his evenings when he was away on business. I listened carefully, alert to any telltale word that didn't ring true, that might tip me off to something I thought I needed to know. It wasn't that I expected him to say, "Well, I think I'll have dinner and see if I can make a date with the waitress after she gets off work." It's that I expected to be able to figure out whether I should worry based on something vaguely out of sync in his words or voice.

All the attempts to guess, to play mental sleuth, to worry as if worry itself might fend off disaster made me emotionally and sometimes physically ill. And none of those efforts ever kept him from doing the things I worried about.

A longtime recovering alcoholic says he is often asked by wives of active alcoholics how to get their spouses to quit lying. He always replies, "Quit asking all those silly questions!"

Today I know my husband can lie to me if he makes up his mind to do so. So why ask for answers I can't be sure I can trust? It's a waste of my emotional energy. I know I can't control his behavior when he is at home, much less when he is out of town. I also know that I am okay no matter what because the God I rely on today has me in the palm of his hand.

KNOWING THAT I AM IN AN EMOTIONALLY SAFE PLACE, TODAY I WILL REFRAIN FROM ASKING QUESTIONS THAT DO NOTHING TO REASSURE ME AND EVERYTHING TO KEEP ME IN DOUBT AND FEAR.

YOUR BODY LISTENS TO
YOUR HEART

Many medical practitioners, both traditional and alternative, today believe that our physical ailments start within us, as unresolved emotional issues. A friend who is a cancer survivor tells me that her oncologist says we all have cancer cells within us, all the time; a determining factor in whether the cells become active is how we deal with stress.

When we refuse to deal with the difficulties in our lives, how much damage are we doing to our bodies? Are we slowly giving disease a fertile breeding ground? Are we killing ourselves with our compulsion to keep the peace or maintain the status quo?

Are our bodies crying out for help already, with a nagging headache or a chronic backache or a stomach that demands antacids on a regular basis?

There are many reasons to resolve the problems in our lives, not the least of which is our physical well-being.

We know that keeping a car in good running order requires more than a weekly trip to the car wash. Likewise, a new dress and a new hairstyle may temporarily boost our mood, but they don't compensate for inner turmoil or neglect from poor nutrition or inadequate rest.

We can work on our emotional well-being with confidence that it will also pay off in improved physical well-being.

TODAY I WILL WORK TO GET HEALTHY FROM THE INSIDE OUT.

JUST LOOK FOR THE EXIT RAMP

The rest of life does not grind to a halt just because we've been hit with an unpleasant jolt about our partner's extracurricular sexual activities.

Our children still get in fights at school, the dog still tears down the neighbor's fence, the doctor still finds something suspicious in last week's mammogram. Life sometimes seems to deliver one direct hit after another. It is easy to become overwhelmed by it all.

When I find myself feeling overwhelmed, it is usually because I'm looking at the big picture. I'm not focused on today, certainly not on this moment. I am unfolding the road map of the entire Midwest and trying to figure out how to cover all that territory tonight, instead of looking for the exit ramp I need at the moment.

We can't tackle all our problems in one day. We can't solve every dilemma in our life with one snap of the fingers. It will take time. And we can do only one thing at a time.

When we are overwhelmed, we can try to decide what needs attention right this minute. Asking for wisdom in weighing our options, we make one decision, select one small action to take. Then we take it. And we move on. We don't agonize over whether we've made the right decision. We just seek guidance again, put one foot in front of the other, and take the next small action.

I WILL MAKE ENOUGH SMALL DECISIONS AND TAKE ENOUGH TINY STEPS TO CHIP AWAY AT EVEN THE BIGGEST PROBLEMS.

HOME FREE

None of us is ever home free.

In love relationships, there is always room for betrayal. Another broken promise down the road, another broken heart.

Even in the midst of our new, hard-won courage, a part of us becomes vulnerable again or we have not truly learned the lesson and gotten on with our lives. If we cannot be hurt, our hearts are probably still too hard, our walls too high.

And because our partner—the same one or a new one—is still simply a flawed human being, hurtful behavior can never be willed away or wished away forevermore.

Today we have a new kind of protection from pain. Today we have a loving group of friends who will see us through anything. We have the kind of spiritual tools that are a framework for handling all of life's problems. We have a close and life-affirming connection with the higher power of our choice.

We have everything we need to deal with life's setbacks. And there will be setbacks. There will be pain. To think otherwise is to believe that living spiritually delivers people of faith from the normal course of life. And evidence abounds that it doesn't work that way. The spiritual way merely offers us refuge.

We are not home free. But we are in a safe haven, and we need never stray so far from it that we can't seek its shelter at a moment's notice.

TODAY I HAVE THE FREEDOM TO LIVE LIFE WITH MY HEART OPEN AND MY ARMS SPREAD WIDE. I CAN RECEIVE JOY WITHOUT FEARING LIFE'S SETBACKS.

UNITY AND AUTONOMY

Two keys to a healthy relationship seem diametrically opposed. Two people in a relationship must strive for both unity and autonomy.

In striving for unity within a relationship, we recognize the importance of sharing common goals. Many of us have run into problems because this shared purpose was implied or assumed. Perhaps we thought the whole reason for family was to provide a safe environment for raising children and growing old together; perhaps he believed it was a firm foundation for a financially secure future. We didn't take time to identify a common vision.

We must take time to discuss, to explore, to agree on our shared purpose. That can be difficult if years have already been invested in opposing viewpoints. But it is time to come together, to reach a consensus. If our old relationship is over, it is time to do this at the beginning of any new relationship.

Unity also asks that when we disagree, we reach a compromise. We don't continue lobbying for our way to prevail. We support the mutual decision.

The other component is autonomy. We are separate people. I do not become him just because we share common goals, and he does not become me. Each of us stands alone, a fully realized human being. We join hands over our common goals. But we are not joined at the hip.

Striving for both autonomy and unity is challenging. It will not always be an easy balance to strike. But the effort to do so will strengthen our life partnerships. It will strengthen us as women.

TODAY I CAN BE ONE HALF OF A PARTNERSHIP WITHOUT LOSING MYSELF AS LONG AS I REMEMBER THAT SHARING COMMON GOALS DOES NOT MEAN GIVING UP MY INDIVIDUAL NEEDS.

THE FINANCIAL BATTLEGROUND

Financial difficulty often keeps company with infidelity. He spends money for his secret life. Suddenly bills are being paid late, and the balance owed is growing instead of being reduced.

In my own home, I contributed to the financial crisis by spending money I didn't have to make myself feel better. On clothes I didn't need, a new car to make him feel indebted to me, cosmetic surgery so I could compete.

Money can also become a power struggle in a relationship at war. *I earned it, I'll spend it however I like. After all you've put me through, I deserve it.* Or my personal favorite, *I'll spend it on me before you spend it on her.*

Family finances can become a very bloody battleground. Just more carnage in a field already littered with the wounded.

First, let us decide that the war over money can end with us. We can be financially responsible ourselves, even if he can't. We can refuse to spend money we don't have. We can begin to establish separate finances so that our circumstances aren't as easily jeopardized by his excesses. We can stop the tug-of-war over money.

Then we can apologize for our part in the financial problems. We can acknowledge where we've been wrong and voice our commitment to behaving differently. And we can do so without making any mention of his contributions to the problem. This is a truce, remember, not another skirmish.

We do all this because we can only clean up our side of the street. We can no more control his spending than we can control his decision to stray.

TODAY I CAN DO MY PART TO CONTRIBUTE TO HEALTHIER FINANCES. IT IS A START. AND THAT IS ENOUGH FOR NOW.

HOW COMMITTED ARE YOU?

Are we passionate about our commitment to our partnership? Passionate despite the blow we've been dealt?

Whether we've uttered traditional vows or made less formal promises to our partner, few of us went into our relationship with the idea that we would bail out at the first sign of trouble. And we clearly felt that our partner had made a similar commitment or we would not feel so betrayed today. We feel in our hearts that our partner broke his commitment.

Are we doing roughly the same thing if we rush too quickly to walk away at a sign of trouble?

No partnership is pain-proof. Difficulties always arise, and adultery is right up there near the top of the worst-case-scenario list. This is a time for us to consider our level of commitment. Just what are we committed to, and why? How far along a rocky path will that commitment take us? Can we renew our commitments together, or is it time to admit that we've been so weakly pledged that it is better, if not necessarily easier, to walk away?

There are many answers, and one is right for each of us.

TODAY I'VE BEEN GIVEN AN OPPORTUNITY FOR SELF-REFLECTION. I WILL TAKE THE TIME TO DETERMINE HOW COMMITTED I AM, AND WHAT I AM WILLING TO COMMIT TO FOR THE FUTURE.

THE IDEAL FAMILY

A woman in the circle wanted a discussion of what a normal family might look like and feel like. We all laughed. We understood that longing. It goes cell-deep for almost all of us.

The truth is, we may be more normal than we think. The selfishness and the dishonesty, the lack of intimacy and the inability to connect or communicate may characterize more families than we realize.

We ended our conversation by deciding there is no normal family. But the truth may be closer to this: There is no ideal family.

What we've been spoon-fed in our culture may not exist. And our drive to find it or create it may cause us more problems than simply accepting the flawed state of our families and committing to working on those flaws.

It may also be worth considering that our present crisis may present us with the opportunity to make progress. Not progress in becoming normal, and certainly not in becoming ideal. But progress in becoming healthier. More realistically happy. Closer to whole. These are attainable goals for a family, even a damaged family.

TODAY I WILL PLACE MY FOCUS ON CREATING A FAMILY THAT IS HEALTHIER, HAPPIER, CLOSER TO BEING WHOLE. I WILL GIVE UP THE MYTH OF NORMAL AND IDEAL.

A MOTHER'S FEAR

Mothers in failing marriages often fear raising their children alone. They fear shortchanging the material and emotional needs of their children. They fear being stretched too thin and losing control.

Single mothers share these tips:

- "Know that you can't do everything. Simplify as much as possible. Each child selects one special activity that requires Mom's taxi, not four. I make sure I'm allotted time for something I want to do also. Children need to see that it's okay for adults to have a life, too. I don't want my children believing they don't count once they're grown."

- "I make a point of never expending any energy whatsoever on hating my ex, on getting back at him, or in any other way focusing on him. I save that energy for myself and my children."

- "Learning to accept help was so hard. But I had to do it. I had to accept help from my children, my parents, my neighbors, even my ex-husband. Amazingly, it has enriched my kids' lives and frees me up for some of the million other tasks in life."

- "First and foremost, I take care of myself, not just my kids. I do things I like. I rest when I need to. I say no when I need to."

We don't have to impress anyone with our supermom routine. We can reach out and hold on to the helping hands of those around us.

IF I HAVE A FAMILY TO RAISE ALONE, I WILL DO THE BEST I CAN AND KNOW THAT IT IS GOOD ENOUGH FOR TODAY. AND I WILL REMEMBER THAT I AM NEVER TRULY ALONE WHEN I ACCEPT THE HELP THE UNIVERSE OFFERS ME THROUGH FRIENDS, FAMILY, AND MY OWN GROWING FAITH.

THE OTHER WOMAN

Confronting the other woman becomes a favorite fantasy for some of us. Sometimes we fantasize about things far more dangerous than mere confrontation.

The other-woman fantasy feeds a lot of needs in us—the need to refute the lies we imagine he must have told about us; the need to make her see how much damage she's done; the need for revenge.

But in truth, confronting the other woman is rarely satisfying.

Confronting the other woman can make us look worse than anything anyone else says about us. In fact, our shabby behavior may confirm for her anything bad she might have heard. It also adds to our treasure chest of unpleasant memories, which is probably already fairly full at this point.

Worst of all perhaps, it lowers us in our own eyes. Rarely does anything come out of such a confrontation that we can be proud of.

Instead of entertaining or fulfilling our fantasies about giving her a comeuppance, we can ask ourselves today what action on our part could further our spiritual goals. We can pray for the willingness to put her out of mind. We can remember that, if he has left us for her, she's attaching herself to a man we all know will cheat and walk out on his partner. Most important of all, we can remember that the other woman is not our concern.

LET ME WORK TODAY ON THE THINGS THAT ARE MY CONCERN—MY SPIRITUAL GROWTH, MY PROCESS OF HEALING, MY FAMILY, MY ATTENTION TO MY OWN WELL-BEING. IF I AM ATTENTIVE TODAY TO THESE THINGS, I DON'T HAVE THE SPACE IN MY HEART TO HARBOR ILL WILL FOR ANOTHER SOUL.

ALICE MAY

DELIVERED BY LAUGHTER

When we face our crisis in the company of others who share our experiences, we learn to laugh at our problems.

One of the most astonishing occurrences for newcomers to the Serenity Group is how often we laugh at our circumstances, our mistakes, the very source of our worst pain. We are all there for a serious reason, and we all take our journey toward healing seriously. We work at our recovery.

But we've also learned how to laugh. I can share about my endless agonizing when my husband played Good Samaritan to a woman whose tire went flat in the rain, only to meet the woman later and discover that she was roughly his mother's age. And we all laugh, because we all understand.

We've learned that nothing provides closure after a good cry or a tense personal revelation like laughter. We know that if we can regain our sense of humor about our lives we are well on our way to reclaiming our health and serenity. We know that our laughter is a sign of our progress. We know that laughter enables us to put these circumstances into a healthier perspective.

MY LAUGHTER DOESN'T BELITTLE MY PAIN OR ANYONE ELSE'S.
WHEN I LAUGH, I AM BEING DELIVERED. EVEN THE DARKNESS
CAN BE BRIGHTENED WITH LAUGHTER.

LONELINESS

The novelist George Eliot wrote, "What loneliness is more lonely than distrust?"

She wouldn't get much disagreement from us. We know far too well the bitterness and despair of being intimately tied to someone we no longer trust. We know, however, that rebuilding trust takes time, that it isn't a process we dare to rush.

So what do we do with our loneliness in the meantime?

We can turn some of our energy and time to our children, who have sometimes been left out or neglected during the crisis.

We can volunteer.

We can join a group—a tennis foursome, a cooking class, a book discussion club.

We can adopt a puppy.

We can ask our three best friends what is going on in their lives and listen.

We can surrender our loneliness and ask for the support and companionship we need to get through this time.

Loneliness can be bitter when we are feeling raw and broken-hearted. To reach beyond our alienation for companionship, we will probably have to make a real effort. We can do it. We are stronger than we think. And we are not alone, even in our loneliness.

TODAY I WILL DO ONE SMALL THING TO CONNECT WITH SOMEONE ELSE. TODAY I WILL ACCEPT THE HOURS THAT ARE LONELY AND TAKE SOME ACTION TO DIMINISH THEM.

A CRACK IN THE FOUNDATION

One of the things he may tell us is that his wandering meant nothing. That it had nothing to do with our marriage and that it was so insignificant we should both forget it and move on.

While it is true that his straying had nothing to do with us, true that it need not destroy our life together, saying that it meant nothing is a lie. Saying it is insignificant is one more lie, whether he realizes it or not.

Betrayal damages families. It damages the betrayed as well as the betrayer. It creates chasms of pain that are difficult to bridge, separating us, alienating us. Betrayal replaces intimacy with distrust, and communication with strained silence or vicious screaming matches.

Betrayal damages everything good in its path. Love, honesty, mutual respect, and self-respect. The security of our children and our financial future. All are at risk when infidelity and betrayal enter the picture.

But the damage cannot be repaired until it is acknowledged.

Do not allow anyone to tell you that this is a minor crack in your life. Do not allow yourself to be convinced that it won't have far-reaching effects. Do not minimize what has happened—it may be a crack, but a crack in the foundation of your life demands immediate attention.

I CAN RECOVER, AND I WILL. EVEN MY RELATIONSHIP MAY RECOVER. BUT NOT BY WHITEWASHING WHAT HAS GONE ON.

YOUR DIFFICULTIES ARE
PERFECT FOR YOU

In our moments of deepest self-pity, we may wish we could trade lives with someone, anyone. Surely it doesn't get any worse than this.

We wouldn't have to look far, however, to realize that there are people whose problems we wouldn't willingly take on. The neighbor with two disabled children. The colleague whose son is addicted to crack cocaine. The young woman whose husband left when she was diagnosed with a crippling and chronic illness.

Our circumstances may be trying and painful. But life is filled with difficulties—some far worse than our own. We can be sure that, if we are honest with ourselves, we would not swap our problems for our neighbors'. Because the truth is, we have been given precisely the problems we need to get us where we need to go. Our problems bring us the kind of growth we need to become the person we are supposed to be.

MY PROBLEMS ARE NO EASIER AND NO WORSE THAN ANYONE ELSE'S. THEY SIMPLY ARE MINE. AND I AM GIVEN WHAT I NEED ON A DAILY BASIS TO LEARN TO LIVE WITH THEM AND GROW FROM THEM.

ALICE MAY

BUILDING NEW DREAMS

Dream home; dream kids, dream man.

We believed we had a dream life, and we've watched it fall apart around us.

It is time to build new dreams. It is time to build them on a more solid foundation.

Today our challenge is to look within and discover what is really important to us. To learn what will truly enrich our lives. If a relationship is a part of that, we are being challenged to find out what will constitute a solid foundation for that relationship.

Dreams are ephemeral, fleeting. Dreams can vanish all too quickly. Instead, we can base the new life we build—whether it is with this same man or not—on solid goals, solid principles.

TODAY REALITY IS MUCH MORE GENUINE, MUCH MORE SUB-STANTIAL THAN A DREAM LIFE.

ENTRUST OUTCOMES TO GOD

Many of us worry at one time or another that God wants us to leave our marriage. We want to do the right thing; we want to carry out God's will. But we can't find the courage in our hearts to walk out on our marriage. Not yet.

One of my spiritual teachers once told me that God is not in the business of destroying marriages. If and when it is time for us to leave this marriage, we will have the wisdom to know the time is right and the courage to take the action necessary. We aren't expected to give up before it's time to give up, but neither are we expected to stay after it is time to go.

When we struggle with the idea that we aren't hearing some important message about our marriage, we can be patient. Each morning we can pray for guidance and place our marriage under the care of the wise and loving spirit that acts in our lives. We can be willing to participate in either healing or ending our marriage. In doing so, we agree to move toward whichever outcome is best. Then we can trust that will happen.

TODAY I WILL BE PATIENT UNTIL MY PATH IS CLEAR.

MATURE LOVE

The marriage counselor asked one woman whether, given all that had happened, she was still in love with her husband.

She hesitated, although she knew the answer. But she worried that her answer wasn't the right answer in a society that encourages Hollywood images of love.

"I'm not sure I even believe in being 'in love' anymore," she said. "Being in love is that initial state of euphoria, where we believe another person is the answer to all our problems. Where we believe that person can save us—from our past, from our fears, from ourselves.

"I don't believe in that anymore.

"What I believe in today is love as a bond that strengthens me and my partner. Love is a relationship that allows me to grow, safely and with confidence, while I watch the person I love grow, too. Love is a place where I can share myself and feel at home.

"It's a place where I feel passion and excitement, too. But those things aren't at the center of love. Emotional fulfillment and growth are at the center of love."

That kind of love not only weathers the worst of times; it grows deeper and more solid during those times.

TODAY I WILL CULTIVATE MATURE LOVE IN MY LIFE BY GIVING UP MY NEED FOR FANTASY.

SHIFTING THE FAMILY BALANCE

Our families are a lot like a gumball machine. We're all packed into a close, confined environment, and we settle into a way of interrelating that leaves each of us leaning on and propped up by someone else.

But if one piece of gum rolls down the chute, it jiggles every piece of gum in the globe. Likewise in our families, none of us changes without affecting everyone else squeezed in with us. The changes can be good or bad, but they shift the balance in our family regardless.

When our partners are unfaithful, everything shifts.

When we respond to that, things shift again.

And as we begin to heal and to find healthier behaviors, more shifts may occur.

Be alert to the changing family dynamics as you and your partner adjust. Know that even your healthier behaviors may generate negative results for a while as less healthy members of the family react. And remember to keep your eyes on your children and do your best to be united on behalf of your children. Provide help and support as they settle into their new spot in the family. Bring in family counselors or ministers or update a school counselor or youth group leader. Do all you can to cushion the upheaval for those in the family who are rightly dependent on you for their security.

TODAY I WILL REMEMBER THAT EVEN HEALTHY CHANGES IN MY FAMILY CAUSE UPHEAVAL. I WILL SEEK SUPPORT FOR MYSELF AND FOR MY CHILDREN DURING THIS TIME.

THE POWER OF DAILY PRAYER

Do we pray when we are in trouble, in pain, in need? Do we pray when it's convenient, when it occurs to us, when we can make the time for it?

Is prayer an afterthought or a last-ditch solution to a crisis?

Prayer will come through, even in those circumstances.

But some of us find that prayer is an even more powerful force in our lives if we use it every day. When things are going smoothly, when we're happy, joyous, and free, when things couldn't possibly be better.

If we pray even at times like these, we know the connection with our spirit is strong for the times when we are in need. We know we won't have to falter or struggle to find our way back to the path that leads to our inner wisdom. We aren't in danger of stumbling in the dark for too long.

And some of us find that, if we pray even when times are good, bad times come around less often.

TODAY I WILL CONSIDER USING THE POWER OF DAILY PRAYER IN MY LIFE. EVEN IF I AM SKEPTICAL, PERHAPS I CAN TRY IT AND SEE WHAT HAPPENS.

CHOOSING UP SIDES

We can't be his partner and his adversary.

Too many marriages become—or start out as—adversarial relationships. We start choosing up sides. Him against me. Saint versus sinner. Winner and loser.

That never works. No one ever wins.

If we make our partner the enemy, we have decided the fate of our marriage before we begin. Before we seek help, before we seek possible healing, we've moved onto the battleground.

So let us remember that, just for today, we can move forward in the hope that we are on the same side. With all the love in our hearts, we can do our part in seeking what's best for all.

Then, even if it turns out that he chooses to become our adversary, we will have strengthened ourselves emotionally and spiritually. And we will discover that we can't be enemies unless we both participate.

TODAY I WILL NOT VIEW MY PARTNER AS THE ENEMY. EVEN IF HE HAS HURT ME WITH HIS BETRAYAL, I WILL NOT COMPOUND THE PROBLEM BY TURNING ON HIM.

CLINGING TO THE ILLUSION
OF CONTROL

When our world is in upheaval, the little changes are sometimes more than we can stand.

We lose it when the grocery store remodels and we can't find the peanut butter. We're filled with outrage when the makeup we've used for years is discontinued, or the city installs a no-left-turn sign at our corner.

Life is full of change, some of it big, some of it small. But when we realize that we're overreacting to the small stuff, it's usually because we are clinging desperately to the illusion that at least some things in our life are under our control.

And it is an illusion. Life goes on. Other people make decisions that shift the flow of our life. We cannot control these things.

When life is particularly difficult, we can't even always control our reactions to these changes. That is when we must remember to ask for the serenity to handle the changes that come our way.

Change is disruptive. But not nearly as disruptive as fighting the change.

TODAY I WILL WORK ON ACCEPTING THE CHANGES GOING ON IN MY LIFE. I WILL RECOGNIZE THE IMPORTANCE OF RELINQUISH-ING MY NEED TO CONTROL THINGS, BOTH LARGE AND SMALL.

GRIEF TAKES TIME

Friends are not always sympathetic when our pain drags on. They may be able to listen and comfort and be there for us for a while. But eventually, some of them may grow impatient that we haven't managed to put it all behind us.

That is natural.

Natural for them, perhaps because they can't really feel the pain we are in or understand our personal grieving process. Natural because our situation makes them uncomfortable or because they miss the old us and want us back.

Natural for us because grief is not a simple cookie-cutter process that we can intellectualize, work through efficiently, and wrap up on a one-size-fits-all timetable.

Grief takes time. It is often ugly and messy and unpleasant to be around. But we need to try not to make it harder by telling ourselves that we should be finished with it by now. With the help of others who have survived this particular kind of loss, we can walk through our grief in the way that is most healing for us as individuals.

TODAY I WILL NOT CARRY MY GRIEF TO THOSE WHO CAN'T UNDERSTAND WHERE I AM. EVEN MORE IMPORTANT, I WILL ALSO REFUSE TO BURDEN MYSELF WITH THE PRESSURE TO BE FINISHED BEFORE IT IS TIME.

ALICE MAY

OPPORTUNITIES TO PRACTICE
NEW BEHAVIOR

The scary thing about seeking to change into a new person is that we can be certain of receiving opportunities to practice the new behaviors we hope will replace our old behaviors.

If we are judgmental, we receive opportunities to practice tolerance and acceptance when we are confronted with situations and people that try our patience. If we hope to be relieved of our dishonesty, we find ourselves in situations that tempt us to tell little white lies or engage in more serious deceptions with people around us. If we tend to wallow in self-pity, life shows us all the reasons we could be grateful instead.

This allows us the dignity of making choices about how we live our lives. It allows us to affirm through our own behavior that we wish to be more honest or more tolerant or more loving, even when our old behaviors would be more convenient.

Meeting the challenges that life sends is our footwork. We needn't expect to get it perfect the first time. We will revert at times to our old behaviors. That doesn't mean we've failed. It simply means we need more practice.

As we practice, we can continue to ask for help. We can ask for courage to behave differently. We can ask for whatever wisdom we need to make better choices. And we can be sure that we will be provided with all that we need to do our part in this important process.

I WILL NEVER BE PERFECT. BUT IF I ACT AS IF I ALREADY HAVE THE GOOD TRAITS I WISH FOR, I WILL EVENTUALLY FIND THAT SOME OF MY LIMITATIONS BEGIN TO FALL AWAY. AND SINCE NATURE ABHORS A VACUUM, I WILL FIND THAT THE GOOD TRAITS I'VE BEEN PRACTICING WILL MOVE IN TO FILL THE EMPTY SPACES IN MY SPIRIT.

DEADLY CONSEQUENCES

Ignoring infidelity can be deadly.

For a variety of reasons, women have sometimes decided to remain in a flawed relationship and to overlook the fact that their partner is straying. Some of us may make up our minds to do the same. And no one can judge us if we conclude that is the best thing for us to do. It is our decision and ours alone.

But in the present day, the consequences of overlooking reality can be deadly.

Some of the diseases that come with indiscriminant sexual behavior are incurable. One of them is fatal. And if we have chosen to remain with a man who cheats, even for the short term, we want to make that call with our eyes open. We want to be clear about the possible consequences and well informed about our options for protecting ourselves.

Making an informed and reasoned decision to stay with a man who is not monogamous is any woman's right; remaining in denial about the possible medical consequences is neither informed nor reasoned.

TODAY I WILL CONSCIOUSLY MAKE THE BEST CHOICE ABOUT HOW TO CONDUCT MY SEXUAL RELATIONSHIP WITH A PARTNER WHO MAY NOT BE EXCLUSIVE. I WILL SEEK WISDOM AND COURAGE.

DOUBLE STANDARDS

Before we judge our partner for his deception and disloyalty, perhaps we can take a closer look at ourselves.

Have we always been as honest as we could have been in our relationship with our partner or with others? Have we lied about money, hedged about our past, covered up actions we didn't want scrutinized?

Have we always been as loyal as we hope our partner will be? Or have we talked about our partner's limitations behind his back, failed to support his endeavors, belittled his dreams?

Our shortcomings in either area don't excuse infidelity. But perhaps looking at our own behavior will help us grow both in compassion for the weaknesses of others and in our willingness to forgive those who sincerely regret their mistakes. We can aspire to greater honesty and deeper compassion in all our dealings with others.

IF HONESTY AND LOYALTY ARE IMPORTANT TRAITS WHEN I CHOOSE A PARTNER, I WILL WORK TODAY TO CULTIVATE THEM IN MYSELF.

GOD ALWAYS ANSWERS

We can choose how we handle an obsessive thought. It works best for me to make my choice as quickly as I recognize the potential for obsession, before it takes root.

On Christmas Eve, I had cookies to bake and thought nothing of it when my husband said he would be gone for a couple of hours on business. But the door had no sooner closed behind him than I was struck with the notion that nobody did the kind of business he'd described on Christmas Eve.

As I measured sugar and flour and creamed butter, my thoughts began to fly. What was he really doing?

I recognized the early stages of an obsession, the kind that could ruin the day, rob me of my serenity, and zap my energy. As I worked on my cookies, I told myself that as soon as I had a batch in the oven, I would go up to my office, sit quietly, and turn my fears over to God. Because no matter what my husband might be doing, it wasn't worth ruining my holiday.

I had no sooner put the cookie sheet in the oven than the phone rang. It was one of my husband's colleagues, hoping to catch him before he left for the appointment he had described to me on his way out the door. The caller unwittingly confirmed everything my husband told me.

The answers to my prayers are not always so immediate or so direct. But I never doubt that God will ease my fears if I turn them over to his care. Because I've seen it work, over and over again.

TODAY IF I HANG ON TO AN UNPLEASANT THOUGHT UNTIL IT BECOMES AN OBSESSION, I WILL REMEMBER THAT IS MY CHOICE. THERE IS ANOTHER CHOICE.

ALICE MAY

ILLUMINATING YOUR PATH

Regrets serve one good purpose in our life today. They illuminate a part of our path, helping us see where we need to set things right and where our footwork takes us next.

For when we have done something that we regret, we now know what needs to be done and how to go about it. We no longer need to cling to regrets. Today we can take constructive action by using the tool of daily awareness.

We can share with someone else what we've done that we regret. We can come clean with our higher power as well. We can ask for guidance in setting things right. Then we can take whatever constructive action is suggested or revealed to us, taking care not to cause further harm just to clear our own conscience. Once we've taken the action we've been guided to take, we can let go of our regrets.

Holding on to regrets can poison the spirit. But when used to guide us to positive action to correct any wrongs we've done to ourselves or others, regrets become another tool for our spiritual growth.

TODAY I WILL EXAMINE MYSELF FOR REGRETS AND TAKE POSITIVE ACTION TO ALLEVIATE THEM.

SUPPORTING HIS EFFORTS TO HEAL

Not all our partners want to change. But even when our partner does want to change, that doesn't immediately make all our problems go away.

Nevertheless, supporting his efforts to change is a powerful step we can take toward healing our relationship.

Our first priority is to take care of our own spiritual and emotional needs. But women who have tried to support their partner's attempts to turn things around have found that they can do so while still taking care of themselves. Here is what they have done:

- "Mostly I've kept quiet. I backed off and kept my nose out of his business. While he was in therapy, I allowed his sexual history to be the elephant in the middle of the living room. Unless the elephant poops again and things start to stink, we walk around it. There's room around the edges of that elephant for both of us to change and grow."

- "I remember that true forgiveness is giving up my right to hurt him for hurting me."

- "My husband said he didn't think he could work on his issues while we were together because of his guilt, because of the pain and distrust he saw in my face. So we separated. I was devastated all over again, but I gave him what he said he needed."

- "I pray for him. That's all I know to do."

TODAY I WILL REMEMBER THAT MY FIRST PRIORITY IS MY OWN WELL-BEING. BUT I CAN FIND WAYS TO SUPPORT A PARTNER WHO WANTS TO CHANGE AND STILL FOCUS ON MY OWN HEALING JOURNEY.

ALICE MAY

THIS DAY IS ALL YOU HAVE

If you were dying, how important would this moment's problems be to you? If you were dying, what changes would you make, what choices?

We are guaranteed only this moment, yet most of us live our lives on hold. We're waiting for something to happen to make us whole and happy. We're waiting for this circumstance to change. We believe that something beyond us, out there somewhere in the future, is going to transform us.

We have this moment. It is all we have. And if we are spending it on regrets, on resentments, on trying to change someone else so our external situation suits us, we are wasting this moment. It is too precious to waste.

TODAY I WILL LIVE AS IF THIS DAY IS ALL I HAVE. BECAUSE IT IS. I WILL MAKE IT COUNT. I WILL FOCUS ON WHAT REALLY MATTERS.

TRUST YOUR SPIRIT

I was finishing a walk on the beach. A strong wind was at my back, nudging me along. As I turned toward my hotel, I saw a woman headed through the sand on crutches, fighting the wind. Each step she took was a struggle.

This was a Gulf Coast beach, too, where the sand is so fine that you sink inches deep with each step. I couldn't imagine how she would make it to the row of beach chairs facing the surf.

But she kept going. It took a long time. Just watching her was exhausting. I kept thinking that not only did she have to make it to the chairs, but sometime later she would have to make the trip all the way back to her hotel.

I wasn't sure I would have had the gumption to make such an effort. But she did, because that was the challenge she'd been handed that day.

Today we have been handed our own challenge.

We aren't sure we have what it takes. The destination looks so far away, the path as uncertain as shifting sand. We're inclined to lay down our crutches and give in.

Don't do it. Don't worry about how long the journey will take. Don't worry about how difficult it will be. Just take one more step. Take a breath. Rest. Remember that the ocean is out there ahead of you. And take one more step.

The human spirit is strong. We are all given challenges we can't imagine facing down. But we can trust our spirit.

WHATEVER MY CHALLENGES TODAY, I WILL TRUST MY SPIRIT. IT IS STRONG. IT WILL SEE ME THROUGH.

ALICE MAY

BEING WITHOUT A RELATIONSHIP

Is it time to think differently about being without a relationship?

We think of it in negative terms. We think of it as a sort of limbo, a wasteland where our life is on hold. As if having a relationship is our sole purpose, the guiding force in our lives.

Can we tell ourselves something different today?

Being unencumbered by a relationship can give us time to determine who we are, without the distraction of seeing ourselves as reflected in someone else's eyes.

It gives us time to find out what we enjoy and where our passions lie.

It gives us a chance to relax and let our guard down. We may still have children or jobs or other responsibilities, but there is one less person with expectations of us. If we allow it to happen, that can become an opportunity to let go of some of our expectations of ourselves.

Being unbound by a relationship also gives us the gift of having no one else to blame when we don't feel good about ourselves. Then we know who has the power to turn that around—we do.

If circumstances have temporarily or for the longer term left us without a partner, let us see that as a blank slate on which we can write whatever we want for this day.

I BELONG TO MYSELF ALONE. IF I AM WITHOUT A PARTNER TODAY, I CAN MAKE IT AN ADVENTURE OF SELF-DISCOVERY AND JOY.

SPIRITUAL HOUSECLEANING

How dirty is it under your refrigerator?

Unless you've just finished spring cleaning or you're a lot more fastidious than I am, it's not something you'd care to reveal. Most of us don't move the fridge on a weekly, or even a monthly basis to scrub away the yuck that collects beneath it. And collect it does.

Most of us, unfortunately, treat our souls a lot like our refrigerators. Things pile up. A tiny lie here, an inconspicuous little resentment there, a big heap of fear or selfishness that grows and grows. Pretty soon, a lot of yuck has collected inside us.

Our process of healing has given us a way to clean up the emotional dirt we've allowed to pile up over the course of our lifetime. Using our self-discovery appraisal and the tool of forgiveness, we've managed to get rid of most of the old garbage. Our souls feel clean.

The problem is, stuff begins to pile up again if we don't take a regular look at ourselves and assess what we find. Each day we need to check for dishonesty or selfishness or fear that has gotten in the way of living a life of the spirit. If we make a clean sweep each day, piles of old grievances and wrongdoings won't collect in the corners, becoming harder to deal with as time passes.

TODAY I KNOW WHAT TOOLS TO USE AND HOW TO USE THEM TO KEEP THE PATH CLEAR BETWEEN THE WORLD AND ME, AND BETWEEN MY SPIRIT AND ME. I NEED NEVER LET THE DEBRIS PILE UP AGAIN, AS LONG AS I PAY ATTENTION TO MY DAILY SPIRITUAL HOUSECLEANING.

REASSURANCE

A young friend struggling to put her marriage back together had doubts about her husband's weekend business trip. What she longed for, she said, was his reassurance that nothing but business would go on.

Her words reminded me that my husband has stopped reassuring me. And most of the time, I don't long for him to say the words designed to ease my fears.

How many dozens of times did he reassure me to cover his deception? How often did I draw comfort from his reassurances when deep in my soul I knew better? And why would I have expected anything but reassurances from him if he had something to hide?

Today I remember that if my husband has nothing to hide, it may not occur to him to reassure me.

Today I remember that his actions are all I need to trust, not his promises.

Today I am grateful that I don't rely on pretty but questionable words for my peace of mind.

TODAY I DON'T NEED OR WANT THE REASSURANCES OF SOMEONE WHO HAS PROVEN UNTRUSTWORTHY. INSTEAD, I WILL FIND ANY REASSURANCES I NEED IN MY NEW WAY OF LIFE AND MY GROWING FAITH. THAT IS REASSURANCE I CAN TRUST.

DROP YOUR RIGHTEOUSNESS

How many of us could eliminate these words from our vocabulary when speaking to our loved ones: *You need to . . . , you should . . . ?*

How many of us could adopt a less virtuous attitude with loved ones we believe are making mistakes? How many of us lecture, then wonder why the people we love won't have a simple conversation with us?

It is so tempting to believe, simply because we have been the wronged rather than the wrongdoer, that we have a direct pipeline to the source of right and wrong. We know what others should do. We know what constitutes good behavior and what constitutes bad. Don't we?

One of the things we can consider dropping on our spiritual journey is our well-meaning certainty that we are righteous. We are not. We are simply women who are doing our best to live a life of value. And we fall short. Just as our loved ones do.

With the right guidance and wisdom, we can direct our own path successfully, but not someone else's. We don't know what anyone else needs to do. When we act as if we do, the most certain result is that we'll misstep ourselves.

TODAY I WILL KEEP MY EYES ON MY OWN PATH. THEN I WILL BE TOO BUSY TO OFFER UNWANTED ADVICE TO ANYONE ELSE ABOUT HIS JOURNEY.

UNKIND WORDS

How much of our pain comes from the painful things our partner has said to us? In moments of anger or desperation or alienation, he may have attacked our worth as a sexual partner, as a mother, as a capable and loving woman.

And we have taken it in. We have listened and absorbed, and anytime we have needed an extra dose of self-flagellation, we have pulled out those words and flung them at ourselves again.

A priest once said to a young woman wounded by her partner's false accusations, "Would you be crying if he called you a chair?"

The answer, of course, is no. There is nothing to hurt us in being accused of something so clearly untrue.

So what hurts us when he says things in the heat of a disagreement, or to deflect his own guilt, is our own willingness to believe what he says.

He has not hurt us with his unkind words.

We have hurt ourselves because we chose to believe his unkind words.

Before we carve his words on our hearts, let us take the time to explore who we really are. Honestly and courageously, let us work to discover who we are. Next, let us use those discoveries to become the people we want to be.

Then any harsh words someone else hurls at us will no longer have the power to make us cry. We will know whether the accusations are true or not. And if they are true, we will know that all we need to do is use our newfound tools to begin changing a little bit today.

TODAY, IF SOMEONE CALLS ME A CHAIR, I CAN LET IT GO, KNOW-
ING IT ISN'T TRUE.

PLACING YOUR CHILDREN
ABOVE THE BATTLE

Let us make a pledge today: We will never use our children as pawns in legal or emotional struggles with our partner.

Let us put it in writing if we must, to ensure our commitment. Let us make this promise to whatever higher power we have discovered, to the women who are helping us through this process, to our family members. Let us do whatever we must to place our children above the battle.

They will be affected deeply by our troubles. We can't keep that from happening. But we can do everything in our power to keep them out of the line of direct fire. We can do that much.

Our children are not a bargaining chip. Our children are not a means for getting back at someone else. Our children are not instruments of guilt to hold over another person's head.

As parents, our job is to protect our children from as much of the ugliness as possible.

So we don't ask them to take sides. We don't pump them for details when they come back from a visit with Daddy and his friend. As much as it may irritate us, we encourage a close relationship between father and child. We speak the kindest truths we know about their father in their presence. We work for a cordial relationship with the father of our children, for the sake of our children.

Our children deserve as safe and healthy a childhood as we can give them. That doesn't mean we stay in a relationship that is killing us body and soul. But it does mean we place their interests above any interest we may have in revenge or greed or spite.

TODAY I WILL CONDUCT MYSELF IN A WAY THAT ENHANCES MY CHILDREN'S SECURITY, KNOWING IT WILL BE IN MY BEST INTERESTS AS WELL IN THE LONG RUN.

ALICE MAY

MY LIMITED THINKING

As I pack in the dead of winter for a trip to a tropical climate, I resist the idea of packing shorts, sandals, and T-shirts. How much warmer can it really be? Surely I'll need my socks and sweatshirts.

I've checked the weather reports on television; I know in my mind that it's in the eighties where I'm headed. But sitting here as the temperature dips into the thirties, watching a little snow accumulate along the fence rails outside my window, I cannot fathom it. I can't feel in my bones that somewhere else it is actually sunny and warm.

This is my limited thinking, and it affects me at other times as well. Wherever I am at the moment, those circumstances become all I can see, feel, or imagine of the world. I cannot fathom that at some point in the future, my world will once again be sunny, warm, happy, easy.

The next time I am bundled up against the elements, I will remember that it is shirtsleeve weather somewhere in the world. And it will eventually return to my neighborhood.

TODAY I WILL REMEMBER THAT NOTHING STAYS THE SAME. DIFFICULTIES COME, BUT THEY ALSO GO. I MAY NOT BE ABLE TO IMAGINE GOOD TIMES COMING AGAIN, BUT THEY WILL.

REFUSING TO JUDGE OTHERS

The women listened as someone recounted a tale of betrayal by the man in her life. Finally, one of the women spoke up: "Men are pigs."

An initial reaction might be to agree. Men have betrayed us. We've seen it happen time and again. But before we attach ugly labels to half the population, let us take a moment to open our minds to the truth.

Yes, some men behave badly in relationships. And some do not. And yes, women are not angels in relationships either.

Do you know women who have cheated on their partner? Married for money? Strung along a man who had money when they cared less for the man than for the good times they could be shown? Do you know women who have stolen a best friend's partner, or at least borrowed him for the night?

We all know them. Some of us have done some of those things ourselves. The truth is, women are sometimes less than admirable, too. And some men are as likely to be honorable as women are.

Lumping all men into a group and assigning them all the negative characteristics of the men who have betrayed us is wrong. It isn't fair to men, and it places us at risk for becoming rigid and unforgiving in our thinking.

TODAY I WILL REFUSE THE CALL TO JUDGE ALL MEN HARSHLY. I WILL EVEN REFUSE TO CONDEMN SPECIFIC MEN WHOSE ACTIONS LEAVE SOMETHING TO BE DESIRED. NEGATIVE JUDGMENT DOESN'T AFFECT THEM BUT LEAVES MY SOUL HEAVY WITH ANGER. I FEEL WORSE—NOT THEM. I WON'T DO THAT TO MYSELF TODAY.

CALMING YOUR DOUBTS

When we have doubts, what do we do with them? Do we ask questions? Demand details? Seek verification?

We can do those things, of course. But one thing I learned long ago is that my attempts to check up on my husband only bog me down in doubt and discouragement. After a time, some of us find more uplifting ways to handle our suspicions:

- "I state my fears in a calm way, being as unaccusing as possible. I don't do it because I expect him to reassure me. I do it to validate my feelings and to remind myself that I have the power to solve my own problems. I do it because I kept quiet for so long, and I want to remember that I never have to go back to keeping quiet just to keep the peace."

- "A phone call to someone who understands this kind of betrayal always helps me get back on track. My husband has turned his life around, and he has no idea I still get stuck in my fears. That's between me, God, and a few women I know I can trust."

- "Prayer is my first defense against doubt and suspicion. I ask God to show me anything I need to know whenever it is right for me to know it. Then I ask him to take away my fears so I can get on with my day."

There are always positive solutions to our negative thoughts and feelings, and we can learn about some of them from other women who are also healing.

TODAY I WILL LATCH ONTO A SOLUTION AND LET GO OF THE PROBLEM.

LET HIM LIVE WITH THE CONSEQUENCES

For too many years, anytime my caught-red-handed partner promised to clean up his act, I jumped at the chance to put my blinders on again. I wholeheartedly gave him my trust over and over, and each time he betrayed me again.

I know today that I can forgive his weaknesses without absolving him of responsibility for his actions. I can give up the idea that he should be punished without pronouncing him redeemed.

Few of us are motivated to make drastic changes in our behavior or our personality unless our actions and our traits cause us enough problems. If what we're doing has few negative consequences, why bother with the difficult process of change?

Learning that it's okay to let him live with the consequences of his behavior is progress for me. And maybe those consequences will someday feel painful enough that he'll be ready to make real changes.

TODAY I AM STRONG ENOUGH TO ALLOW SOMEONE I LOVE TO LIVE WITH THE CONSEQUENCES OF HIS BEHAVIOR. I CAN DO SO WITH COMPASSION, NOT BITTERNESS, IN THE KNOWLEDGE THAT IT IS BEST FOR ME AND BEST FOR THE PERSON I LOVE.

ALICE MAY

A LINK IN THE CHAIN

Some of us begin to feel better; the tools and principles that saw us through our crisis begin to lose their urgency. Sure, it helped to turn to God and establish our lives on a spiritual basis. It certainly helped to connect with women who shared our difficulties.

But our difficulties are over now. Either things have returned to normal or we've established a new normal.

We don't need our tools or our principles the way we once did.

That may work for some people. But it hasn't worked that way for me, or for others who have walked through this difficulty with me. I've found that after a taste of healthy, spiritual living I am unwilling to go back to my old ways of doing things. I've found a way of life that is rewarding and wholesome. I don't want to give it up.

And there is something more.

Today I want to become one of those women who was there for me when I was in pain. I want to provide comfort and support for other women who are just beginning this difficult journey. I want to share with others how the tools have worked for me.

This desire, I now know, is the final stage of my journey. The stage of giving.

Yes, it might be easier to put this behind me and not expose myself to constant reminders of the past. But I want my experiences to count for something. And the best way I know to accomplish that is to become a link in the chain of hope and healing. When I do that, I find that the reminders of my past reveal to me how much I've grown, how far I've come. The reminders aren't painful, they are affirming.

TODAY I WILL SEEK WAYS TO USE MY NEWFOUND STRENGTH AND HOPE IN THE LIVES OF THOSE WHO DON'T YET HAVE HOPE FOR THEMSELVES.

GIVING FROM THE HEART

Helping others is something I always managed to get wrong. I either helped at the expense of my own needs, overwhelming myself and resenting those I helped, or I decided I knew exactly what others needed and bulldozed them on the way to my solution.

My spiritual journey teaches healthy ways to help the people around me, using the spiritual principle of service, or giving.

Some spiritual guides I've learned from believe that the sole purpose of our journey is to fit us for maximum service in this life. But those of us who have trouble finding a healthy balance in our lives must learn to distinguish service from caretaking.

One important difference is the spirit in which the action is taken. We are being of service when we give expecting nothing in return—nothing. Not gratitude, not praise, not approval, not a kind deed in repayment. True service is an act of the heart.

Another way to differentiate between service and caretaking is the willingness of the recipient. Have we been asked for our help? Or are we barging into someone's life with a solution we've come up with on our own, certain we can provide precisely what that person needs? We are being of service when we wait for someone to request help and then give only the help we were asked for. That kind of service leaves recipients with dignity, the dignity of making choices and decisions on their own.

TODAY I WILL GIVE PURELY FROM THE HEART—NOT BECAUSE I WANT GLORY AND NOT BECAUSE I HOPE TO FORCE MY SOLUTIONS ON SOMEONE WHO MAY HAVE NO INTEREST IN THEM. WHEN I GIVE FROM THE HEART, MY GIVING WILL BE RETURNED IN UNEXPECTED ABUNDANCE.

ALICE MAY

THE LIE OF URGENCY

If it's urgent, it's not from God.

We decide we must act. Now. We must have the answer. We must reach a decision or change our life or tell someone off. And the only time we can do these things is now.

Chances are, when we feel that urgent compulsion to act, it's all about satisfying our own will. Chances are, God isn't anywhere on the scene.

When our higher spirit has a hand in our life, we can be calm because our actions will achieve good just as easily the next day or the next week as they will at this moment. We can rest assured that the perfect moment will arrive, and it doesn't have to be now. We can be confident that we will be given plenty of opportunities to contribute to good in this life. We needn't worry that we'll miss the chance.

IF IT'S URGENT, IT ISN'T FROM GOD. THE SOURCE OF MY WISDOM NEVER ASKS ME TO RUSH WHEN IT IS TIME TO STEP ONTO THE PATH.

WORK IS LOVE

She was a highly sought-after massage therapist at a pricey spa, but she worked me over so quickly and so aloofly that I felt as if I'd been through an assembly line.

In contrast, the checkout clerk in the grocery store often notices when I'm not in good spirits and, with caring in her voice, encourages me to smile. I feel her concern, and it never fails to turn my day around.

If we are preparing to enter or return to the workforce, an awareness to take with us is that any job provides us with an opportunity to be of service. Some of us fear starting at the bottom, taking a job that won't pay much and won't challenge us. But the challenge comes in remembering that even the most mundane work allows us to touch the lives of others in a positive way. And when we allow our spirits to become engaged with the spirits of those we serve, the amount on our paycheck is only a small part of what we receive in return for our day's work.

We may greet people at a discount store or teach or design homes or cut hair. But we can decide whether to do our job like the preoccupied massage therapist or the encouraging grocery clerk. Whatever we do, we can do it with love. We can do it from the heart. With a smile and a gentle word. We can look people in the eye and acknowledge their humanity. When we do that, our own spirits are fed no matter what kind of work we do.

TODAY I CAN FIND REAL SATISFACTION IN KNOWING THAT NO MATTER WHAT WORK I'VE BEEN GIVEN TO DO, MY REAL JOB IS LOVING OTHERS THROUGH MY WORK.

ALICE MAY

FEELING SEPARATE

My pain was greatest on those days when I was utterly alone with it.

I would lock myself in my office, my bedroom, or the bathroom and huddle into a tight ball, feeling abandoned by the world. There was no one to talk to, no one who could understand what I was going through, no one who had ever felt such abject betrayal and pain.

Today I know how wrong I was. I was alone only because I had not yet learned how to reach out for the solace and companionship available to me. I had not yet learned that most of my fear and pain is born in the illusion that I am separate. The illusion that I am adrift, alone, abandoned. That I will never be connected to a source of love, warmth, comfort.

The word to zero in on is *illusion*.

So many things that have caused me difficulty in my life are just that—illusion. And this is yet another—the illusion that I am alone and disconnected.

In reality, I am connected in many profound ways. To all the good energy in the world. To other women, to my family. To the spirit of love I now see all around me. It is up to me to reach out, to be willing to act on that connection.

NOW THAT I SEE ALL THE WAYS IN WHICH I AM CONNECTED TO AND LOVED BY OTHERS, I KNOW THAT I NEED NEVER FEAR LOSS OR ABANDONMENT AGAIN.

GROWING YOUR WINGS

A friend at a bereavement workshop heard this story of a child who stumbled upon a cocoon.

The little boy watched, growing impatient as the emerging butterfly struggled, making so little headway that the boy became convinced it was stuck. The child decided the butterfly would die without his help, so he went into the house for a pair of scissors. Very gently, he made the tiniest snip in the cocoon.

The butterfly was free.

But the little boy noticed something strange about the butterfly. Its body was puffy and larger than a typical butterfly. Its wings looked clipped and unformed. Although it tried valiantly, the butterfly never flew.

The reason, of course, is that the struggle is part of the butterfly's process. The struggle to be free of the cocoon is what develops the wings. Without the struggle, the butterfly would never become the beautiful creature God intends it to be. Without the struggle, it would never fly. And neither will I.

WHEN I RAGE AGAINST MY CIRCUMSTANCES, I WILL TRY TO REMEMBER THAT, LIKE THE LARVA, I AM SIMPLY BEING PREPARED TO FLY.

GLIMPSES OF REAL LOVE

What does real love feel like? Some of us have such doubts, have spent so much time living in what we now label phony love or unhealthy love that we fear we wouldn't know real love if it brought us a thirty-pound box of chocolates on Valentine's Day.

By surrounding myself with people who also are dedicated to growing emotionally and spiritually, I've gained glimpses of real love in recent years. For me, real love feels like this:

I am free to behave with the carefree and innocent abandon of a child, without fear of ridicule or judgment.

I am free to make a mistake, big or small, admit it, and make amends without having it held over my head now or in the future.

I am free to allow others to see the parts of me that are unlikable or unappealing without fear of being abandoned or condemned.

I can share my moments of grace and growth and sheer joy with a certainty that they will be honored and appreciated.

These are some of the ways I experience love today. Not through giddy ecstasy or blind adoration, but through genuine support and unconditional acceptance. I first experienced real love in my interactions with the women who have supported me through this crisis. But I am learning to carry over that kind of love to all areas of my life.

TODAY I WILL ACCEPT NO SUBSTITUTES FOR REAL LOVE. I WILL RECOGNIZE IT WHEN IT IS GIVEN TO ME BECAUSE IT LIBERATES ME AND LIFTS ME.

APPROPRIATE ANGER

Good girls do get angry.

Some of us have been taught otherwise. But we don't need anyone's permission or approval to feel our anger. Under the circumstances, anger is normal. Acknowledging it and expressing it are healthy. The challenge is to release our anger in constructive rather than destructive ways.

Some of us have learned that what allows our anger to grow destructive is either suppressing it or expressing it at the wrong time, in the wrong way. We have learned to vent our initial rage in safe ways, so that we can express it calmly but firmly to those who need to hear it.

We can exercise, exhausting ourselves and our rage. We can clean the house until it sparkles. We can fill our surroundings with soothing music. We can practice deep breathing. Some of us find release in creativity— we sing or paint or write until our emotions are spent.

After we've vented the worst of our fury, it is safer to express our anger and hurt to those who are closest to us. Most of us first talk to other women we trust, discussing what we want to say and how we can say it best. Then we tell our partner how we feel. Expressing ourselves this way is good.

But we are ready to do that only when we've given up the idea that it will change him or his behavior, and only when we can do it without being vindictive or destructive ourselves.

Anger is potent and volatile. We want to exercise care in handling our anger, neither stuffing it nor misdirecting it nor destroying with it. We can manage our anger if we first acknowledge it and express it safely.

TODAY I WILL ACCEPT MY ANGER AS NORMAL. I WILL TALK TO PEOPLE I TRUST AND FIND A WAY TO RELEASE IT THAT IS HEALTHY FOR ME. THEN I CAN EXPRESS IT HONESTLY, BUT NONEXPLO-SIVELY, TO OTHERS AS WELL.

ALICE MAY

SINKING SPELLS

Some mornings, even long after the worst is over, crawling out of bed and getting on with our day seems like a task too hard to handle. Our spirits are lethargic, even if our bodies are rested. We feel no joy in the prospect of the new day ahead. We find no hope that the day will bring the true peace that seems to elude us.

Sinking spells are to be expected. It is doubtful that many of us can experience a traumatized relationship without having days when we would do anything rather than rise and plod through another day of fear or sorrow or doubt.

When I have a sinking spell, I've learned that the longer I lie there, the lower I sink. The more times I close my eyes and try to will myself back into the oblivion of sleep, the more debilitating the depression becomes.

But if I get up when I feel like staying down, if I shower and eat a good breakfast and say my morning prayers, my body soon forgets that my spirit is low. If I seek to be of service that day, then go on about my daily work, I always encounter opportunities to give something good back to the world around me.

By walking through this day even when we feel like taking things lying down, we find our spirits grow lighter as the day ticks by. We smile. We laugh. We find something to be grateful for. In trusting that a positive approach to life will lift us, we are given the joy, the hope, and the energy our spirits need.

TODAY I WILL RECOGNIZE THAT EVERYONE HAS SINKING SPELLS, AND THAT THEY'RE NOT AN INDICATION THAT I'M DOING SOME-THING WRONG. IF A DAY BEGINS BADLY, I WILL TAKE POSITIVE ACTION TO TURN THINGS AROUND. IT'S NEVER TOO LATE TO START MY DAY OVER.

YOUR BODY DOES NOT DEFINE YOU

Does it help to obsess about our bodies? Does it motivate us to eat well or exercise faithfully? Does going to extremes in an attempt to achieve unrealistic results make us desirable? Or does obsession simply drive us to binge dieting and compulsive workouts?

We know the answer. But can we stop obsessing if we want to?

Yes, if we can learn to place our sexuality and our physical selves in the proper perspective in our lives.

A part of me always believed that as long as I was desirable, it followed naturally that I would be loved. And conversely, if I wasn't physically desirable, I wasn't worthy of love. All that came crashing down on me after my partner's infidelity. My self-esteem plummeted, and I was consumed by the nagging fear that I would never be loved again.

In sharing my fears and hurt and feelings of inadequacy with others, I came to see that this was my opportunity to learn where my true value lies. This was my chance to believe, on a soul-deep level, that I am worthwhile and lovable no matter what I look like on the outside.

It took work. It took a willingness to stop listening to my negative and negating self-talk. It took being open to what is really valuable about myself. It required that I change the way I think and behave.

And it took time.

But one day I realized that it no longer mattered to me what my body looked like. It didn't matter if I had gray hair or firm breasts or fab abs. What mattered was my heart, my spirit. I was free. Free to define myself in some way other than my sexuality and my physical attractiveness.

TODAY I WILL SEE BEYOND MY PHYSICAL SELF TO THE PARTS OF ME THAT REALLY MATTER—MY HEART AND MY SPIRIT. I WILL KNOW THAT THERE I AM ALWAYS BEAUTIFUL.

ALICE MAY

TRIAL AND ERROR

Can you remember teaching a child to tie her shoestrings? How many times did she have to be shown? How many times did she have to do it badly before she could tie her shoes? And even after she learned, there was a long period when her shoes came untied a dozen times a day because she still wasn't very good at it. You could've done it better, but it was more important for her to learn than for you to avoid the aggravation of trailing shoestrings.

In fact, having to retie her shoes a dozen times a day was part of the process that taught her, finally, how to get it right.

Life is changing, and we're being asked to learn new skills in response to this crisis. We won't get all of them right immediately. We'll keep making mistakes, and those mistakes will catch up with us, and we'll be tripping over our shoestrings plenty.

Learning is like that. Growing is like that.

Don't be discouraged when you can't detach perfectly or forgive wholeheartedly or live unfailingly by the guidance of your inner wisdom. We will make mistakes. We'll get it wrong and try again. Don't be discouraged and don't disparage yourself. Trying again is how we learn to get it right.

WHEN I MAKE A MISTAKE, I WILL WATCH HOW I TREAT MYSELF AND ASK WHETHER I WOULD REACT THE SAME WAY TO A CHILD LEARNING TO TIE HER SHOESTRINGS. THEN I WILL ADJUST ACCORDINGLY.

TRUST THE PROCESS

Even after almost three years, during which time my husband had done everything he could to restore our relationship to wholeness, I still harbored bitterness in my heart.

After that much time, I still hated the beach because I hated the glistening young girls in their skimpy little suits. I hated young love, too, wherever I saw it. I hated hand-holding and adoring eyes and kisses that couldn't wait for privacy. I hated love songs and mushy movies and just about anything else that celebrated what I thought I'd lost.

I was bitter and cynical. I was not healing.

Then infidelity erupted again, leaving me reeling.

And what came out of that crushing blow was the healing I had been unable to find. We both began to heal because the second episode of unfaithfulness gave us the courage to dig deep enough to discover what was beneath this destructive pattern in our lives.

We reached a new level in our healing as a couple. And I was able to move beyond the bitterness I hadn't been able to let go of before. Today the girls on the beach are simply girls on the beach; they no longer seem like a threat to my happiness. I am free of bitterness and regret. And that freedom is worth the pain it cost me to get there.

Healing does not come easily, and its price tag is rarely small. But never give up on it. At some point, when things are their worst, healing is beginning. Healing will occur if we stay on the path. Give it time. Trust the process.

TODAY I WILL TRUST THAT PURSUING MY NEW WAY OF LIFE WILL EVENTUALLY LIFT MY BITTERNESS AND MY GRIEF. WHEN I CAN SEE THE TRUTH ABOUT MY LIFE, I WILL BEGIN TO EXPERIENCE THE GIFTS IN HEALING.

ALICE MAY

THE OTHER WOMAN AS STEPMOTHER

Sometimes our spiritual reserves are severely tested. Sometimes the other woman becomes stepmother to our children. This can be the bitterest pill of all, especially if our children grow fond of her.

Remaining neutral at such a time requires hefty doses of both maturity and grace. This is a time when even those of us who have conducted ourselves valiantly can be overcome by jealousy or a compulsion to strike out. *Anything*, we think, *anything but this.*

We do have tools at our disposal at times like this. It is up to us to use them. And we do so not to benefit her, but to benefit ourselves and our children.

We can pray to be more concerned with what is best for our children than for our own bruised egos. We can detach, finding a place in our hearts for an emotionally neutral zone where we can go when we must interact with her or hear about her. We can make up our minds not to seek details, thus limiting the information we have to obsess over. We can turn our attention to our own lives, our own interests, our own work.

We can take the high road.

The advantage to us is that we won't be responsible for damaging our relationship with our children or their relationship with their father. The advantage to us is that we are filled with grace each time we choose a loving action over a spiteful one. The advantage to us is that we find peace sooner rather than later.

IF THE OTHER WOMAN PLAYS A LARGER ROLE IN THE LIVES OF MY CHILDREN THAN I WOULD LIKE, TODAY I WILL REMEMBER THAT MY ATTITUDE AND MY BEHAVIOR HAVE AN IMPACT ON MY SERENITY AND WELL-BEING, AS WELL AS THAT OF MY CHILDREN. I WILL MAKE GOOD CHOICES ON OUR BEHALF.

20–20 HINDSIGHT

As we grow a little healthier, most of us look back and wish we'd done things differently.

Some of us question whether we forgave too quickly. Some of us wish we'd paid attention earlier to the warning signs that something was wrong. One wife and mother thinks back twenty years in wishing for changes; she's already teaching her children how to make better choices in partners.

Surely something, we think, could have saved us some of this pain, could have smoothed out our lives just a bit.

But one woman, who is in the middle of a painful and sometimes unpleasant separation from her husband of twenty-plus years, said, "I wouldn't trade anything for my growth. I know I'm a better person today for having been through it. Some people think my life is ruined, but it isn't. I have a wonderful life."

The things that have happened to us—the betrayals, the anguish, the shame, the rock-bottom despair—were necessary to get us where we are today. Sorrow is the price we paid for ultimate serenity.

Most of us, once we have tasted grace and serenity, believe the price was worth it.

TODAY I CAN LOOK BACK AND FIND A MEASURE OF PEACE DESPITE THE PAIN I'VE EXPERIENCED. I UNDERSTAND THAT MY DIFFICULTIES HAVE BEEN STEPPING-STONES TO GROWTH, AND I AM CONTENT WITH THE TRADE-OFF.

LEND A HELPING HAND

Our spiritual journey asks us to be willing to share our experiences and our hope with someone else who is in the early stages of her journey.

Some of us are reluctant to do so because we're aware of how limited we still are, how far from perfectly we practice the new principles we're trying to live by. We're hesitant because it would surely be easier to put this all behind us rather than set ourselves up for constant reminders.

Yes, our wisdom is limited. But if we offer ourselves in service, we will be given all the tools we need to help someone else. If we are willing to help someone else without expecting strokes for our egos, what we give will be of value to someone else.

And the time we spend helping others will bring blessings to us as well.

In being available to walk beside others who are beginning their journey, we will gain many things. We will learn patience. We will learn how to comfort another person without being weighed down by her emotional baggage. We will learn how to love unconditionally. We will learn to accept others where they are. We will learn that what is right for us may not necessarily be right for someone else. We will learn to be trustworthy and dependable. We will learn to open our hearts again.

HELPING OTHERS HAS MANY REWARDS. TODAY I WILL WELCOME THE OPPORTUNITY TO DO SOMETHING FOR SOMEONE ELSE AND GRATEFULLY RECEIVE MUCH IN RETURN.

THERE IS ENOUGH LOVE

My cat was a seven-month-old stray when we adopted her. She was skittish and timid, but she started gaining weight as soon as she came home with us. Too much weight.

The problem was that anytime I filled her food bowl, she ate every bite before walking away. Trying to correct the problem by feeding her less or refusing to feed her again that day if she gobbled up her daily allotment first thing in the morning only made the problem worse. Because depriving her in those ways only seemed to reinforce her belief that this food could be the last she ever saw.

Deep inside, she believed what experience had taught her: There is not enough food. There will never be enough food.

I finally learned to keep her bowl full, no matter what. And within a few months, she learned that she could come to her bowl anytime and have plenty to eat. She no longer overeats. But I still make sure her bowl is always full.

Those of us who have been abandoned by those we love, who have had love snatched away and were left to starve, believe deep in our souls that we may never be loved again. That there isn't enough love in the world to keep us safe.

There are dangers in that belief. One is that we may beg for love, as my cat used to beg for food even though she'd eaten plenty. When we beg for love, especially when we beg for it in places where there isn't any love for us, we will inevitably be left unsatisfied and desperate.

Or when our bowl is full, we may be so consumed with doubt and fear that we can't see the love that is right in front of us.

TODAY I WILL REMEMBER THAT THE WORLD IS FULL OF LOVE. I CAN LEARN HOW TO RECOGNIZE LOVE, ACCEPT IT, AND GIVE IT.

ALICE MAY

HITTING BOTTOM

Twice in one day, I heard the same tearful plea from two different heartbroken women. When would their husbands be able to see the damage they were inflicting? When would they open their eyes to the fact that their unfaithfulness was a disease in their souls and throughout their families?

No one can answer that question, of course. We know it takes hitting an emotional bottom. But what that bottom is and how we get there is different for each of us. For some, it can be as simple as seeing the disbelief and pain in the eyes of one who has trusted you. For others, it requires losing everything—home, children, partner. Sometimes again and again.

What is important for us to remember is that we hit our emotional bottoms in our own time, in our own way. Some of us turned away from the truth time and again because it was too painful to consider. Some of our partners will do the same.

We can do nothing to make him capable of seeing his actions as others see them. We can only concentrate on our own healing and take steps to meet our own needs. Some of the actions we take may help him with his process. If we refuse to live the lie any longer, for example, it may become harder for him to continue covering up his behavior. But our partner heals on his own timetable, and it isn't always in sync with ours.

Regardless of where he is in his process, we can be okay if we use the tools we're learning. We are no longer living in darkness. We can make healthy choices.

I HAVE HIT BOTTOM, AND I AM ON MY WAY UP. I MAY HOPE THAT IS TRUE FOR OTHERS IN MY LIFE. BUT MY INFLUENCE WILL NOT MAKE THAT HAPPEN.

POST-TRAUMATIC STRESS

Do you feel as if you've been engaged in a war?

That isn't far from the truth, according to a marriage therapist interviewed recently in my local newspaper. Living through infidelity is like living through a war, this expert said, so don't be surprised when the continuing emotional danger leaves you with a very real case of post-traumatic stress syndrome.

Infidelity rocks our world. It knocks the foundation out from under us. It kills something very precious to us. It leaves us without allies, or at least without the ally we've counted on for some time.

Do not underestimate the stress you have been under. Do not underestimate how long it will take you to recover. Recognize that you will need help to move forward.

That doesn't mean you're weak. It means you accept the reality of a circumstance that is in many ways as painful as the death of a spouse. A circumstance as traumatic as any battlefield.

Put yourself in good hands. Rest. Recover.

You will heal. Your life will be restored. But the battle is over. Let it go. Rest.

TODAY I DON'T HAVE TO MINIMIZE WHAT I'VE BEEN THROUGH. BETRAYAL IS TRAUMATIC, AND THE PROCESS OF HEALING DIFFICULT. I WILL ACKNOWLEDGE THE STRESS I'VE BEEN UNDER AND BE GENTLE WITH MYSELF.

DIVERSIFY

We are so accustomed to turning to our partner for all our needs. We need a hug? He's there for us. Encouragement? Financial backup? Companionship? We have a partner, and that makes for a built-in answer to all our needs.

And now that partner is unavailable to us for many of those needs. Maybe he's moved out. Maybe we simply can't go there with our needs. Not yet. The bottom line is, our source of many of life's essentials is now no longer there.

And our needs are greater than ever.

What do we do now?

What we do now is something we would have been wise to do all along—we diversify. We embrace our new awareness that one person cannot meet all our needs. We learn that our lives will be filled with plenty if we surround ourselves with a variety of people who can fill our needs while we fill theirs.

I have one friend who walks with me. One who gives me a tough talking-to. One who listens while I muddle through my own confusion. One friend loves to take care of my cat when I'm out of town, and one likes to shop whenever I'm in the mood. One loans me books, and one will stay in with me on Sunday nights to watch TV movies. I have tons of friends who give me hugs and encouragement and love. And I can turn to any of them, anytime.

With so many sources of support, I am never without. No matter what happens between my partner and me, I have a bounty of love and companionship and emotional intimacy.

TODAY I DON'T EXPECT ONE PERSON TO FULFILL ALL MY NEEDS. I AM WILLING TO ACCEPT WHAT I NEED FROM MANY PEOPLE IN MY LIFE.

Surviving Betrayal

EXPECTATIONS

More than once she has confronted our group with her question, "Aren't I entitled to have certain expectations? Isn't that what marriage is all about?"

In our society, yes, that is what we've been taught marriage is all about. It is all about those unspoken expectations we bring to the relationship.

The sex will be all that the women's magazines promise. Our children will be models of behavior and accomplishment, and we will always agree on their upbringing. Our future will be secure. He will be loyal and faithful and supportive.

Those are more than hopes and dreams. They are expectations. Expectations no marriage can live up to completely.

And therein lies the problem.

If we have expectations, we are setting ourselves up for disappointment. Worse, for bitterness and resentment. Even reasonable expectations can leave us hypervigilant and vulnerable to losing our peace of mind at another person's whim.

We would be better off to live in this day only, making the best of our present circumstances, growing because of our difficulties. We would be better off to take the pressure off our loved ones, including our straying partner, and trust that things will work out the way they are supposed to work out. We would be better off to know our own boundaries and to ask for the courage to protect them.

Those changes leave room within us for peace and forgiveness and unconditional love.

TODAY I WILL TRY TO REPLACE MY EXPECTATIONS WITH HOPE AND FLEXIBILITY.

ALICE MAY

MOMENTS OF JOY

The moments of pure joy will take us by surprise.

If we are faithful in our spiritual seeking, we will find ourselves overtaken at unexpected moments by joy. Not ecstasy or happiness as we have come to identify them. Not those giddy, sky-high moments when our blood is rushing and our skin is flushed with pleasure. But joy.

Joy. Quiet contentment that seeps through us, softly. A sense of wellbeing that surpasses anything we've ever experienced or hoped for. A lightness of spirit that strips even our worst experiences of their power to wound us further.

Those moments of pure joy don't come just because events in our lives are going right. In fact, I've experienced them most often at times when outcomes were still uncertain and circumstances still appeared gloomy. But the moments of joy came anyway, filling me, expanding me, lifting me. They aren't a product of success or triumph or another person's response to us. Joy simply comes to us, unbidden, as a result of living a spirit-filled life. Joy is a by-product of cultivating compassion in our hearts. Joy comes to us when we have given up fighting life and accept the flow of life's ups and downs instead of struggling against them.

Fleeting at first, joy is given to us for a moment here and there, grows more frequent, then lasts longer as we continue our spiritual discipline.

TODAY I WON'T SEEK JOY. BUT I WILL PREPARE A PLACE FOR IT IN MY SOUL.

TRIGGERS

We're feeling pretty good. No outward signs of trouble. We may even be experiencing healing or returning trust or growing faith that some source beyond ourselves is acting in our best interests.

In the midst of that serenity, we are blindsided when emotional insanity strikes again.

Nothing external changes, but we're suddenly filled with fear. The urge to interrogate or snoop or engage in whatever unhealthy behavior plagued us at the worst of times is too powerful to resist. We lapse into our old craziness. And we don't even know why.

Such a slip is a reminder that our diseased thinking is insidious and potent.

Sometimes, however, something has triggered our relapse. A hang-up when we answer the phone. The anniversary of a painful event. A new neighbor who is younger or prettier than we ever hope to be. Triggers are powerful. They are also quite often irrational, based in emotion and grounded in the past.

When something triggers us, let us remember that yesterday is over. Its reality has nothing to do with today, with this moment. We can choose to dwell in that old reality, or we can stay in today. In this moment, we can ask our partner for reassurance, if that feels safe. We can call someone who shares our experiences and talk about our feelings until they lose their power over us. We can choose a healthy response to our emotional triggers.

TODAY I WILL RECOGNIZE A TRIGGER AS OLD STUFF. I WILL REC-OGNIZE A RELAPSE AS QUICKLY AS POSSIBLE AND WALK AWAY FROM IT.

ALICE MAY

LIFE IS GOOD

Life is good.

My friend repeated the words many times as we walked. She repeated them not out of a need to convince herself, but out of a profound and hard-won understanding that they were true.

Life is good.

Often, when she said it, the words peeved me. Sure, *her* life was good. Lots of people have the good life. But not me.

Still, I kept my lips sealed and allowed her to savor her time in the sun. If she wanted to believe life is good, I would certainly not enlighten her.

We kept walking. I kept making progress in my spiritual journey. Prayer. Meditation. Daily awareness. Invitations to openness and honesty to enter my life, through journaling and sharing and being accountable for my actions.

Some days when she sighed that life is good, I almost believed her. When people backed off a little, when the crisis abated, life was good.

We've been walking for years now. On her spiritual journey, she is miles ahead of me. But she stays by my side while I continue my struggle and my surrender. And the longer I remain on the path beside her, the more pairs of Nikes we run into the pavement together, the more I can see the truth.

Life is good.

Life teaches me what my soul longs to know. Life coaxes me toward love and joy. Life unfolds before me and reveals just enough of God to keep me safe and seeking.

TODAY I WILL KNOW THAT LIFE IS GOOD. EVEN IF I DON'T FEEL IT AT THIS MOMENT, I CAN TRUST THAT IT IS SO. LIFE IS GOOD.

SCAR TISSUE

Can the distance between our partner and us ever be healed? Or will the chasm that gapes between us continue to separate us?

At first, the distance between us can be a blessing. There is so much negative feeling—pain, anger, distrust—that not connecting may be more comfortable than drawing too close. Being close could sharpen feelings that are barely manageable already.

But now the difficulties between us are diminishing. Things are beginning to feel resolved. We've worked through the events that caused our problems, we've applied solutions. The healing in our relationship is very real, and so is the hope.

But the distance is still there. And more pronounced for being side by side with our hope. We begin to fear that it is permanent. We begin to fear that this is the scar tissue our relationship will always bear.

This is a stage of our healing. Like all the other stages, it serves its own purpose, and it takes whatever time it takes. We may not understand its purpose today, and we cannot rush the process. We cannot force a solution to present itself because we cannot be sure what the outcome is intended to be.

But we can continue using our tools. We can behave in a kind and loving way, hoping our emotions catch up with our actions. We can do no further harm. We can inventory what is going on inside us, looking for remnants of anger or mistrust. We can deal with what we find. We can be open and honest with ourselves and with our partner.

This stage of our journey is serving some purpose we cannot see. And this, too, shall pass.

TODAY WE CAN PRACTICE PATIENCE AND ACCEPTANCE. OUR INNER WISDOM HAS BROUGHT US THIS FAR. WE CAN TRUST THE SOURCE OF OUR WISDOM AND COURAGE A LITTLE LONGER.

ALICE MAY

STRIVING TO BE CHEERFUL

What face do we show our friends, our co-workers, our family? Are we still allowing ourselves to play the martyr, walking around with a grim expression, the long face of the victim?

While we now know it is good and even necessary to express our true feelings instead of masking them, that isn't permission to become perpetually glum.

If we choose to conduct ourselves as the eternal victim, many things will happen. Our friends will grow weary of our behavior and begin avoiding us. Our co-workers may opt out of opportunities to include us in their projects or their socializing. Being around someone who is depressed, even justifiably so, is depressing, and few people endure it willingly for long.

We don't have to pretend to be something we're not. But we can make an effort to be as cheerful as we're capable of being when we're around friends or colleagues. We can attempt to focus, for those few hours, on the progress we are making or on those parts of our life that are still good and intact. We can smile when it is appropriate, no matter how tempting it is to demonstrate to the world how desperate our circumstances are.

We have people with whom we can share our pain, people who are safe and who understand our problems. Let us save our despair for them. And let us cross over to the sunny side of the street whenever possible with the others in our life.

I NO LONGER NEED TO HIDE MY TRUE FEELINGS, BUT I DON'T NEED TO WEAR THOSE FEELINGS ON MY SLEEVE EITHER. I WILL REMEMBER THAT, EVEN IF THINGS ARE STILL BAD, SOME DAYS THEY ARE BETTER THAN THEY HAVE BEEN. I WILL ALLOW MY PROGRESS TO SHOW ON MY FACE.

FACING YOUR PROBLEMS

What do we gain when we run away from our problems? And is it really more than we lose?

What we gain is fleeting and false. We gain the illusion of peace of mind, or control. We can believe for a while that our problems are behind us, or that they were never very serious to begin with. We gain the contrived certainty that we can keep life's harshness at bay, that we are brave enough, good enough, wise enough to manage whatever comes our way. Or that someone will rescue us before it's too late.

We can believe, for a little bit longer, that we can defeat life.

All of it is false.

Life and its difficulties still nip at our heels, waiting patiently for us to slow down or stumble. Life will catch up with us. Life always has the power to defeat us as long as we believe we have all the power we need to battle it alone.

What we lose when we run from our problems is the opportunity to learn—to learn humility in the face of our own limitations; to learn how to listen to the voice of our own spirit; to learn that life's difficulties light the way to healing.

TODAY I WILL TRY TO STAND STILL LONG ENOUGH TO FACE MY PROBLEMS. I WILL REJECT THE FLEETING AND THE FALSE, THE ILLUSIONS THAT LIFE TEMPTS ME WITH. I WILL ACCEPT THE GIFTS THAT COME WHEN I QUIT RUNNING AWAY.

PRIDE

When our relationship begins to heal, we can let our pride stand in the way of the good times that could be ours again.

I am afraid of holding my husband's hand when we run our errands together, as we so often did before. I am afraid to be caught looking into his face with obvious love. I am concerned, wherever we are and whatever we're doing, about the appearance of having too much fun with him.

And it's all about pride. All about my wounded ego.

What if someone who knows all that has gone on sees me giving myself completely to this relationship again? What will they think of me? What kind of fool will they take me for?

What others think of us and our relationship is none of our concern. Others' opinions should never influence how we conduct ourselves. The only explanations we owe are to ourselves and to our higher spirit. And in allowing the opinions of people outside our relationship to influence us, we are giving power to people who cannot see inside our heart or our partner's.

If our reluctance to take part wholeheartedly in our relationship is really about what others will think, we can let that go. It is not their concern. Their opinions are not our concern.

TODAY I WILL LET GO OF THE PRIDE THAT MAY HAMPER MY HEALING. I WILL REMEMBER THAT I NO LONGER NEED TO LEAD MY LIFE BASED ON WHAT OTHERS MAY THINK. TODAY I WILL DO MY BEST TO MAKE DECISIONS BASED ON MY GREATER GOOD, NOT ON MY DESIRE TO HAVE OTHERS THINK WELL OF ME.

RECEIVING OBSESSIVE ATTENTION

During one of the rockier patches following my husband's infidelity, I asked him to move into a spare room. I turned a cold shoulder to all his attempts to reach me and soften my attitude. His remorse and his promises had always won me over before, and I was determined this time would be different.

The more I focused on myself and my healing journey, the more he focused on me. And the more he tried to connect, the further I retreated.

Feeling my negative reaction to his attempts to influence my behavior was a good lesson for me. It helped me see how unpleasant it can be to become the sole focus of another person's energy and efforts. He was obsessed with changing my reactions to him. I felt pressured, manipulated, and suffocated.

Now if I am focusing my emotions and energy on an attempt to change, influence, attract, or gain the approval of another person, I remember my discomfort when I was on the receiving end of such attention. I remember my natural impulse to flee. I remember how all my partner's efforts had just the opposite effect from what he was after.

TODAY, IF I AM FOCUSED ON SOMEONE ELSE, I WILL REMEMBER HOW EASILY SUCH ATTENTION CAN BACKFIRE. AND I WILL BACK OFF.

THE DISCIPLINE OF SPIRITUAL GROWTH

Spiritual growth is about discipline, not burning bushes.

Even if we've been blessed by a profound spiritual experience, we cannot count on that onetime event to maintain our spiritual connection. If we want to develop our spiritual muscles, we must put them to work as surely as we must give our abs a workout if we want them to strengthen.

We must practice our way to spiritual growth.

We can spend time each day in prayer and meditation, even if it's only two minutes at first. During that time, we can talk to God about our plans for the day, asking for help rather than outlining what we expect him to do for us. We can write a letter to God about our feelings. We can read inspiring passages that connect us to inner wisdom. We can adopt a mantra or an affirmation that supports the phase of our growth that we struggle with at the moment. We can sit quietly and listen for peace.

After starting our day that way, we find ourselves more God-conscious as the day unfolds. We see God acting in our life. We are also aware of all the times we take the reins ourselves and cut God out of the picture.

I know a man who often talks about the early days of his spiritual quest. He practiced his spiritual routine grudgingly but persistently, certain it was a waste of time. He was startled one day to realize that he had grown closer to God anyway, just as if he had been sincere. His experience tells us that spiritual practice works, even if our hearts are not completely in the work.

Our spirituality can be an afterthought in our life. Or it can be a vital tool. The choice is our own, and we can carry out that choice through our actions.

TODAY I WILL HAVE A SPIRITUAL ROUTINE. I WILL WORK TOWARD MAKING IT A DAILY PRACTICE.

Surviving Betrayal

MOVING TOWARD GRATITUDE

Are you grateful for the infidelity?

It sounds impossible, but look for the gift inside the betrayal. It will help you on your healing journey. Keep changing those things inside you that continue to hold you back. Keep practicing forgiveness until it seeps into your soul and becomes unconditional love. Keep offering your help to other women who need it.

One day you will wake up in amazement at how light you feel, unburdened by the insecurities and fears and untruths you've lugged around all your life. You will walk through a day in which you are free of bitterness. You will know the freedom of loving others with no strings attached.

And you will experience a soaring, splendid moment when your worst experience and the way you worked through it builds a bridge between you and another woman, a bridge that links her pain to her healing. Aside from childbirth, that may be the most transcendent moment any of us are given here on earth, that moment when we know our experiences are helping someone else move toward the light.

When that happens, you will be grateful for everything that has happened to you. That has been our experience, over and over again. Hold that hope in your heart. Know that we are telling you the truth about these gifts. Know that you will never again wish to turn back.

TODAY I WILL TRY TO BELIEVE THAT GRATITUDE WILL COME. I WILL TRUST THAT I WILL HAVE THE SAME UPLIFTING EXPERIENCES OTHER WOMEN HAVE HAD IF I CONTINUE PRACTICING THE PRINCIPLES THEY PRACTICE.

NO NEED FOR ILLUSIONS

I don't want my illusions back.

I don't want to believe his love makes my life worth living. I don't want to believe anymore that if he just loves me enough he will never again hurt me. I no longer need to believe that men are the weaker sex, at the whim of their hormones and thus deserving of indulgence when they give in to their weaknesses.

I don't want to be blind to all the ways I've made myself easy to deceive. I don't want to buy into anyone else's illusions about me either—that I am strong or that I have it together or that I have all the answers.

I don't want to believe that marriage is the pot at the end of my rainbow.

My illusions are gone. I have examined them one by one and determined that they hold me back. I have buried them, along with any regrets or shame that accompany them. There is more joy in reality than in any of the fairy tales I've been taught, and there is no bitterness in seeing them die.

TODAY I AM CONTENT TO LIVE IN REALITY. I HAVE NO NEED OF ILLUSIONS. I AM GLAD THEY ARE GONE.

SPEAKING UP

A marker of how far I've come is my willingness and my ability to say whatever needs to be said without fear of the consequences.

Some of us have had trouble speaking up on our own behalf. We have found it hard to speak our own truth or to be honest about our feelings because we were afraid of what might happen. We were afraid of his anger or his withdrawal. We were afraid of disapproval. We were afraid he might get drunk and out of control, or turn his sarcasm on us. We were afraid he would find someone more agreeable. We were afraid he would leave us.

As we grow, we understand that his reactions to our truths cannot hurt us. We understand that if he overreacts, it is likely that he is looking for an excuse to indulge his whims and sooner or later any excuse would have served. We understand that our truth frightens him, and that frightened people often attack.

But the most important understanding we have today is that speaking our truth is too vital to accommodate or compromise any longer. The consequences of not saying whatever needs to be said are more profound and damaging than any of the consequences of speaking up. We finally understand that being alone with our courage and our truth brings more happiness, more health, more freedom than living with another person in silence born of fear.

When we recognize this, we have grown. When we can act on it, we are living in faith.

TODAY I WILL TRY TO SPEAK UP ABOUT ONE SMALL THING IN MY LIFE. I WILL FACE THE FEAR THAT COMES WITH SPEAKING UP AND FEEL THE FREEDOM THAT COMES AFTERWARD.

ALICE MAY

OTHER-SHOE SYNDROME

We all believe that if only things would turn the corner, if only we could see the light at the end of this tunnel, we would be okay. We could stop obsessing. We could stop living in fear. We could learn to trust again.

So why is it that, when things look up, we can't? We're as fearful or obsessive as ever. Maybe worse. Our hypervigilance may kick in all over again.

The other shoe is bound to drop. And we're determined to be ready for it.

Allowing ourselves to accept the good things that come our way is hard for many of us. We don't trust the good things in life. We almost seem to fear that accepting the good makes us even more likely to be blindsided by the bad.

Living in this moment is the best antidote to other-shoe syndrome. What is happening right this moment? Is everything okay just for today? Are there tangible, concrete threats to our home, our heart, our contentment, or are we only looking at fears? Do we have facts about any circumstances that we need to address or correct?

We can live in the reality of this moment. We can trust that yesterday has been dealt with. We can trust that our spirits will be strong enough if we need to deal with more tomorrow. We can trust that life has given us this moment of calm to enjoy, even if it is only the calm before another storm.

AT THIS MOMENT, THERE IS NO OTHER SHOE. AND THIS MOMENT IS ALL THAT MATTERS.

REDIRECTING YOUR
SEXUAL ENERGY

If we choose to abstain from sex for a time, what do we do with our sexual energy?

Many of us direct our extra life force into pursuing our spiritual growth. We take additional time to journal about our self-discovery process. We spend time getting in touch with people with whom we hope to set things right. We nourish relationships with women in our support group.

Others of us use the energy to rejuvenate. To rediscover our ability to be creative or just have fun. We ask our son to teach us how to play his drums. We climb a tree for the view. We join a community choir or organize visits to nursing homes. We put up a trellis and plant morning glories. We teach our grandchildren to skip rope. We roll up the rug and pretend we can dance. We clean house for the elderly neighbor who broke her hip.

Sex is one of life's great gifts, an experience to cherish and just plain delight in. But there are many other experiences in life to cherish. If we can't think of any we would enjoy pursuing, it's a good sign that we are overdue for exploring some of them.

TODAY I WILL SAVOR MY SEXUAL ENERGY AND FUNNEL IT INTO SOME ACTIVITY THAT WILL FEED ME BODY AND SOUL.

PRINCE CHARMING

Why are we so dumbfounded when our infinitely charming partner cheats?

Weren't we drawn to him in the first place by some of the same characteristics that make him such a likely candidate for infidelity? His genuine admiration for women? The easy way he carries on conversations or the intensity he focuses on us when we speak? Didn't we love him for understanding us? For the way his smile seemed to lift us right off our feet?

Men who cheat are often charismatic. They are appealing, and they know how to make it work for them.

Why are we surprised when they do precisely that?

We can be more careful today about separating charisma and desirability from traits that have real substance. We can be careful not to be carried away again by his magnetism at a time when he might love to charm us right back into a false sense of security.

Today we can look for staying power. We can look for a history of loyalty. We can look for strength instead of charm. Honesty and humility and a commitment to spiritual growth might be higher on our list than a ready smile, a knack for setting people at ease, or an ability to have the right word always on the tip of his tongue.

His appealing ways may make our heart race. But they aren't necessarily substance. Let us beware of charisma until we can be confident what lies beneath it.

TODAY I WILL SEEK THE WISDOM AND THE COURAGE TO OUT-GROW MY NEED FOR ANOTHER PRINCE CHARMING.

HOW DO YOU TREAT YOURSELF?

How much we value ourselves is revealed less in what we say or think than in what we do for ourselves.

Do we feed ourselves well? Or do we indulge our weaknesses and ignore our nutritional needs?

Do we rest when we are tired, overworked, or injured? Or have we denied our feelings for so long that we are incapable of recognizing pain or exhaustion?

Do we challenge our minds? Do we seek a balance of work and fun? Or do we allow ourselves to go overboard in one direction or another? Too much self-indulgence is as harmful as excessive responsibility.

Do we moderate our spending, finding a way to live within our means? Or do we either deprive ourselves or indulge ourselves by spending money we don't have?

Do we respect our own opinions or constantly allow others to override our decisions?

Others are not the only ones in our life who may devalue us. We may do it to ourselves, in the name of discipline or freedom or a host of other smoke screens.

TODAY I WILL LOOK HONESTLY AT HOW I TREAT MYSELF. I WILL CONSIDER WHETHER I WOULD WANT MY DAUGHTER TO TREAT HERSELF THIS WAY. I WON'T FLINCH FROM THE TRUTH, BUT I WON'T USE IT TO BEAT MYSELF UP EITHER. I WILL USE IT AS A CATALYST FOR POSITIVE CHANGE.

ALICE MAY

STUCK IN YOUR MISERY

If we become trapped in our resentment over what has gone on, we may perpetuate the misery in our family. We may make it impossible for ourselves to move on by constantly focusing on and reacting to the past and the problem.

Perhaps we continue to do little things to monitor where he is and who he's with. A dozen phone calls to his office. Probing until he recounts every detail of day. And if he grows weary of it, perhaps we speak up and remind him that this is all his fault.

We may diligently get in little digs about how poorly the children are doing in school since the crisis at home, or about the sorry state of our finances. Or we may try to be his counselor or adviser as a way to keep him under our thumb. Perhaps we talk encouragingly about forgiveness and second chances but make it clear through our actions that we still blame him.

If we are stuck and hanging on to the old baggage of our relationship, we can try to recognize it. We can acknowledge the ways in which we could be perpetuating the damage.

TODAY I WILL WORK ON MOVING FORWARD, FOR MY SAKE AND FOR THE SAKE OF MY ENTIRE FAMILY. I WILL LEAVE YESTERDAY'S BAGGAGE ALONE AND RESPOND ONLY TO WHAT IS GOING ON TODAY. I WILL RECOGNIZE THE DIFFERENCE BETWEEN GETTING STUCK AND ALLOWING MYSELF TIME TO HEAL.

GOOD-BYES

Our partner's infidelity sometimes seems to rob us of everything that ever mattered in our lives. Our home. Our family. Our treasured belongings. The things that appeared to give our life meaning and pleasure are lost to us, through divorce.

We must say good-bye to our old life. Rooms that hold our fondest memories. Gifts and keepsakes, mementos of family trips and special holidays. We must pack up, sell off, divide things. Each good-bye is another little death.

We are right to honor our grief over giving up the bits and pieces of our lives. We are entitled to tears and anger as we say good-bye. We didn't ask for this, and it may well be one of the worst things we have to endure in our lives. We may be far from ready to look on our new beginning with hope or optimism.

We can only say our good-byes in the best way we can manage. We can draw around us people who support and encourage us. We can look with gratitude at the things we do take with us. Our children perhaps. Our knowledge that we've conducted ourselves with dignity and honor during the worst moments of our lives. Our strengthening faith. Our certainty that we will ultimately rebuild a happier, healthier life.

TODAY I CAN SAY GOOD-BYE. I CAN CRY. AND I CAN TURN MY HEART TOWARD THE NEW DAY AHEAD.

ALICE MAY

327

BAD MEMORIES

She spoke with a quaver in her voice. "This is not the memory I would have chosen for myself."

Heads nodded around the circle. We all empathized. Every head in the room was full of ugly memories, memories that had often consumed most of our waking moments. Memories that would not seem to fade. Memories that tainted other memories that should have been precious.

What do we do with unpleasant memories? How do we loose their hold over us?

Most of us find it does no good to try and will away the bad memories. So we give it time. We grieve, willingly and thoroughly. We build new associations to replace old ones. We make new memories. We acknowledge an ugly memory when it rears its head, but refuse to give it our undivided attention for more than a few minutes.

And we remember the rest of what the young woman with the quaver in her voice said, and acknowledge the truth in it. "This is not the memory I would have chosen for myself. But I know now that I wouldn't have gotten here, to this new way of living my life, in any other way."

TODAY I WILL REMEMBER THAT MEMORIES HAVE NO REAL HOLD OVER ME. I CAN ACKNOWLEDGE BAD MEMORIES, ACCEPT WHAT WAS, AND TURN MY ATTENTION TO WHAT IS.

SABOTAGING YOURSELF

We will not allow this bad experience to sabotage any future relationships we may have with men.

To make sure we don't play this relationship out with others in the future, we must be willing to continue learning everything this situation has to teach us. We must be willing to heal thoroughly, and at our own pace. If we shortchange this process in any way, our unfinished emotional business can resurface later as we seek to get on with our life and make a new start.

Other men are not responsible for what our partner has done. And by walking through this situation and our own healing journey, we will be able to feel that in our hearts and souls if and when we are ready for a new relationship. We will trust ourselves to attract and recognize healthy people. And we will not need to live under any shadows from this betrayal.

TODAY I AM WILLING TO DO THE WORK TO BE FREE OF ANY LONG-TERM DAMAGE FROM THIS RELATIONSHIP. I WILL BE A WHOLE, HEALTHY PERSON WHEN THIS IS OVER. I WON'T NEED TO FEAR MY NEXT RELATIONSHIP, AND I WON'T NEED TO CONTINUE BLAMING ALL MEN FOR THE ACTIONS OF ONE.

THE RIGHT COMMITMENTS

We want a commitment from him if we are to stay and continue working on this relationship. We want something we can believe in, something that will restore our confidence in the relationship, and in him.

We want him to say he'll never stray again. We want a promise that makes us believers.

Isn't that the bottom line?

And isn't that asking him to make a promise that is too easy for any of us to break? A promise he may have already made, and broken? Then why would we even consider setting ourselves up for more heartache by hoping for or insisting on such a promise?

Are there other commitments we could consider making together instead?

Could each of us commit to being more honest with one another? Perhaps not absolutely honest today, but increasingly honest as time goes on? What constitutes dishonesty in each of our minds? Could we get very clear about how we stand on lies of omission or twisting words to achieve a version of the truth that we can hide behind?

Can we make a mutual commitment to share more openly, not judging, not withholding? Can each of us make a commitment to trying to see our own behavior as our partner might view it?

We can make many healthy commitments if and when each of us is ready to work on the relationship. We can find the ones that don't require us to be perfect and don't set either of us up for a fall.

TODAY I WILL LOOK FOR COMMITMENTS THAT FOCUS ON IMPROVEMENT RATHER THAN ABSOLUTES. I WILL DO THAT TO SAVE MYSELF DISAPPOINTMENT. I WILL DO THAT BECAUSE PROGRESS IS POSSIBLE AND PERFECTION IS NOT.

SEEK AND FIND

If we seek God, we have already found God.

The finding is in the seeking. And the seeking is lifelong, a daily ritual for many of us. Prayer. Growing quiet and listening for the voice of wisdom in our hearts. Making choices that reflect our limited understanding of our higher spirit. This is seeking. This is as close as we may ever come to finding.

For we can never hold a higher power in our hands, can never see the enormity of spiritual truths, can never understand the complex and miraculous machinations of the world of the spirit.

Those things will always elude us. Our relationship with our higher source must always be one of mystery and of seeking to solve the mystery. The answers come not in solving them, but in accepting that the best we can hope for is to keep asking, seeking, striving.

WHEN I ASK, I AM IN THE PRESENCE OF A HIGHER SPIRIT. WHEN I SEEK, GOD HOLDS ME IN HIS HANDS. I STILL DON'T HAVE ALL THE ANSWERS, BUT I HAVE EVERYTHING I NEED.

THE POWER TO HEAL

During my mother's last years, she had major surgery four times. Following her final surgery, her incision became infected. When that happens, they open the incision and allow it to heal naturally. No sutures, just a clean dressing twice a day.

At first, I couldn't imagine cleaning and dressing an open stomach wound. But I did it because it had to be done. And as I watched the incision gradually growing pink and healthy, closing up millimeter by millimeter, I developed awe for the power of healing that nature had created in each of us.

In five or six weeks, the incision was healed.

God has placed in each of us the power to heal; it is our nature to heal when we are wounded. We can see this miraculous process at work in our physical bodies. And just because we can't see the process at work in our hearts and souls is no reason to suppose the spirit of creation neglected to endow us with an equally miraculous mechanism for emotional healing as well.

TODAY I WILL TRUST THAT I HAVE BEEN GIVEN ALL I NEED TO HEAL. AS I MUST CLEAN AND DRESS A WOUND FOR THE MIRACLE TO TAKE PLACE PHYSICALLY, SO MUST I TAKE CERTAIN ACTIONS FOR THE MIRACLE TO TAKE PLACE IN MY HEART AND SOUL. I WILL DO MY PART. IN TIME, I WILL HEAL. GOD HAS ALREADY SEEN TO IT.

YOUR HEART'S DESIRE

Write in your journal today a vision of your ideal life. Don't hold back. We're talking heart's desire, so let your imagination soar. Write it all down, then put today's date on it.

And come back to it in five years.

If you continue along a spiritual path, you will be amazed at what will have happened.

If you limited yourself to only those things on today's wish list, you will have shortchanged yourself. You would have settled for far less than life can provide.

How often I have heard people say they are filled with wonder by the abundance life holds when we live the life of the spirit. An abundance, often, of the material things we hunger for—jobs, homes, relationships, money, luxuries. But most particularly an abundance of those things that really matter, the things that might not come to mind early in our spiritual journey. Love and friends and purpose, the joy of being of service, peace of mind.

Trust that your higher power wants only what is best for you. Trust that life's plan for enriching your life is better than your own. Trust that you will be cared for.

TODAY I BELIEVE I CAN LIVE MY HEART'S DESIRE. IT WILL HAPPEN FOR ME, AS IT HAS HAPPENED FOR OTHERS, IF I CONTINUE ON THE PATH I AM ON.

GIFTS AND PROMISES

One of my friends loves to encourage those who are losing heart by saying, "Don't give up before the miracle happens."

Actually, the miracles are many. Some of us call them the gifts of healing. Others call them promises. Each stage of the healing journey offers promises, or gifts. Here is what we can expect:

- Surrender: As we accept our inability to cope on our own and seek help, we will lose our sense of being isolated and alone. We will no longer believe that we must fight the world single-handedly.

- Self-discovery: We will find courage in facing the darkest parts of our hearts and souls. Our self-confidence will begin to return, and our panic is replaced with a calm assurance that we are being helped.

- Unburdening: As we share with others, as we mend fences, regret and pain over the past will slip away. Our shame will leave us, and we will begin to see that we are worthy of love.

- Daily awareness: A capacity for serenity and joy will fill us. We will experience all of our emotions without being ruled by them.

- Giving back: We will regain our hearts. We will know how to love others without giving ourselves away, and we will be able to accept the love others give us.

As we continue our journey, we will be blessed beyond our imaginings. That is a promise.

TODAY I WILL CONTINUE MY HEALING JOURNEY, WATCHING IN AWE AS MY SPIRIT IS LIFTED AND MY LIFE IS ENRICHED.

STAY IN TOUCH

Don't lose touch just because the worst is over.

Don't lose touch with the women who have supported you and loved you through this, because they will be there for you in any crisis you face.

Don't lose touch with the new principles you've learned, because they will bring you gifts every day you practice them.

Don't lose touch with your heart, because it will guide you well and keep you pointed toward your higher spirit.

Don't lose touch with yourself, because that has happened once before and it's too painful a lesson to repeat.

Don't lose touch with your faith, with the personal higher power you know today, because faith is the foundation for all that is good and enduring and enriching in your life today.

TODAY I WILL STAY IN TOUCH WITH ALL THAT IS GOOD ABOUT MY NEW LIFE. I WILL REMEMBER THAT MY NEW SOURCES OF STRENGTH ARE MINE EVERY DAY, IN EVERY SITUATION. I WILL STAY IN TOUCH.

ALICE MAY

YOUR PARTNER

Today we can choose a new partner in facing all that life brings. Today our partner is God.

Our partner is a good and faithful companion, and a wise and patient guide. Our partner never falters just because the path has grown narrow. Our partner loves us unconditionally, flaws and all, and wants only the best for us.

God is our partner. And God is always available. He is never too busy, never too stressed, never out of town when we need him. God is patient with our foibles. God is never jealous or petty or argumentative. God is always encouraging and fair.

Our new partner always brings out the best in us.

Today our life is filled with ease and comfort, joy and serenity, even in the face of difficulties, because we have found a partner who always knows exactly what we need, no matter what the circumstances.

TODAY I HAVE NOTHING TO FEAR BECAUSE MY PARTNER GIVES ME STRENGTH, COURAGE, AND WISDOM TO HANDLE LIFE'S DIFFICULTIES. MY PARTNER IS GOD.

BUILDING A HEALTHY RELATIONSHIP

Once we have given up the myth of a happily-ever-after union, we are free to explore marvelous possibilities. What do we want this partnership to be, now that we are no longer hampered by unrealistic, unattainable ideals?

Together, we can design the foundation of a partnership firmly grounded in reality. We can set goals for our family. We can decide together what our shared values are. We can agree on the boundaries that keep us safe while encouraging intimacy. We can learn our individual triggers and negotiate ways to sidestep them. We can decide what our relationship will look like and how each of us can contribute to that.

And because of all we've been through together, we now have a clear commitment to our own growth and mutual support. There is a solidness in our partnership that we never could have achieved in our days of starry-eyed devotion.

On this side of the darkness, we can see ourselves and one another just as we are. We understand the struggles each of us faces, and we appreciate the strengths we bring to the table. We are freer with one another because neither is burdened with the other's daunting expectations. We know we can be loved in all our frailty and imperfection.

Our partnership is tempered, forged into a tougher alloy by the fires that failed to consume it.

TODAY I RECOGNIZE WHAT GOES INTO A HEALTHY RELATION-SHIP. I CAN ALSO SEE THAT DIFFICULTIES IN ANY RELATIONSHIP CAN CONTRIBUTE TO ITS STRENGTH.

CONTINUOUS CHANGE

I paused beside the pond, beneath a sunny, cloudless sky. It was a still day, a quiet path. I sat beside the water to soak up the serenity.

Within a very few minutes, I saw what had not been apparent as I walked past. Although the water appeared undisturbed, it was never still.

The faintest of breezes rippled its surface, creating a continuous pattern of motion and change. A flitting dragonfly made the water shimmer in the sunlight. Beneath the surface, a turtle stirred up mud. And at the water's edge, birds twittered and chirped and squawked. The pond was never still. It didn't offer me the same view for thirty seconds in a row.

Yet it never lost its serene appearance.

Like the water, my life is never still. Things are always flitting or rippling or squawking through my life. And like the water, I might grow stagnant if things were perfectly still.

TODAY I WILL TRY TO ACCEPT THE RIPPLES IN MY LIFE WITH THE CALMNESS OF THE POND. I WILL SEE THE DISTURBANCES AS A CHANCE TO AVOID STAGNATION. AND I WILL BE GRATEFUL FOR THE OPPORTUNITY TO SHIMMER IN THE SUNLIGHT.

GIVING GOD ROOM TO WORK

Here is how I regained my trust: by completely and wholeheartedly giving up the idea that I ever needed to trust my partner again.

Here is how I regained my marriage: by completely and wholeheartedly giving up the idea that I could do a single thing to save it.

Here is how I regained my joy: by completely and wholeheartedly giving up the idea that any circumstances in my life would restore my happiness.

Everything I have surrendered into my higher power's hands has been returned to me. Everything I have given up trying to fix by myself has been restored. Not quickly. Not easily. Because I haven't surrendered quickly or easily. I have surrendered haltingly, grudgingly. Each time I surrendered only when I had reached a place where the single alternative left to me was surrender. My bag of tricks was empty. So I surrendered. A little. Then a little more. Until, finally, it was all surrendered.

And then it was returned to me.

Not through my own efforts. But because I have finally given a higher spirit room to work miracles in my life. In my marriage. In my heart. In my soul.

WHEN I GIVE UP THE STRUGGLE, I WIN THE WAR. IN SOME WAY THAT I MAY NOT BE ABLE TO FORESEE TODAY, ALL PARTS OF MY LIFE WILL BE RESTORED IF I REMAIN WILLING TO SURRENDER.

THINK BEFORE ACTING

Today we can stop and think before we react. We can think before we speak, before we make a decision, before we act.

We can think about the repercussions of what we are about to say or do. We can think about how it might affect us or our children or others we love.

We can think about how others might instinctively react to what we are about to do. We can consider the possibility of setting in motion a backlash that grows in intensity and ugliness, until it is beyond control or recall. We can think about doing our part to stop that spiral of events before it begins.

We can think about what the actions we are considering would say about us and the kind of person we are. Is this a statement we want to make about ourselves? And we can think about the kind of person we could become if we made a habit of the kind of action we are considering.

We can think about what a higher source of wisdom might counsel if we had a direct line to that source.

Once we think about these things, we will know in our hearts and our heads whether we are choosing the right course of action or not. If the course we're on is a destructive or unwise one, we can think again. Then we can act.

TODAY I WILL THINK ABOUT MY ACTIONS BEFORE I TAKE THEM. I WILL THINK, NOT OBSESS. AS I THINK, I WILL LISTEN TO THE WISE INNER VOICE I'VE LEARNED I CAN RELY ON. AND I WILL KNOW THE RIGHT COURSE OF ACTION.

TEMPTATIONS IN HELPING OTHERS

Once we have healed a bit, we will be gifted with the opportunity to help someone else who is just facing her problems. She will be in pain. She will be confused and uncertain and eager to be rescued.

Life has placed her in front of us so that our experiences can guide her to the same healing and growth we have found. That opportunity holds for us both blessings and temptations.

We will be tempted to give her advice. We know what worked for us, and we will believe with all our hearts that the same thing will work for her. This isn't necessarily so. We can teach her the tools that worked for us, that led us to the answers that were right for us, but we cannot know how she should use those tools. Because we can't see into the future. We can't save her, we can only guide her. And that is enough.

We will be tempted to tell her what she wants to hear instead of what we know to be true. She is already so distraught that we want to offer comfort without saying anything that might disturb her more. But we are here to share the truth about what it takes to heal, not to enable her to remain a victim by offering nothing but consolation.

And it is especially tempting to think we are wise, that we know all there is to know about her circumstances, about healing, about the spiritual life. We do not. We only know what we've been taught; we only know how the tools worked for us. If we begin to think of ourselves as a guru of some sort, we cannot help her, and we can only hurt ourselves.

WHEN SOMEONE ASKS ME FOR HELP, I WILL TRY TO BE HUMBLE AND TO REMEMBER THAT ALL I CAN SHARE IS MY EXPERIENCE, STRENGTH, AND HOPE. I AM NOT RESPONSIBLE FOR HER HEALING.

ALICE MAY

WANTS VERSUS NEEDS

My eyes land on something appealing, and my first thought is, "I need that."

I need it to make myself look good. I need it to elevate my status in your eyes. I need it because I think it will make me feel better, make me happier, make my life more complete.

The truth is, most of what we think we need we actually only want. We desire it. We long for it. And worst of all, we ascribe to it powers it can't possibly have—like the power to make our life perfect.

This, of course, is the same kind of thinking that caused problems for our partner and for us. The same kind of thinking that led him astray.

It can only do the same for us.

Today we can learn to distinguish between our needs and our wants. We can learn that most things we desire are simply wants and we will do perfectly well without them. We can learn to say, "I don't have to have this today." And when we do that, we will be able to recognize that we probably don't have to have it tomorrow either.

Our needs are simpler than our wants—food, shelter, fulfilling work, a connection with others and with our own spirit. But our wants, ah, our wants are unlimited. Elaborate. Ever expanding. Costly, and not just in dollars, but in what we pay personally for satisfying them. Sometimes it is our boundless wants that keep us in a relationship that is killing us, body and soul.

TODAY I WILL REMEMBER THAT NOT EVERYTHING I WANT IS SOMETHING I NEED. I WILL TRY, JUST FOR TODAY, TO DO WITH-OUT A FEW OF THE THINGS I THINK I WANT. I WILL LISTEN TO MY SOUL FOR SIGNS THAT I AM MORE EASILY SATISFIED THE LESS I CATER TO MY WANTS.

EXPRESSING YOUR LOVE

Our expressions of love may have been rejected often enough that we repress the urge now. That may have started before the infidelity, before our marriage even. Some of us simply have trouble showing our love.

Just for today, we can be aware of how often we hold back. How often we decide not to take some action, large or small, to show another person that we love him or her. Have we held back when we felt the urge to touch the arm or cheek of someone we love, including a child or a sibling? Have we swallowed words of affection? Have we decided not to call, not to leave a note, not to make the gesture that tells someone he or she is on our mind?

Also, we can pay attention to the ways in which we do try to show our love. Do we express worry? Do we give advice? Do we do things that we believe grow out of our love but in reality grow out of our fear, gestures that look and feel more like nagging or smothering than love?

Can we say the words? Can we smile when someone we love comes into the room? Does touch come easily for us? How many times have we given hugs today? Can we give someone a few minutes of our undivided attention?

We may be justified in shutting down the ways we express love to the people who have betrayed us. But most of us don't know how to shut our emotions off and on at will. So others—our children, friends, parents, siblings—may experience the fallout if we lose our ability to express our love. And so will we.

TODAY I WILL LOOK FOR WAYS IN WHICH I CAN EXPRESS MY LOVE TO ALL THOSE I ENCOUNTER. I CAN SHARE MY FEELINGS OF LOVE WITH DIFFERENT PEOPLE IN DIFFERENT WAYS, AND THAT WILL KEEP ME ON SAFE FOOTING, EVEN WITH THOSE WHO DON'T ALWAYS FEEL SAFE TO LOVE.

ALICE MAY

SAY YES TO LIFE

In the preface to her book *Amazing Grace: A Vocabulary of Faith*, Kathleen Norris says that the vocabulary of faith begins when we learn the word *yes*.

Yes.

It is easy to reject. It is easy to say no to things unfamiliar, frightening, challenging. It is easy to say no when we've been hurt. It is easy to say no to anything that makes demands of us. Demands that we grow, that we change, that we move beyond our safe limits.

It is easy to say no to love. To taking a new chance. To starting over.

But if we are to go beyond this place where we are stuck in our misery, we must say yes.

We must say yes to a new way of life. Our old lives have been disrupted and destroyed to one extent or another anyway. A new life is upon us already, and resisting it will only prolong our pain. Instead, we can say yes.

We can embrace the new life we didn't ask for and still may not want. We can say yes to love, new or renewed. We can say yes to faith. We can say yes to God. We can say yes to the challenges of becoming aware of who we are and why we are. We can say yes to a journey few of us embark on willingly.

TODAY I WILL SAY YES TO MY JOURNEY OF FAITH.

INTENSIVE SELF-CARE

If we decide to continue in a close relationship with a man who is not yet ready to be exclusive, we are faced with a challenge. We must learn not to allow his behavior to harm us or rob us of our serenity.

To stay in the relationship and continue the roller-coaster ride of ups and downs we've been on invites poor physical health, declining mental health, and a toxic environment for everyone in our home.

But it *is* possible to release him to his unhealthy choices without being dragged down with him. It is possible to say, in our heart if not aloud, "Do what you must. I love you, and it is sad that you choose this path. But I am choosing to disengage from the insanity we've created. I am choosing both to love you and to love myself enough to seek spiritual health."

If we stay in this relationship, we can do so with the understanding that we cannot change him. We can do so knowing that we will need ongoing support from people who can love us without judging our circumstances. We can do so remembering that our own well-being prohibits us from nagging, manipulating, judging, checking up on him, or otherwise attempting to control his behavior.

I REMAIN WITH A PARTNER WHO CONTINUES TO MAKE UNHEALTHY CHOICES BY LIVING IN THIS DAY ONLY; BY FOCUSING ON MY OWN LIFE, WORK, AND BEHAVIOR; BY DISCOVERING AND FEEDING THE THINGS THAT REMIND ME OF MY OWN VALUE. I OWE MYSELF THE INTENSIVE SELF-CARE NECESSARY IN THESE CIRCUMSTANCES TO MAINTAIN MY SERENITY.

ALICE MAY

DEFLECTING YOUR ANGER

My favorite targets for anger during my lowest days were sales clerks. Bank tellers were good, too, but it was more satisfying to make a scene in a department store.

Deflecting our wrath onto someone else—someone we feel safer alienating—is a common reaction. Common, but counterproductive. Anger is a by-product of our difficulties, and allowing it to come out sideways is destructive and demeaning.

It may feel safer to unleash our temper on someone we'll never see again. Someone who is powerless, as powerless as we feel. But turning our fury on a mail carrier, our secretary, our dog, our children does nothing to alleviate the anger or its underlying cause. When we've vented anger in that way, we invariably spend the rest of the day justifying and hanging on to our rage just to assuage the guilt and self-loathing we always feel after one of our tantrums.

Equally as bad, we distract ourselves from what really needs our attention—the true source of our anger and the actions we need to take to improve our situation.

This journey asks us to look at our role in our difficulties. Focusing on the real source of our anger and the spiritual solutions will be more productive and healing than scattershot rage.

IF I AM TEMPTED TODAY TO DISTRACT MYSELF WITH SIDEWAYS ANGER, I WILL FOCUS ON SOME FOOTWORK THAT IS PART OF MY HEALING JOURNEY. I WILL FOCUS ON THE TRUTH ABOUT MY EMOTIONS AND REMEMBER THAT MY GOAL IS SERENITY.

NO ONE TO FORGIVE

A friend left a phone message recently apologizing profusely for not returning a call I'd made months ago. I smiled. There was nothing to forgive. Although I'd thought of my friend several times during that period, I'd never had a moment of resentment. I'd simply assumed that when the time was right, my friend would call.

At that moment, I realized there is no one in my life I need to forgive.

I'm not hanging on to a single grudge or resentment from the past; I've dealt with all of those, thanks to the spiritual principles I now practice. Once I was able to see the flawed humanity that creates hurtful situations, how could I continue attaching blame?

And once I've seen that truth, how can I attach blame when something happens today?

When a friend slights me or a neighbor levels my recycling bin with his SUV or a colleague elbows me out of a project, my heart remains peaceful today. There is no room in my heart for anger or bitterness. My friend, my neighbor, my colleague, all are human. Not perfect.

So who is there to blame? And if there is no one to blame, there is no need to forgive.

Saying I no longer blame is not the same as saying I don't hold people responsible. Sometimes there are consequences, and today I have healthy enough boundaries to allow people to live with the consequences of their behavior. My neighbor may need to pay for my recycling bin; my colleague may no longer be privy to my professional ideas if she uses them behind my back.

But I don't have to waste time and energy on blame.

TODAY I WON'T POISON MY SPIRIT WITH ILL WILL OVER THE ACTIONS OF THE LESS-THAN-PERFECT PEOPLE IN MY LIFE. MY HEART IS TOO LIGHT TO BE WEIGHED DOWN WITH BLAME.

ALICE MAY

FORGIVENESS THROUGH PRAYER

When I first began to work on spiritual solutions to my problems, I believed it was okay to hate those who had done the unforgivable. I didn't realize how much resentments poisoned my spirit.

The person I resented most was the other woman. I blamed her, hated her, and fantasized about making her pay. But it wasn't long before wiser women than I helped me see that holding on to my bitterness was keeping me both stuck in the problem and emotionally ill.

I became willing to let it go, but I didn't know how. And I didn't like it one bit when I was told to pray for her.

Prayer for the other woman was the last thing I wanted to do. What I really wanted to do was take out an ad in the local paper telling everyone what she'd done, to ruin her reputation, maybe even her career. But I'd seen others who were further along the path on their healing journey, and I wanted to be more like them. So I made up my mind to do what other people told me had worked for them. I would trust the process.

I prayed for her. Every day. I prayed to be able to see her as God saw her. I did it grudgingly, the words like dust in my mouth. But I did it.

About two months after I started praying for her, I started thinking about her, as I often did. But my thoughts that day veered in a new direction. It came to me that if anyone else had been hurt as much as I had been by my husband's deceit, it was her.

At that moment, I realized that God had indeed answered my prayers. I could see her as another hurting person who had made lousy choices in life, just as I had. This woman had no more power over me. I was free. Prayer had worked a miracle.

TODAY I CAN TAP INTO MIRACLES, USING THE TOOLS I'VE LEARNED ON MY JOURNEY. I WILL USE MY NEW TOOLS AND WAIT FOR MIRACLES.

ONE DAY AT A TIME

Who knew how to live one day at a time? Who knew it was a good way to live even? Certainly not me. I spent all my time dwelling either in yesterday's pain or tomorrow's fear. Today was devoured as I relived painful old memories or entertained terrifying what-ifs.

But nothing productive, nothing positive can be accomplished when we are living in the past or the future. The only place where we can act to change our life, to heal our pain, to rediscover the self that has been lost, is in this present moment.

In the here and now, we can pray for help.

In this moment, we can pick up the phone and find comfort in the wisdom of other women. We can find a small pleasure to lift our spirits—a favorite song, the breeze on our face, a walk around the block.

One day at a time, our problems are not insurmountable. One day at a time, our problems are not as bad as our fear wants us to believe they are. One day at a time, we are being cared for. We can manage this one day.

TODAY I WILL REMEMBER TO KEEP MY HEAD AND MY HEART WHERE MY FEET ARE. FOR THAT IS WHERE I CAN TAKE THE POSITIVE ACTION NECESSARY TO CHANGE MY ATTITUDES, MY FEELINGS, AND MY LIFE.

ALICE MAY

A BAD LIFE VERSUS A BAD DAY

I used to believe I was having a bad life. A tragic life, in fact. A life crippled by failed marriages and sorrow and disconnection because of other people's wrongdoings.

Granted, my life had been sprinkled with some successes, some accomplishments, some happiness. But I believed the truth was that I was having a bad life.

Today I can see the truth, and it isn't what I once believed.

I may be having a bad day, but I am not having a bad life.

Today I can see that I am and always have been blessed with riches. With talent and opportunities to express it. With people who love and treasure me. With good health and a strong body and mind. With work that feeds my spirit and with challenges that keep me growing.

I have a good life.

And that leaves me room to have a bad day. A bad year even, when some of the things that make up my life fall apart. But today that won't negate all the wonderful things that make up the rest of my good life.

I AM NOT HAVING A BAD LIFE. I MAY BE HAVING A BAD DAY. I CAN SURVIVE A BAD DAY.

HE IS NOT A FIXER-UPPER

He is not a project.

He may be our partner, friend, lover, confidant, and the family lawn maintenance professional.

But he is not a fixer-upper.

If we took him into our life in order to change him, we made a mistake.

If we've made it one of our life's goals to help him see the error of his faulty thinking, we need to set new goals.

If we believe it is our job to make him more ambitious, better dressed, a regular churchgoer, a more attentive father, or a man who knows how to sort laundry, we are wrong.

We can do none of those things. Even at our most persuasive, we can't even make him want to work on any of those areas of his life himself.

And neither can we make him into a man who will never again be unfaithful.

He can make all those changes, and more, if he sincerely wishes to and seeks help. But we cannot do it for him. And all our efforts to influence him sometimes make him cling all the more stubbornly to his old ways.

TODAY I WILL ALLOW MY PARTNER THE DIGNITY TO DECIDE FOR HIMSELF WHO HE CHOOSES TO BE. I WILL BE GRATEFUL FOR ALL MY LOVED ONES WHO ALLOW ME THE SAME DIGNITY. TODAY I WILL REMEMBER THAT HE IS NOT A PROJECT.

ALICE MAY

LIFETIME LOVE

He talked of his love for his deceased wife with such tender fondness that it brought tears to my eyes. Not because I appreciated the beauty and the tragedy of his story, but because all I could do was pity myself.

My perfect love had been damaged. It no longer had that glow.

But as I listened to this man I did not know, I realized that the love he described had no resemblance to the movie-script love I was imagining. The kind I thought I coveted. The love he described, the love he still carried in his heart years after her death, was a love built on living through life's little hells together. It was built on shared pain, the anguish of mistakes, the acceptance of imperfections. Their love was about two people, side by side, supporting and encouraging and being there for one another when the going got tough.

The kind of love you never get if you cut and run the first time life deals you a blow.

We have the opportunity to build that kind of lifetime love now, either in this relationship or in one we may be given in the future. We have the opportunity to prove ourselves loyal and stalwart and reliable. Things still may not turn out as we would hope, with an enduring and inspiring love. Our only certainty is that no such love is possible if we don't do our part to weather the storms.

TODAY I RECOGNIZE THAT BUILDING A LIFETIME OF LOVE ASKS ME TO FACE AND FIND HEALTHY SOLUTIONS TO THE PROBLEMS LIFE BRINGS. I CAN DO THAT TODAY, WHETHER IT SAVES THIS RELATIONSHIP OR NOT.

SAFE IN GOD'S HANDS

"Do I believe that God has me in the palm of his hand?" My friend repeated the question. "Yes, and I can tell you exactly how I came to believe it. It wasn't an event, it was a process.

"My first hint came when my first child was born. I knew, as I held him in my arms, that I couldn't handle motherhood alone, that there had to be a source of help beyond me. And there was, always.

"Next, years later, as my father was dying of AIDS, I realized even through my grief and helplessness that there must be a plan I couldn't see. And I tried to trust that.

"Then, a few years ago, I had the opportunity to spend two weeks with some members of my family in a safe, nurturing environment. They were all deeply spiritual, and during that time I developed the strongest sense that God really did hold me in the palm of his hand.

"A week after I returned home, I discovered a pornographic video in my husband's briefcase. And I was no longer able to deny the serious problems we'd been hiding from for so long."

My friend drew a deep breath. There was no pain in her eyes as she spoke. "Some people might have seen that as a cruel joke. But I understood that it was God's way of preparing me emotionally for some very turbulent times. God wanted me to know, before I had to face the truth about my husband, that I would be safe and cared for."

TODAY I WILL LOOK FOR ALL THE MANY WAYS IN WHICH GOD REMINDS ME THAT I AM SAFE AND CARED FOR. GOD'S MESSAGES TO ME ARE ABUNDANT. I WILL BECOME MORE ATTUNED TO SEEING AND HEARING THEM.

ALICE MAY

GOD'S WORLD

In God's world, everything is just as it is supposed to be. I am exactly where I am supposed to be.

When my life blew up in my face, that message infuriated me. It so enraged me that I blacked it out with a fat marker when I came across it one morning in my favorite meditation book.

If this is what God has in mind for me, I thought, *then to hell with God.*

As always, however, I received what I needed when I needed it. Shortly after my little temper tantrum, I came across a typewritten message someone sent me after my mother died. The passage said that my higher spirit wants more for me than earthly happiness. That spirit wants better for me than an easy life, pleasant days, unchallenging relationships.

My higher power wants my greatest good. And in God's world, my greatest good is spiritual growth.

Not cars with leather upholstery or his-and-hers perfect children or a spouse out of a 1950s sitcom. Not shallow, earthly happiness, but spiritual growth.

My pain, my shame, the betrayals and humiliations and losses I've suffered, are exactly as they are supposed to be. I am exactly where I am supposed to be. I am being given the opportunity to develop courage and wisdom and faith.

TODAY I WILL BE GRATEFUL THAT GOD WANTS MORE FOR ME THAN SUPERFICIAL, TEMPORAL HAPPINESS. I WILL BE GRATEFUL FOR THIS OPPORTUNITY I'VE BEEN GIVEN TO LIVE IN A SPIRITUAL WORLD. I WILL BE GRATEFUL THINGS ARE EXACTLY AS THEY ARE SUPPOSED TO BE.

FINDING YOURSELF

We are on a journey to awareness. We seek to become aware of who we are and how our choices and attitudes in life affect our happiness. We seek to become aware of spiritual good as it occurs in our lives.

On our journey, we will find parts of ourselves that we have lost or ignored or buried beneath a lifetime of denial and dysfunction.

On our journey, those of us who have been fearful will find courage through faith.

Those of us who have shut down our feelings will find our hearts filling with love and pain and an abundance of emotions.

Where we have been perfectionists, we will learn the joy of our purely human failings.

Where we have sold our souls for the approval of others, we will find the confidence to please only ourselves and our higher spirit.

Where we have been alone, we will share our journey, joining hands with others who will love and accept us just as we are. And just as we are becoming.

I AM ON THIS JOURNEY TO RECOVER MY BEST SELF, MY WISE SELF, MY TRUE SELF. TODAY I SEE GLIMPSES OF THE WOMAN WHO HAS BEEN LOST ALONG THE WAY, AND I LIKE WHAT I SEE.

LISTEN AND LEARN

If we can do nothing else today to improve our circumstances, we can listen.

We can listen to our children. We can ask them how they feel about the disruption in their home, then listen to their concerns and fears.

We can listen to another woman who has survived. We can ask what helped her most and listen carefully. We can listen to another woman who is new to her pain. We can listen with gratitude for our own growth. We can listen with an open heart.

We can listen to the world around us. A splash in the birdbath, clothes tumbling in the dryer, neighborhood children hawking lemonade on the corner. And we can connect with this moment.

We can listen without judgment. We can listen with our hearts open to learning something that will help us grow or lift us up. We can listen and learn.

WHEN I LEARN TO LISTEN, I AM LEARNING TO COMMUNICATE BETTER. I AM LEARNING TO HONOR OTHERS. I AM LEARNING TO HEAR HOW AND WHERE WE ARE ALIKE.

LIVING SIMPLY

One of the harsh realities of divorce or separation is that most women end up far less secure financially. Our finances may have been secure before, but they may be very shaky now.

Learning to live with less is one more experience that may be difficult, but it isn't automatically bad for us. Learning to live with less doesn't necessarily translate into depriving ourselves. It may help us see the value and the pleasure in living simply. It may lead us to a slower pace of life, over time, or a greater awareness of the things in our life that have true and lasting value far beyond the material. It may give us greater opportunities to connect with our children when we are less distracted by pricey possessions and activities.

Abundance is not a bad thing, but neither is simplicity. And we may actually learn that what we thought was abundance was merely excess.

TODAY I WILL WELCOME THE OPPORTUNITY TO LIVE A LIFE LESS CLUTTERED BY THE MATERIAL, LESS DRIVEN BY ACQUISITION. I CAN LIVE MORE SIMPLY AND NEVER BE DEPRIVED.

ALICE MAY

GOD IS GENTLE

Some of us who already had faith when we began our healing journey find that our beliefs change as we seek to live out of that faith on our journey.

This is especially true for those of us who sometime in the past came to believe in a punishing God. One woman who resisted spiritual solutions put it this way, "I actually believed that God would not help me unless I first helped myself by leaving my husband.

"I saw God as a parent so demanding he would say to a child with a broken leg, 'I'll help you, but you've got to get rid of the bike you fell off of first.'

"I had to learn from watching and listening to others that God is more loving that that."

Most of us on the journey to healing come to rely on a higher power who does not condemn us for our mistakes, much less someone else's. We learn that if we turn to a higher spirit with our fears, our pain, our worries, or even our mistakes, that spirit is available with comfort and love and guidance. The God we have found is gentle with us in our difficulties. Not punishing.

If you don't know a God who treats you with all the loving kindness of a warmhearted parent, look again. Perhaps you have confused God with others in your life who delight in demanding too much and putting you down when you can't deliver.

GOD DELIGHTS IN LIFTING ME UP. TODAY I WILL LOOK FOR A GENTLE GOD.

THE OPPORTUNITY TO LEARN

What can we learn from hard times?

Can we learn more compassion for others?

Can we learn to be more conscious of how our decisions and our actions affect others?

Can we learn to appreciate all that is good in our world instead of focusing solely on what is bad?

Everything in our life is our teacher, if we are open to the lessons. The people we encounter, the people we love, the random events in our day, the defining moments that become the major mileposts in our life—all offer us the gifts of insight and growth and enrichment. And this sad and harrowing experience is no different. It, too, can teach us something valuable that we couldn't or wouldn't learn any other way.

What can we learn from hard times? Can we learn to walk tall and speak clearly on our own behalf? Can we learn how to make vital connections with other human beings who also suffer and grow? Can we learn how to look inward and see ourselves more clearly?

The answer, of course, is yes.

TODAY I WILL ACCEPT THE CHALLENGE TO LEARN FROM ADVERSITY. I WILL BE GRATEFUL FOR THE OPPORTUNITY.

ALICE MAY

STRONG, NOT TOUGH

Being strong is not the same as being tough.

We learn to be tough to protect ourselves, to weather bad situations with a minimum of damage. To be tough is to develop a thick skin, to build a high wall, to brandish emotional weapons as hurtful as the ones others may have used against us. To be tough is to deny feelings until they vanish. To be tough is to beat off any emotional involvement that has the potential to hurt us.

Today we can do better than tough. Today we can be strong.

To be strong is to detach with love by remembering that others' poor behavior is not aimed at us and that our reaction to it is up to us. To be strong is to be compassionate when others are weak. To be strong is to surround ourselves with people who can support us. To be strong is to know ourselves and love ourselves and to be committed to growth. To be strong is to have resources beyond ourselves for dealing with life's harsh realities.

TODAY I DON'T HAVE TO BE TOUGH TO SURVIVE. TODAY I CAN BE STRONG. THAT LEAVES ME ROOM TO BE GENTLE AND LOVING AS WELL.

CRACKED VESSELS

The peasant went to the river each day for his family's water. He brought it back in two pitchers, suspended from the ends of a pole he balanced across his back and shoulders.

One of the pitchers was perfect and arrived at his home each day filled with water for drinking and cooking and bathing. The other pitcher was cracked, and by the time the peasant reached his home the second pitcher was often already half empty.

One day the second pitcher expressed its remorse for being less than perfect and asked the peasant why he bothered hauling water in a cracked vessel. The peasant replied by retracing his daily path to and from the river. The side of the road where the perfect pitcher hung was dry and dusty. But on the side of the road where the cracked pitcher dribbled out water each morning, a riot of wildflowers bloomed bright and fragrant.

The perfect pitcher served its own valuable purpose. But so did the cracked vessel.

WHEN WE WONDER WHETHER WE ARE CAPABLE OF A POSITIVE CONTRIBUTION BECAUSE WE HAVE BEEN SO BROKEN BY OUR PAIN, WE CAN REMEMBER THAT EVEN CRACKED VESSELS ARE RESPONSIBLE FOR MUCH THAT IS BRIGHT AND BEAUTIFUL.

ALICE MAY

YOU CAN STOP PRETENDING

We don't have to show the world a smile all the time.

How often have we forced ourselves to smile, to laugh, to respond with a lie when the world asked how things were going? How often have we choked on our unhappiness rather than reveal ourselves to the world?

We don't have to do that today. Today we can be honest, while still safeguarding ourselves from those who don't belong in the middle of our business.

We can say, "Things are shaky right now, but thank you for asking."

We can say, "I don't wish to talk about it right now, but I appreciate your concern."

We can quit pretending our lives are perfect, and we can set boundaries at the same time, two healthy behaviors that may still feel new to most of us. We can also cry to those who understand our pain.

If asked, we can say, "Life is difficult, but I'm in good hands."

I DON'T OWE ANYONE EXPLANATIONS ABOUT PERSONAL MATTERS. BUT I OWE MYSELF MORE THAN A FACADE, MORE THAN FUTILE ATTEMPTS TO DENY MY PAIN. TODAY I AM FREE TO FEEL WHAT I FEEL AND TO SHARE WHAT I WANT WITH THE PEOPLE I KNOW ARE SAFE.

RESPONDING TO A LAPSE

Long after this is over, months or even years after we believe we have left this behind, something will creep up on us and sting us. A bad memory. A self-defeating belief. A haunting fear.

This may happen whether we are still in the relationship that spawned these feelings or have moved on to a new and apparently healthier relationship. Or no relationship at all. Things may seem better than they have ever been.

When we are stung by the past, it doesn't mean our situation is hopeless. It doesn't mean we are in for a long bout of depression or heartache. It doesn't mean the sky is about to fall.

The sick thinking and diseased emotions that accompany betrayal are powerful. They don't release their hold on us easily. Sometimes we simply will be ambushed by a troubling memory or an old fear. Our sick thinking will take one more shot at us.

We can respond positively, and with confidence. We can acknowledge the thought or feeling for what it is—a part of our past that would like to regain a foothold. It is strong, but it is not stronger than our new-found courage or our active faith.

The same tools that saw us through our crisis will see us through this momentary lapse. Prayer. Meditation on solutions that lead to serenity. Contact with someone who was helpful in our earlier crisis. Reaching out to offer comfort to someone still grappling with fresh pain.

BECAUSE I HAVE MY SPIRITUAL DISCIPLINE, A BAD THOUGHT OR A PAINFUL FEELING NEED NOT OVERWHELM ME AGAIN.

REWRITING THE PAST

We cannot rewrite the past.

We cannot change a single thing that has happened in our lives. Unfaithfulness has touched our world and altered both our interior and exterior landscapes. Nothing is the same as it was. And we can do nothing to change that.

But today is ours to shape. Tomorrow is unexplored territory. We can achieve the delightful, the challenging, the inspiring, the marvelous. Because this day is ours.

We have our new tools for living. We have a new way of viewing the world. We have new ways of participating in relationships. We have gifts of the spirit that enable us to create a bright and joyful future.

TODAY I WILL GIVE UP ANY ATTEMPTS TO REWRITE THE PAST. I WILL FOCUS ON ALL THE MARVELOUS POSSIBILITIES THIS DAY HOLDS, KNOWING THAT I CAN CREATE A REWARDING, FULFILLING FUTURE.

YOUR MIRACLE IS OUT THERE

Waiting somewhere along the journey of help, hope, and healing is a miracle for each of us.

The miracle is waiting at different places along the path for each of us, and the miracle is a little different for each of us. But there is a miracle. One for you. One for me.

I know this because I've seen it happen. Over and over again. I've been personally involved in dozens of lives as women struggled down this path. And I have never seen it fail.

Each woman who stayed on the path found a miracle.

Some found their miracle during their self-evaluation, some as they shared their stories with others, and some as they embarked on the challenging task of seeking forgiveness. Others found it as they followed through on a commitment to make the process a part of their daily spiritual journey. Or when they reached out to others.

For some, the miracle was sudden and powerful. For others, it unfolded slowly but steadily.

For some, the miracle was courage, or a new purpose in a life that had been directionless. For others, it was an active relationship with a living God, or self-esteem for the first time in their lives. For some, it was a glorious second chance at love.

Some of us have been blessed with all those things, and more. But all of us have been blessed.

My miracle is out there. It is waiting for me. I will stay on the path. I will do the footwork. My miracle will find me.

ALICE MAY

INDEX OF TOPICS

Index